THE CAVE OF FONTÉCHEVADE

This book provides a summary of the discoveries made during the course of excavations at the Paleolithic cave site of Fontéchevade, France, between 1994 and 1998. The excavation team used modern field and analytic methods to address major problems raised by earlier excavations at the site from 1937 to 1954. These earlier excavations produced two sets of data that have been problematic in light of data from other European Paleolithic sites: first, the Lower Paleolithic stone tool industry, the Tayacian, that differs in fundamental ways from other contemporary industries and, second, the human skull fragment that has been interpreted as modern in nature but that apparently dates from the last interglacial, long before there is any evidence for modern humans from any other site in Europe. By applying modern stratigraphic, lithic, faunal, geological, geophysical, and radiometric analyses, the interdisciplinary team demonstrates that the Tayacian "industry" is a product of site-formation processes and that the actual age of the Fontéchevade I fossil is compatible with other evidence for the arrival of modern humans in Europe.

Philip G. Chase is a senior research scientist at the University of Pennsylvania Museum of Archaeology and Anthropology. He is the author of *The Emergence of Culture* and *The Hunters of Combe Grenal*, as well as numerous articles and chapters on Paleolithic archaeology, zooarchaeology, and the origins and evolution of symbolism and culture.

André Debénath is professor and director of research at the University of Rabat and professor emeritus at the University of Perpignan. He specializes in the Paleolithic of the Charente River Basin, France, and of Morocco. He has excavated numerous sites in both countries and has published more than 200 articles and several books.

Harold L. Dibble is professor of anthropology at the University of Pennsylvania and curator-in-charge of the European Section at the University of Pennsylvania Museum of Archaeology and Anthropology. Editor of the journal *PaleoAnthropology*, he is the author of 12 books and has directed excavations in France, Morocco, and Egypt for more than 25 years.

Shannon P. McPherron is an archaeologist in the Department of Human Evolution at the Max Planck Institute for Evolutionary Anthropology. He has codirected Paleolithic field projects in France, North Africa, and East Africa, and he has published on lithic analysis, site formation processes, and the use of computers in archaeology. He is coauthor, with Harold Dibble, of *Using Computers in Archaeology: A Practical Guide.*

The Cave of Fontéchevade

RECENT EXCAVATIONS AND THEIR PALEOANTHROPOLOGICAL IMPLICATIONS

Philip G. Chase

University of Pennsylvania Museum of Archaeology
and Anthropology

André Debénath

University of Perpignan Via Domitia

Harold L. Dibble

University of Pennsylvania

Shannon P. McPherron

Max Planck Institute for Evolutionary Anthropology

CAMBRIDGE
UNIVERSITY PRESS

CAMBRIDGE UNIVERSITY PRESS
Cambridge, New York, Melbourne, Madrid, Cape Town, Singapore, São Paulo, Delhi

Cambridge University Press
32 Avenue of the Americas, New York, NY 10013-2473, USA

www.cambridge.org
Information on this title: www.cambridge.org/9780521898447

First published 2009

Printed in the United States of America

A catalog record for this publication is available from the British Library

Library of Congress Cataloging in Publication data

The cave of Fontéchevade : recent excavations and their paleoanthropological
implications / edited by Philip G. Chase . . . [et al.].
    p. cm.
Includes bibliographical references and index.
ISBN 978-0-521-89844-7 (hardback)
1. Fontéchevade Cave (France)   2. Antiquities, Prehistoric – France – Fontéchevade
Cave.   3. Stone age – France – Fontéchevade Cave.   4. Human remains
(Archaeology) – France – Fontéchevade Cave.   5. Tools, Prehistoric – France –
Fontéchevade Cave.   6. Excavations (Archaeology) – France – Fontéchevade
Cave.   7. France – Antiquities.   I. Chase, Philip G.
GN776.22.F65C38   2008
936.4–dc22   2008005649

ISBN 978-0-521-89844-7 hardback

To the memory of Antoine Debénath

Contents

Foreword

Anta Montet-White

In 1994, the authors of this book undertook new excavations at the Cave of Fontéchevade, a site best known for its human remains and the uncommon artifact assemblages recovered by Germaine Henri-Martin in the 1950s. Henri Vallois attributed the skull fragments to an early form of *Homo sapiens,* which he designated as presapiens, and the artifact assemblages associated with them were labeled "Tayacian" by Henri Breuil, who had also confirmed the relatively early (interglacial) date based on faunal association. Henri-Martin's interpretation of the cave as a campsite marked by the presence of large hearths was supported by observations and arguments in line with accepted views of her time. However, progress in recovery and analytical techniques and changes in perspectives and theories lead present-day researchers to challenge earlier findings and sometimes overturn the interpretations proposed by previous generations of archaeologists. The latest work at Fontéchevade is a vivid illustration of this process.

Discovered at the end of the nineteenth century, the cave was first excavated in the years before World War I, and although visited occasionally by professional archaeologists, it was abandoned to looters for some 20 years before becoming Germaine Henri-Martin's research focus in 1937. She worked at the site off and on until 1955. The site was then considered closed until the new team, whose results are described in this monograph, decided to undertake a new series of investigations. In short, there have been three distinct episodes of active fieldwork at Fontéchevade, each one reflecting the resources, technical capabilities, and concerns of its time.

Before World War I, the field of Paleolithic archaeology in France was dominated by a small number of professionals, but it also welcomed a large number of amateurs, as the many discoveries of the late 1800s and the archaeological exhibits presented at world's fairs had excited considerable public interest. Centers of systematic research began to develop in several regions. Peyrony, Breuil, and Capitan focused on the Périgord and the Pyrenees. The Charente received recognition thanks to the work at La Quina of Germaine's father, Léon Henri-Martin (who was born Henri Martin but changed his name to Henri-Martin). Regional and national *sociétés savantes* published the latest findings, which were presented at regular meetings. The pioneer work of Breuil and Peyrony focused primarily on the temporal ordering of cultural stages defined by specific assemblages of bone or stone artifacts. Their writings remain the best testimony of research at the time.

At the same time, geologists, other natural scientists, and educated amateurs, among whom were medical doctors, teachers, and priests, surveyed and collected artifacts and often engaged in the excavation of cave sites. There was little control or restriction, other than securing the permission of the landowners. The collected artifacts were considered the property of the excavators and/or the landowners, and private collections multiplied. The sites were often excavated rapidly and completely, the objective being to procure collectible items, while other bone and stone artifacts were discarded. For example, the Saint-Périers, amateur archaeologists with a great deal of field experience, dug a trench through the Fontéchevade Cave in one day; they then abandoned the site, which they judged to be without interest. Artifact assemblages were sometimes sold but often ended up in small museums with little or no provenance or context information. Some researchers presented summaries to local or regional *sociétés savantes*, but there again the proportion of published results was small indeed. Few followed the example of a Denis Peyrony.

Durousseau-Dugouthier did extensive work in the Fontéchevade Cave between 1902 and 1910, collecting series of artifacts and bone, but he kept no notes. Vallade, who followed in 1913 and 1914, did keep some records, but his concern seems to have been to identify cultural layers on the basis of index fossils. He was content to bring some support to the classification and ordering of Paleolithic manifestation proposed by Breuil. Between them, Durousseau and Vallade emptied the cave of all visible layers that contained Mousterian and Early Upper Paleolithic assemblages.

Gemaine Henri-Martin's work was of a very different nature. She was a musician by vocation who came to Paleolithic archaeology somewhat reluctantly to maintain the research lab founded by her father at Le Peyrat and to continue the work he had engaged in the region; it was from him that she received most of her training. She maintained contacts with professionals in a determined effort to keep up with progress in the field. She sought the advice and collaboration of other researchers, most noticeably that of Henri Breuil, who was the recognized authority in the field. He was the one to whom she turned to corroborate her interpretation of the lowermost material, recovered under the Mousterian. She was quick to consult Henri Vallois for the analysis of the human remains.

Working in what was decidedly a man's world, she sought continued support and frequent and regular exchange of ideas with women who were active in the field. Among her closest friends were Suzanne de Saint-Mathurin, an erudite amateur archaeologist who discovered the sculptured friezes at Angles sur l'Anglin, and Dorothy Garrod, a professional noted more especially for her work at Tabun (Israel) and Bacho Kiro (Bulgaria). Garrod spent a considerable amount of time at Le Peyrat making use of the comparative collections stored in Henri-Martin's laboratory. Henriette Alimen inspired much of the research done on site formation and sediment analysis that became a major section of Henri-Martin's published report.

In her introduction to that report, Henri-Martin (1957) acknowledges the financial support that she received from state organizations. Compared to modern project budgets, the sums she had at her disposal were minimal, being only enough to compensate one, sometimes two, laborers for a few weeks and to purchase essential equipment or provide protection to the site. She had no crew, working by herself except for the occasional help of neighbors and students. She worked at sites located near her house, as a bicycle was her only mode of transport. Similar situations prevailed at most of the sites I visited in the early and mid-1950s, including Combe Grenal, where Bordes was working, and even more so at Caminade, where Denise de Sonneville-Bordes was excavating. The field school at Arcy-sur-Cure was something of an exception, as it had a relatively large crew of student volunteers. It is perhaps worth mentioning that, in spite of very limited resources, F. Bordes and A. Leori-Gourhan, each in his own way, managed to reinvent excavation methods, developing and enforcing standards that were to transform the field. By the late 1950s, the situation had evolved, and some projects at least enjoyed financial support that enabled them to accommodate larger teams of students. However, Henri-Martin's excavations had closed by then.

Her excavation techniques were much improved compared to those of her predecessors at the site. Yet she did not keep up with the dramatic changes introduced by the new generation of professional archaeologists who transformed the field in the late 1940s and early 1950s. She was cognizant of the changes in excavation and recovery techniques but continued to practice methods learned in the 1930s. She discussed grid systems, the use of Cartesian coordinates to locate artifacts in situ, and other related topics with her friends and with students she encountered. She did divide the site into sectors, and eventually, in an effort to follow the new guidelines, she established a grid. Yet, she recorded exact coordinates only in the case of unusually important items. Her concern was to identify and follow natural stratigraphy, but she was most comfortable working on a slant rather than a vertical exposure. She kept careful notes of daily progress, but provenance information was limited to unit and level. She did, however, under Alimen's influence, engage the collaboration of many specialists who provided sediment analyses that were then up to date. And to her credit, she completed and published a detailed report of her work.

The work of Chase, Debénath, Dibble, and McPherron belongs to a completely different era. The project, conducted in the 1990s, almost 50 years after that of Henri-Martin, was well funded and well staffed, as modern projects tend to be. The excavation methods they introduced or developed are at the cutting edge of recovery techniques. More important perhaps, the problem orientation and the whole theoretical framework within which their archaeological fieldwork operates have been completely transformed. They started out questioning every conclusion proposed by Henri-Martin: What part did natural processes play in the formation of the site of Fontéchevade? Are the chipped stones human-made? Is the Tayacian a real variant of the early Middle Paleolithic? Are the proposed dates and interpretations acceptable?

Henri-Martin's interpretations may or may not withstand the test imposed by modern archaeology. However, one should remember that the work she accomplished was a step in the development of our understanding of prehistory, and when viewed in the context of its time, her well-published contribution remains significant. And as the field is alive and well, current views may not, in turn, resist the scrutiny of future generations of archaeologists.

Acknowledgments

We thank the National Science Foundation and the University of Pennsylvania Museum of Archaeology and Anthropology for funding of the Fontéchevade excavations. The Leakey Foundation funded the radiometric dating. (We thank Don Dana for his continued support.) M. Perrin and the staff of the Musée d'Archéologie Nationale, Saint-Germain-en-Laye, provided invaluable assistance and access to the material excavated by Germaine Henri-Martin.

We are grateful to all of the residents of the village of Orgedeuil for their generous hospitality, especially M. and Mme. A. Buffet, the owners of the site, not only for permission to excavate there but also for their interest and assistance.

Finally, we thank all the students and volunteers, without whose hard work the excavations would never have taken place. Thanks also to Dr. Galina Sorokina and Brad Evans for their drawings.

List of Authors and Contributors

AUTHORS

Philip G. Chase
University of Pennsylvania Museum of Archaeology and
Anthropology, Philadelphia, Pennsylvania, United States.
Email: pchase@sas.upenn.edu

André Debénath
Université de Perpignan, Via Domitia, Perpignan
(Pyrénées-Orientales), France, and Muséum National d'Histoire
Naturelle, Paris, France. Email: Adebenath2b@aol.com

Harold L. Dibble
Department of Anthropology, University of Pennsylvania,
Philadelphia, Pennsylvania, United States.
Email: hdibble@sas.upenn.edu

Shannon P. McPherron
Max Planck Institute for Evolutionary
Anthropology, Department of Human Evolution, Leipzig, Germany.
Email: mcpherron@eva.mpg.de

CONTRIBUTING SPECIALISTS

Laurent Chiotti
Département de Préhistoire du Muséum National D'histoire
Naturelle, Les Eyzies-de-Tayac (Dordogne), France.
Email: lchiotti@mnhn.fr

Brooks B. Ellwood
Department of Geology and Geophysics, Louisiana State University,
Baton Rouge, Louisiana, United States. Email: ellwood@lsu.edu

William R. Farrand
Department of Geological Sciences and Exhibit Museum of Natural
History, University of Michigan, Ann Arbor, Michigan, United
States. Email: wfarrand@umich.edu

Henry P. Schwarcz
School of Geography and Earth Sciences, McMaster University,
Hamilton, Ontario, Canada. Email: schwarcz@mcmaster.ca

Thomas W. Stafford, Jr.
Stafford Research Laboratories, Inc., Lafayette, Colorado, United
States. Email: twstafford@stafford-research.com

Virginie Teilhol
Direction Scientifique et Culturelle du Paléosite, Saint-Césaire,
France. Email: v.teilhol@paleosite.fr

Jean-François Tournepiche
Musée d'Angoulême, Angouléme (Charente), France, and
Université Bordeaux I, Talence (Gironde), France.
Email: jftbill@aol.com

PART I

INTRODUCTION, BACKGROUND, AND METHODOLOGY

Philip G. Chase
André Debénath
Harold L. Dibble
Shannon P. McPherron

1

Introduction and Background

INTRODUCTION

This monograph reports on excavations carried out in the Cave of Fontéchevade (Charente, France) in the Universities of Pennsylvania and Perpignan from 1994 through 1998. The site had been excavated sporadically since the late nineteenth century, but is best known from the work of Germaine Henri-Martin (1957) conducted from 1937 to 1954. In total, these earlier excavations uncovered a very small Châtelperronian assemblage, along with an Aurignacian and Mousterian, all of which overlay a deep set of beds with a Tayacian industry. Bronze Age burials and occupation beds were also uncovered near the back of the cave.

The site of Fontéchevade has figured prominently in the paleoanthropological literature for many years because of two principal discoveries made by Henri-Martin. The first was a portion of hominin frontal bone designated Fontéchevade I, which, because it lacked a supraorbital torus, appeared quite out of place for a specimen that was originally thought to date to the last interglacial. Taken together with Fontéchevade II, a partial calotte that displays a more archaic appearance, this specimen was used to argue for the existence of an independent presapiens line of more modern humans in Europe during the early Upper Pleistocene (Heberer 1951, 1955; Vallois 1958), an interpretation that conflicts with what is now known about the fossil record in France and the rest of Europe.

The second puzzle is the Tayacian, a rather enigmatic stone tool industry named after the village of Les-Eyzies-de-Tayac, which is near the site where the industry was first described (Bordes 1984).

However, the industry is best documented at Fontéchevade, which has become, though not the eponymous site, the de facto-type site of the industry. Like the hominin fragments, the Tayacian fits poorly with the rest of what is known about the lithic industries of the Lower and Middle Paleolithic of southwestern France. Given the nature of the industry, and the fact that it is often found in geological contexts that indicate considerable frost fracturing or sediment movement, the suspicion has gradually arisen that it is, in fact, less an industry than a product of taphonomic processes. As we report, that is the primary interpretation that results from the present research.

THE SITE AND ITS HISTORY

The site of Fontéchevade is located in the extreme eastern part of the Department of the Charente (Fig. 1.1) in the Commune of Montbron, immediately adjacent to the hamlet of Fontéchevade. Although the hamlet is located in the Commune of Orgedeuil, the cave itself is just beyond the commune boundary.

The north-facing cave (Fig. 1.2) opens onto the valley of a small unnamed tributary of the Tardoire. This stream is intermittent until it joins a spring about 100 m upstream from the cave. The Tardoire is a small river that eventually joins with the Bonnieure and flows into the Charente near the town of Mansle. Its valley contains several important Paleolithic sites. The small stream in whose valley Fontéchevade is located flows into the Tardoire opposite the site of Montgaudier (Bouvier, Cremades and Duport 1987; Debénath 1974; Debénath and Duport 1986; Duport 1969, 1976) less than 1.5 km from Fontéchevade. The caves of La Chaise (Debénath 1969, 1974, 1976; Schwarcz, Blackwell and Debénath 1983) are located only some 2 km down the valley from Montgaudier, about 2.7 km from Fontéchevade.

The external morphology of the cave is somewhat peculiar (Fig. 1.3). The overlying plateau forms a point jutting north into the valley, and it is at this point that the cave's mouth is located. The effect is that the sides of the cave are actually exposed to some extent. Since the initial formation of the cave, there has also been a gradual retreat of the dripline, which has left part of the lateral sides still standing outside of the mouth. Today, following Henri-Martin's excavation, which removed virtually all of the material outside of the dripline, one enters the cave initially within a kind of canyon and then proceeds ultimately to the cave itself.

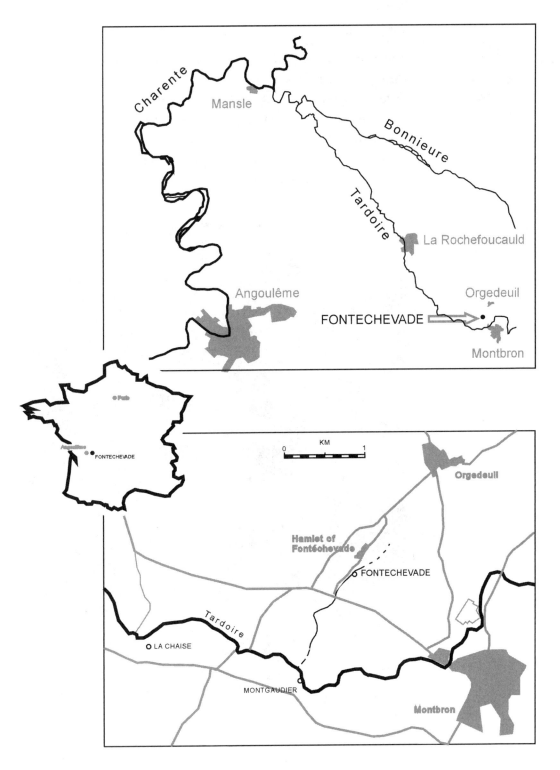

Figure 1.1
Map showing the location of Fontéchevade.

Early excavations

The history of early excavations at the site is known primarily through the writings of Henri-Martin (1957:21–23, 36–39), who collected information about those who had worked at the site before her. The first of these was apparently a teacher at the Collège de La Rochefoucauld named Plaire. His excavations were described by a later excavator, Vallade, in an unedited manuscript given to Henri-Martin (1957:21–22). According to this manuscript and the sketch

Figure 1.2
Photograph of the mouth of Fontéchevade Cave.

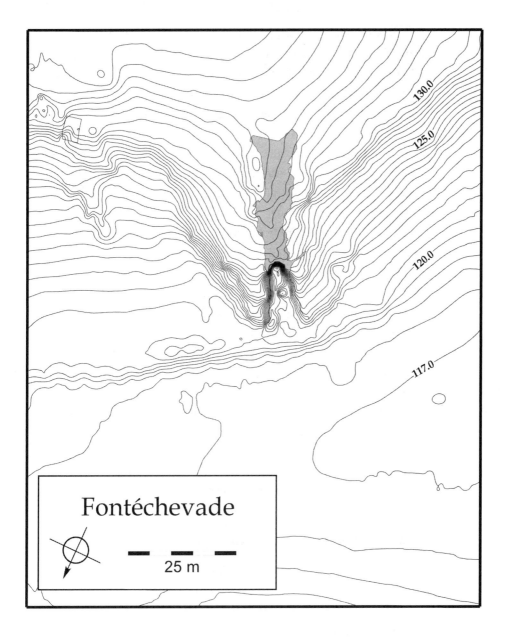

130.0

125.0

120.0

117.0

Fontéchevade

25 m

map of his excavations, Plaire excavated an area about 2 m in diameter directly in front of the dripline. The dates of his excavations are
unclear, but may have been as early as the 1870s.

Plaire was followed by L. Durousseau-Dugontier, who excavated
the interior of the cave in his spare time from 1902 to 1910. He found
pottery and Aurignacian and Châtelperronian industries. He also
found, according to Henri-Martin (1957:22), a human calotte and
"some other human debris." Eventually, the family of Durousseau-
Dugontier turned over his collections to Henri-Martin.

Figure 1.3
Topographic map of the
cave and its immediate
vicinity.

More systematic excavations were carried out by Vallade in 1913 and 1914 and reported in an unpublished manuscript given to Henri-Martin. He excavated from about 1 m inside the dripline outward and apparently located the excavations of both Plaire and Durousseau-Dugontier. His excavations were important because they produced the only conclusive evidence for the presence of Châtelperronian at the site (Henri-Martin 1957:209 and see Chapter 10). The great majority of the Châtelperronian artifacts recovered belong to his collections, which were given in part to the Museum of Angoulême and in part to a M. Lugol (Henri-Martin 1957:22), who lived near the town of Mansle (Charente). These collections were later studied by Henri-Martin herself. Vallade recognized three beds (Lower, Middle, and Upper) containing Châtelperronian, Aurignacian, and Gravettian, respectively. He also found a bed with unbroken animal bones marked by hyena teeth that Henri-Martin (1957:37) believed must have been a Mousterian bed.

Another pair of amateurs, M. and Mme. De Saint-Périer, spent a single day at the site in 1921, excavating a trench at the entrance to the site (Henri-Martin 1957:22). They recorded a stratigraphy that included a meter-thick Aurignacian "hearth." Henri-Martin attempted a correlation between their reported stratigraphy and her own (Henri-Martin 1957:37–38). Later, P. David, a prehistorian who had worked many sites in the area during the course of his career, put in another series of test pits (David 1933).

Excavations by Germaine Henri-Martin

Henri-Martin began excavations at Fontéchevade in 1937 and continued until 1954, but with interruptions during World War II. She first excavated a series of test pits, and then, in 1946, she began major systematic excavations, which destroyed all traces of earlier excavations in or at the entrance to the site (Figs. 1.4 and 1.5). Because the finds from most of her test pits were eventually included with those from the later full-scale excavations, she did not report on their contents separately. Briefly, Test Pit 1, which was 3 m² by 3.8 m deep (Henri-Martin 1957:56–57), was located in the field approximately 10 m in front of the cave and was apparently sterile. Test Pit 2 was located directly in front of the cave and consisted of a trench 3.5 m wide by 4 m long by slightly more than 2 m deep that cut into the talus in front of the cave. This trench today is covered

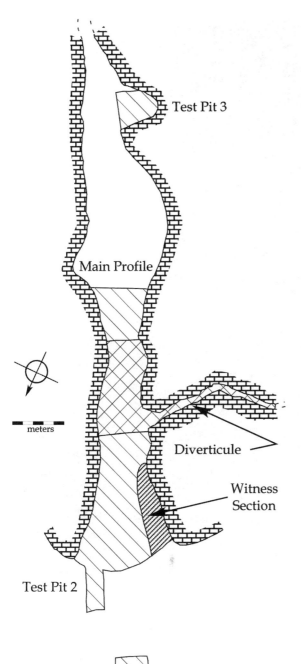

Test Pit 3

Main Profile

Diverticule

Witness
Section

Test Pit 2

Test Pit 1

Figure 1.4
Plan view of the interior
of the cave indicating
areas of the cave exca-
vated. (Redrawn from
Henri-Martin [1957]
fig. 7.)

by a tractor road that passes directly in front of the cave. It, too,
was apparently sterile (Henri-Martin 1957:57). Test Pit 4 was located
60 m east (upstream) from the cave, on the same slope into which
the cave penetrates. It measured 2 by 1.3 m in area and 1.6 m in
depth. This test pit does not appear on any of her maps or plans, but

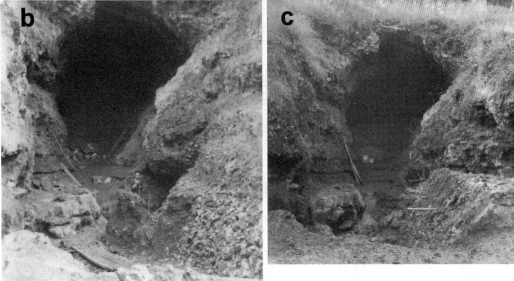

it produced a tooth of a small horse and an "atypical" worked flint (Henri-Martin 1957:59). Test Pit 5 was located upslope from Test 4, at the base of a small "microcliff" formed by a bedrock outcropping. It was of the same dimensions as Test 4 and was archaeologically sterile (Henri-Martin 1957:59–60).

Test Pit 3 (referred to simply as the "Test Pit" in this report) is the only one that remains, having been placed approximately 25 m behind the dripline, west of the midline of the cave, behind a small pillar. It was approximately 3.5 by 4.0 m in area and 3 m deep, although, in keeping with Henri-Martin's policy of not leaving

Table 1.1. Stratigraphy of Henri-Martin's Test Pit 3

AB	An upper bed, 0.3 m thick, disturbed by burrows, with a mixture of pottery and Aurignacian lithics. In her profile of the Test Pit (Henri-Martin 1957:58, fig. 12), she designated this as Bed AB, which is consistent with her designation of beds throughout the cave. Because she excavated to the bottom of AB throughout the cave, the Test Pit in fact begins at the base of this bed, and at this point AB is continuous with deposits in the rest of the cave.
C1	A bed approximately 0.6 m thick from which she recovered a Mousterian industry and rare faunal remains. This was underlain by a thin stalagmitic floor.
C2	A sandy horizon from which she recovered a few "atypical" flakes and the highly fossilized bones of aurochs, horse, and hyena.
D	A bed 0.75 m in thickness consisting of uncemented blocks. In the upper portion, the spaces between the blocks were filled with sand from the overlying bed.
E	A bed with Tayacian industry but no diagnostic fauna.

vertical cuts, the pit became narrower as it descended. She describes six beds in Test Pit 3. Her designations of the beds are taken from her profile drawing of the pit (Fig. 1.6 and Table 1.1).

Her primary excavations of the cave began approximately 18.5 m in front of the dripline and extended more than 20 m into the cave, leaving a sloped section that is referred to in this report as the "Main Profile" (Fig. 1.7). Laterally, she removed all sediment between the cave walls everywhere she excavated, except for a small area approximately 1–2 m wide and 5 m in length just in front of the dripline, which she referred to as a "Témoin" (called the "Witness Section" in the present report). However, the depth of excavations varied. She reached bedrock from about 1 m in front of the dripline to about 3 m behind it. From about 4 to 5 m behind the dripline, she left a sloping

Figure 1.6
Henri-Martin's drawing of her Test Pit 3. (Redrawn from Henri-Martin [1957] fig. 12.)

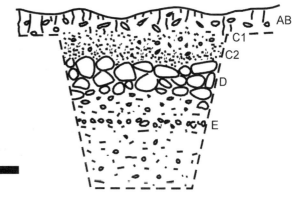

AB	BACKDIRT
C1	MOUSTERIAN
C2	MOUSTERIAN OF ACHEULIAN TRADITION
D	ROOF FALL
E	TAYACIAN

5 m

Figure 1.7
Photograph of the
Main Profile within the
cave following Henri-
Martin's excavations.
(From Henri-Martin
[1957], plate III. Used by
permission of Elsevier
Masson.)

profile some 2.5 m in height. In front of this profile, she removed all
the upper beds and all or most of the Tayacian. Behind this profile,
she removed less than 2 m of sediments (Fig. 1.8).

From the upper beds (A-AB; Table 1.2), Henri-Martin recovered ceramics that Riquet (Henri-Martin 1957:282–285) interpreted as
probably dating to the late Bronze Age or Hallstatt I. In 1965, Henri-
Martin planned to extend her Test Pit 3 near the back of the cave,
but the discovery of a bracelet and bones in a burrow stopped the
project. R. Joussaume then undertook excavations in the southwest
corner of the accessible part of the cave, west of the Test Pit (Joussaume et al. 1975). These revealed disturbed burials of three individuals (see Chapter 6) intruding into a "Mousterian bed" (Joussaume
et al. 1975:61) between two stalagmitic formations. Also recovered
were six undiagnostic fragments of pottery, as well as one complete
and one fragmented bracelet and a fragment of rod, all of bronze,
which Joussaume et al. (1975:66) dated to the late Middle Bronze
Age or early Final Bronze Age. Henri-Martin herself (1957:68) raised
the possibility that fragments of human bones from the upper beds
of the cave – a metatarsal from a disturbed Mousterian context excavated by her, a child's mandible and isolated molar excavated by

Durousseau-Dugontier, and a fragment of radius excavated by David and attributed by him to the Aurignacian – might therefore date to the Bronze Age.

Henri-Martin found only two small remnants of Bed B against the west wall of the cave (1957:33–39). These remnants were each about 0.5 m wide and 2.0 to 2.5 m long, averaging 0.6 m thick, and they had been truncated by earlier excavations. In contrast, the sandy Bed C1, which contained a "Mousterian with points," was found over the entire area excavated by her. On the slope in front of the cave, this bed was somewhat out of place, but elsewhere Henri-Martin considered it undisturbed. She reported a "very poor glacial fauna, including reindeer" in this bed (Henri-Martin 1957:40). Vallade found wooly rhinoceros ("*Rhinoceros ticorhinus*") in what she believes to have been this bed (Henri-Martin 1957:41).

Bed C2 (Henri-Martin 1957:41–43) was found inside the current dripline of the cave. Outside of the dripline, it was found brecciated along the walls, and it eventually became sterile and graded into Bed C1. At its base, on top of the underlying roof-fall, she found a poor and unevenly distributed Mousterian with points, along with an equally poor fauna that included horse, aurochs, and hyena. Because these faunas have not been published, it is not clear what basis was used to assign the bovines to *Bos* rather than to *Bison*.

The most striking component of this stratigraphy was the mass of largely brecciated roof-fall, Bed D (Henri-Martin 1957:43–46). It would appear that Henri-Martin removed all of this bed, for no remnants of it exist today. The bed was sterile, except on the slope in front of the cave. Here, the breccia was "dislocated," sand from Bed C1 had worked its way into the interstices, and Henri-Martin found some artifacts and bones (Henri-Martin 1957:44). For Henri-Martin, Bed D represented an important chronological break in the deposition of the site, which she correlated to a deterioration of climate marked by the beginning of the Würm glaciation. This meant that the underlying deposits pre-dated this event and so were considered to be of Riss-Würm Interglacial age and therefore much older than other Middle Paleolithic deposits.

These underlying sediments were lumped into a single homogeneous unit, Bed E, which was arbitrarily subdivided into Beds E0, E1, and E2, with further arbitrary subdivisions within the latter two designated as E1′, E1″, E2′, E2″, and E2‴. E1′ (and E0) were 0.5 m thick; all the others, 1.0 m thick (Henri-Martin 1957:31, note 6). The

Table 1.2. Henri-Martin's stratigraphic designations for her main excavations

A-AB	Humus and disturbed beds with mixed industries and pottery fragments
B	Middle Aurignacian
BS	Horizon of small cemented blocks
C1	Mousterian with points
C2	Mousterian with bifaces
D	A sterile bed of blocks (roof-fall), in large part cemented
E0	Upper beds of the Tayacian
EI	Upper beds of the Tayacian
EI'	Upper beds of the Tayacian
E1"	Upper beds of the Tayacian
Cave Bear Horizon	
E2	Lower beds of the Tayacian
E2'	Lower beds of the Tayacian
E2"	Lower beds of the Tayacian
E2'''	Lower beds of the Tayacian

only natural break noted in this deep set of deposits was what she referred to as the Cave Bear Horizon, which served to divide Bed E into an upper (E0 and E1) and lower (E2) series of beds. Although, in her opinion, the entirety of Bed E (up to 7 m thick) was remarkably uniform, she did admit the existence of local variations, and she described some of the differences among them (Henri-Martin 1957:50–51, 54–55). The Cave Bear Horizon was a somewhat heterogeneous layer that included intercalated brecciated silt and sand. It was truncated in front of the cave by the slope and pinched out or graded into the rest of E some 4 m inside the present dripline. The fauna of this bed was the same as the rest of E, except for a larger frequency of cave bear bones. These bones were unbutchered, but she reported that some were burned (Henri-Martin 1957:52–53).

Less than 2 m inside the present-day dripline, there is an entrance to a small passageway that leads from the main cave in a generally westward direction. She excavated approximately 13 m of this "Diverticule," which proved to be sterile. However, where it branched off from the main cave, at a depth between 5.5 and 6.0 m, she recovered numerous bones that showed no trace of displacement (Henri-Martin 1957:55–56).

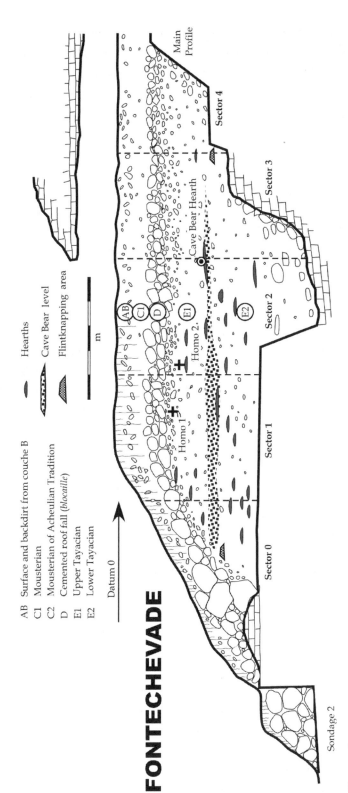

FONTECHEVADE

AB Surface and backdirt from couche B
C1 Mousterian
C2 Mousterian of Acheulian Tradition
D Cemented roof fall (*blocaille*)
E1 Upper Tayacian
E2 Lower Tayacian

— Hearths
▨ Cave Bear level
▨ Flintknapping area

— m

Datum 0

AB C1 D E1 E2

Homo 1
Homo 2.
Cave Bear Hearth
Main Profile

Sector 0 Sector 1 Sector 2 Sector 3 Sector 4

Sondage 2

Figure 1.8
Longitudinal section of Fontéchevade showing the extent of Henri-Martin's excavations and the locations of Fontéchevade I and Fontéchevade II. (Redrawn from Henri-Martin [1957].)

THE PLEISTOCENE HUMAN REMAINS FROM FONTÉCHEVADE

Two important discoveries of Pleistocene hominid remains, generally referred to as Fontéchevade I and II, were made at the site in 1947. Fontéchevade I was discovered in the laboratory in a block of breccia. The block came from a depth of 2.4 to 2.6 m below her datum, which put it in Bed E0 (Vallois 1958:7). Fontéchevade II was found in place some 2 m farther toward the mouth of the cave and slightly lower down, in Bed E1″.

Fontéchevade I (see Fig. 6.3 in this book) consists of a fragment of frontal that includes glabella, the medial portion of the left superciliary arch, and a small part of the squamous portion above these. What is remarkable about this piece, given its presumed age, is the complete absence of a frontal torus. This, as well as the thinness of the squamous portion, gives it a very modern appearance. Fontéchevade II (see Fig. 6.5 in this book) consists of the upper part of the frontal bone and portions of the left and right parietals and is much more consistent with what is known about Neanderthal cranial variation.

Vallois's is the most thorough study of these specimens to date (Vallois 1949, 1958). His analysis in effect set the agenda for the ensuing controversy in two ways. First, he assumed that the two specimens, Fontéchevade I and Fontéchevade II, represented the same biological/taxonomic population (although they clearly came from two different individuals). Second, in his interpretation of the morphology and taxonomic status of "Fontéchevade man," he placed these specimens on a presapiens lineage that included both the Swanscombe calotte and anatomically modern Upper Paleolithic and present-day humans. Given that the presumed age of the deposits in which they were found put them chronologically earlier than other Neanderthal finds, he considered that this lineage must have evolved alongside but separately from Neanderthals.

Vallois's presapiens interpretation of the Fontéchevade remains generated a great deal of debate and discussion during the mid-twentieth century. Although Heberer (1951) accepted a presapiens interpretation, Howell (1951, 1957, 1958) objected to it on several grounds, including his assessment that only Fontéchevade I suggested a modern affiliation, and he questioned whether both were truly contemporary. At about the same time, Drennan (1956) also cited some of the same similarities between Fontéchevade and Neanderthals that Vallois had noted, suggesting that the Fontéchevade specimens represented a pedomorphic variant of Neanderthals, an interpretation that was developed further for Fontéchevade I by

Trinkaus (1973). Several others – Brace (1964), Weiner and Campbell (1964), and Corruccini (1975) – also questioned the modern aspects of Fontéchevade II, interpreting it instead as falling within the variation of Neanderthals (see Chapter 6 for a more complete discussion).

Thus, after considerable debate, most authors consider that Fontéchevade II can be comfortably assigned to a Neanderthal taxon. There are two other possibilities for Fontéchevade I, however. One is that it is a juvenile Neanderthal who died at an age before the development of the supraorbital torus. The second is that this particular individual dates to a more recent time and is, therefore, actually a fully modern *H. sapiens*. Given the fragmentary nature of the specimen, it would be difficult to determine which of these interpretations is correct based on morphology alone, and the application of fluorine tests by Oakley and Hoskins (1951) as a means of correlating the two specimens is far from conclusive. New absolute dates from faunal specimens found stratigraphically close to this specimen suggest, however, that it is more recent than had been assumed (see Chapter 7 and Chase et al. 2007).

THE TAYACIAN

Although the Tayacian was first recognized at the site of La Micoque, Henri-Martin's excavations at Fontéchevade yielded an even larger assemblage of this type, and ultimately Fontéchevade became the reference site for this industry. In spite of a relatively long history of research, with numerous examples found in other sites throughout Europe, North Africa, and the Levant, the Tayacian is not without controversy.

As recounted by Bordes (1984:57), the naming of the Tayacian came about with little fanfare. After the excavations at La Micoque by Hauser before World War I, Peyrony went back to the site in 1929 and discovered a series of beds that underlay the so-called Micoquian horizons (Peyrony 1938). In these layers were some assemblages that generally lacked the kind of refined bifaces that had come from Hauser's excavations; they consisted instead of large flakes and rough flake tools. Being a bit undecided as to what to call this industry, Peyrony took the advice of the Abbé Breuil, who happened to pass by the site for a visit on his way to the nearby village of Les-Eyzies-de-Tayac and who suggested naming it for that village.

At the time, the problem faced by Peyrony was that it was difficult to deal with a non-handaxe industry that preceded the Mousterian. In the previous century, de Mortillet (1869, 1883) established a unilineal scheme for the Paleolithic based on the kinds of artifacts represented rather than on paleontological grounds alone (Lartet 1861; Lartet and Christy 1865–1875). De Mortillet's sequence began with the Chellean and Acheulian, which contained bifaces; followed by the "Epoch of Le Moustier," or the Mousterian, which was a more flake-based industry; and subsequently the Solutrean and Magdalenian, which had more sophisticated lithic assemblages and bone tools. Later, Commont (1910, 1913) continued the refinement of the unilineal ordering of the Paleolithic based on his work in the Somme Valley in northern France.

It was Breuil (1932; Breuil and Lantier 1959) who proposed the existence of two major contemporaneous Lower Paleolithic phyla, the Clactonian (composed of flake tools made on unprepared blanks with large, unfaceted platforms) and the Acheulian (which contained significant percentages of bifaces of various types). By isolating two independent "phyla" in the Lower Paleolithic, it was thus possible to have non-biface industries preceding the Mousterian, and for Breuil, the Tayacian was then just one variant of a number of "Pre-Mousterian" industries.

In the extreme paleontological perspective that was prevalent in archaeology at the time, the Tayacian was thus seen as a direct descendant of the Clactonian, and it preceded, chronologically, the Micoquian. The linkage to the Clactonian was based on the fact that the Tayacian had similar sorts of large, wide flakes, but there were also more evolved aspects to the Tayacian in that it exhibited a higher degree of platform faceting and less pronounced bulbs of percussion. In turn, the Tayacian was seen to have eventually evolved into the Levalloisian, which still later merged with the Acheulian to produce the "Cave Mousterian."

Thus, for Breuil, the Tayacian was a flake industry without handaxes, with some degree of platform preparation, but lacking the degree of core preparation that would enable it to be called Levallois. It dated to a time before the final Acheulian and exhibited a style of flaking reminiscent of the Clactonian (Breuil 1932).

In subsequent years, the Tayacian seemed to appear everywhere. In the Levant, Garrod (Garrod and Bate 1937:89–90) noted the presence of the Tayacian in the lowest level of Tabun, Neuville (1951; see also Perrot 1968) described it in the sequence at Oumm Qatafa, and Solecki (1968) described it at the site of Yabrud. In North Africa, it was found at the sites of Bahsas (Howell 1959) and Sidi Abderamman

(Biberson 1961; Neuville 1951). In Central Europe, the Tayacian was found in the Kulna Cave in the Moravia province of the Czech Republic (Valoch 1968). In France, a number of assemblages were attributed to this industry, including the lower levels of Combe-Capelle Bas (Fitte 1948), Baume-Bonne (Lumley 1960), and Mas des Caves (Le Grand 1994), just to name a few. Although most published references to Tayacian are historical, the term is still used today (e.g., Abbazzi et al. 2000).

As noted by many authors of the 1940s and 1950s, there was an early controversy as to the homogeneity of the Tayacian. Fitte (1948), for example, suggested that there was one facies that was focused on the production of large flakes (seen in the basal levels of Combe-Capelle Bas [cf. Dibble 1995]) and another facies of small, thick, and irregular flakes (apparent at La Micoque and La Ferrassie, for example). Others (e.g., Bourgon 1957) started referring more to the typology of early industries in assigning them to the Tayacian, emphasizing the production of notches, denticulates, so-called Tayac points (convergent denticulates), and pieces with abrupt and alternating retouch. After some time, as more and more assemblages were found and named Tayacian, the heterogeneity of this industry became such that it was effectively in "a state of classificatory limbo" (Bordes and Bourgon 1951; but see also Peyrony 1950; Rolland 1986:124). The situation grew even worse as several new names appeared in the literature that more or less described the same phenomenon: Howell (1959) suggested the name "Tabunian" for the examples from North Africa and the Levant; Solecki (1968) named the Tayacian-like assemblages from Yabrud the Shamshi industry. The material from Combe-Capelle Bas, now dated to between 50 and 60 kyr (Valladas et al. 2003), is likewise now seen as a lightly reduced variant of what is known, on technological grounds, as the Quina Mousterian (Dibble and Lenoir 1995).

Not everyone was convinced, however, that the Tayacian reflected only human modification. Bordes himself (1953, 1984; Bordes and Bourgon 1951) believed that at least some of the typological nature of the industry, especially the abrupt and alternating retouch, was a result of post-depositional processes that damaged the material. Indeed, at many of the sites mentioned previously, layers that exhibited such assemblages were also shown to be geologically disturbed. Bordes (1953; Bordes and Bourgon 1951:17) also showed by experimental trampling (cf. McBrearty et al. 1998) that it was very easy to produce such "tools" naturally. In fact, one of the categories of "tools" organized by Germaine Henri-Martin and stored presently in the Musée d'Archéologie Nationale (formerly the Musée National des Antiquités) at Saint-Germain-en-Laye, was labeled by Bordes as "podoliths."

To a large extent, one of the problems of the "Pre-Mousterian" in general and the Tayacian in particular, namely their early age, has largely been done away with because recent work has radically altered notions regarding the chronology of the Middle Paleolithic. Traditionally, the Mousterian was thought to date from only the early part of the last glacial, with some occurrences of earlier last Interglacial industries termed "Pre-Mousterian" (Bordes 1947, 1952; Laville et al. 1980). The revised chronology, based on correlations of marine and terrestrial sequences (Laville 1988; Laville et al. 1983; Wolliard 1978), now suggests that the date of the onset of the Würm (OIS 5d) is 115 kyr, extending the duration of the Würmian industries by as much as 50 percent. Moreover, assemblages absolutely characteristic of the Middle Paleolithic are now known to date to OIS 8, or about 250 kyr (Clark 1988:239; Gilot 1984; Kolfschoten and Roebroeks 1985; Laville 1982; Schwarcz and Blackwell 1983; Tuffreau 1982; Tuffreau and Sommé 1988; Wendorf and Schild 1974), which eliminates any logical need for a separation between Mousterian and Pre-Mousterian. Nonetheless, the peculiarities of the assemblages demanded some sort of explanation.

HENRI-MARTIN'S INTERPRETATION OF THE USE OF THE CAVE DURING THE TAYACIAN

There are three classes of raw materials present in the Tayacian lithic assemblages: flint (occurring in very limited quantities), quartz (mostly in the form of cobbles, although some have flakes removed from them), and a very poor-quality local chert that erodes directly from the bedrock of the cave itself. The quartz cobbles and the flint came from elsewhere, though there are large numbers of quartz cobbles on the overlying plateau. Henri-Martin also reported a number of hearths (some of which contained cave bear bones) and localized flintknapping scatters.

The interpretation put forward by Henri-Martin was that hominins associated with the Tayacian entered the cave with some flint that they transported from elsewhere, along with quartz cobbles. They came to the site with the express intention of using the cobbles as hammerstones to exploit the chert eroding out of the cave itself. Thus, for her, Fontéchevade was, in effect, a locus of raw material exploitation, with most of the archaeological materials being manufactured on the site itself. Henri-Martin (1957:231–244) also believed that people lived in the cave year-round and carried out certain domestic chores there based on the appearance of what she interpreted as hearths.

The problems of Fontéchevade

Henri-Martin's excavations produced two sets of data that fit rather uncomfortably with what is known from elsewhere about the Paleolithic and about human evolution in Europe in particular. First, Fontéchevade I, the very modern-looking frontal bone from the upper part of her Bed E, is out of place chronologically, if Bed E dates to the last interglacial (OIS 5e), as she believed. Based on its modern appearance, its early date, and its proximity to the more archaic calotte, Fontéchevade II, Vallois posited the existence of a presapiens line in Europe (Heberer 1951, 1955; Vallois 1958). However, this supposition is at odds with everything else that is known about the arrival of anatomically modern *Homo sapiens* in Europe. Second, Fontéchevade is the de facto type site of the Tayacian, an enigmatic stone tool industry that fits poorly with other known lithic industries in southwestern France during the Lower and Middle Paleolithic. Because of its nature and because it is frequently found in geological contexts indicative of either sediment movement, frost fracturing, or both, it is plausible to ask whether it is less an industry than a product of taphonomic processes (Dibble et al. 2006).

Both the archaeology and the hominid remains thus present problems that must be solved if we are to get an accurate picture of what really happened in terms of both lithic technology and human evolution in the Lower and Middle Paleolithic of France; the nature of both suggests that the answer to both puzzles may lie in the geological forces at work in the cave during and after the deposition of the archaeological and fossil remains, and in the interpretation of the stratigraphy and of the formation processes.

It is clear that many of the most important implications of Henri-Martin's excavations at Fontéchevade depend on her interpretation of the stratigraphy, of the nature and integrity of the deposits, and of the formation processes at the site. However, recent advances in archaeological methods demand that these interpretations be reexamined.

Since Henri-Martin completed her work at the site, methods of excavation and dating have undergone tremendous improvement. Moreover, systematic research into taphonomy and site-formation processes post-dates her excavations at Fontéchevade (Behrensmeyer and Hill 1980; Bonnichsen and Sorg 1989; Brain 1981, 1985; Dibble and Lenoir 1995; Dibble et al 1997; Efremov 1940; Fosse 1995; Giacobini 1990–1991; Hill 1978; Lyman 1987, 1994; Nash and Petraglia 1987; Potts 1988; Schick 1986; Shipman 1981; Sutcliffe 1970; Villa 1982). This means that the methods and tools available to archaeologists, geologists, and paleontologists today are far more sophisticated than those that were available to her. It also means that Henri-Martin, like most excavators of her time, was much less aware of potential problems that can affect archaeological sites and their deposits than archaeologists are today. As a result, she rarely documented the reasons for her interpretations in a way that makes it possible to evaluate them today. Consequently, certain key findings or interpretations may be open to question.

Stratigraphic and site-formation problems

First, there are essentially four ways to resolve the dilemma posed by Fontéchevade I:

1. The specimen is actually a Neanderthal, contemporary with Fontéchevade II.
2. Fontéchevade I is a presapiens, contemporary with Fontéchevade II.
3. Fontéchevade I was intrusive or out of stratigraphic context and was not actually contemporaneous with either Fontéchevade II or the Tayacian industry and interglacial fauna.
4. The upper part of Henri-Martin's Bed E is younger than has been believed, in which case both Fontéchevade I and Fontéchevade II are much younger than the last interglacial.

Researchers have investigated and debated the anatomy and taxonomic status of the Fontéchevade I and II specimens, but to date there has been much less investigation of the stratigraphic integrity of their context (cf. Oakley and Hoskins 1951). In addition, there have been no radiometric dates available for the beds of Fontéchevade from which they were recovered.

Second, Henri-Martin interpreted the site as primarily a long-term, year-round workshop for the exploitation of the low-quality chert from the cave walls. (This is true whether occupation was permanent or intermittent.) This construal depends on her interpretation of the Tayacian as a real industry, on her interpretation of the stone-working scatters, on her interpretation of the relative intensity of human versus carnivore contributions to the fauna found in the cave, and on her interpretations of various other phenomena, such as her belief that quartz cobbles were used as hammers and anvils to knap chert (Henri-Martin 1957:164).

In the years since Henri-Martin excavated at Fontéchevade, it has become clear that it is very easy for an excavator to misinterpret or over-interpret what is observed in the course of excavations (Chase and Dibble 1987; Dibble et al. 1997; Jéquier 1975; Leroi-Gourhan 1964). This is particularly true because we now realize that the effects of natural processes on the archaeological record are much greater than was understood during the time of her work. The only solution is to document in detail – at the time of excavation – the empirical grounds for one's interpretations. This was not, however, the custom in the decades when Fontéchevade was being excavated, and so it is difficult to know whether Henri-Martin's interpretations were valid based on the evidence that she published.

For example, her record of the stratigraphy is apparently not based on detailed measured drawings. Various profiles she provides differ in empirical detail but not in concept, so we must conclude that what she recorded was not what she saw in terms of changes of color, individual blocks of roof-fall, and the like, but rather her *interpretation* of what she saw. If one compares the profile published in her site report (Fig. 1.8) with profiles published elsewhere in 1951 and 1958 (Fig. 1.9), it is clear that the drawings are entirely schematic in nature. In addition, the hearths she recorded were not drawn based on measurements, and neither their locations nor even their number can be taken as raw data. Moreover, her stratigraphic profiles of the cave, both transversal and longitudinal, show a simplicity and uniformity over considerable depths and horizontal distances. Her two lower Tayacian Beds E1 and E2, respectively, spanned some 1.5 and 3.0 m vertically and some 20 and 23 m along the longitudinal axis of the cave. Although such a simplicity of stratigraphy is not impossible, it is not the norm for cave fill. Combined with the questions raised by the nature of her drawings, her stratigraphic profiles raise the possibility that modern excavation techniques might find

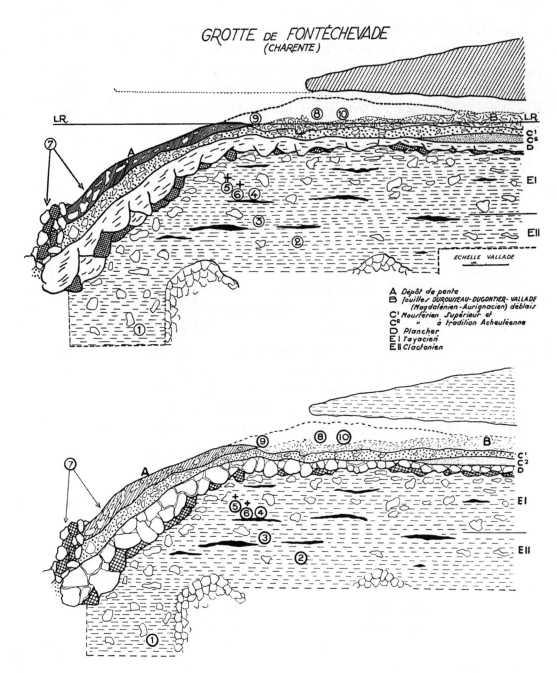

GROTTE DE FONTÉCHEVADE
(CHARENTE)

A Dépôt de pente
B fouilles DUROUSSEAU-DUGONTIER-VALLADE
   (Magdalénien-Aurignacien) déblais
C¹ Moustérien Supérieur et
C²   "   à tradition Acheuléenne
D Plancher
E I Tayacien
E II Clactonien

ECHELLE VALLADE

Figure 1.9
Stratigraphic drawings
of Henri-Martin's exca-
vations published in 1951
(top) and 1958 (bottom).
Compare with Figure 1.8.
(From Henri-Martin
[1951] and Vallois [1958],
fig. 1. Reproduced by
permission of Elsevier
Masson.)

the stratigraphy of the cave more complex than she appreciated. This
in turn implies that she may have been unaware of some of the depositional and other complications that could cast doubts on some of
her interpretations of the site.

In general, the same observations must be made about her horizontal plans of the locations of "hearths" and "knapping areas"
(Fig. 1.10). Although in the text she numbered the hearths and
knapping areas, there are no indications of such numbers in the

plans. Although she provided inventories of two of these hearths and a low-resolution photograph of another, she provided no measured drawings of the areas of sediment affected by heat or plots of the artifacts. Given that both worked and unworked chert were scattered throughout the sediments, documenting the existence of knapping areas would have required three steps: (1) plotting the material associated with a knapping area, (2) comparing it with the contents of the surrounding sediments, and (3) eliminating any natural cause for the accumulation of lithic material in this particular area. Because she provides no documentation of any of these steps, we are left with her interpretation of what she saw without the empirical data to support or refute it. The same is true of the uneven distribution of bones in the site, a phenomenon she interpreted as evidence for human activity rather than for carnivore accumulation.

THE 1994–1998 EXCAVATIONS

We decided to reopen the site for several reasons. The first was simply that so few details were known about the geological and chronological context of the assemblages and of the hominins excavated by Henri-Martin. For such an important site, it was imperative

Figure 1.10
Henri-Martin's plan drawings showing hearths and knapping areas. (Redrawn from Henri-Martin [1957].)

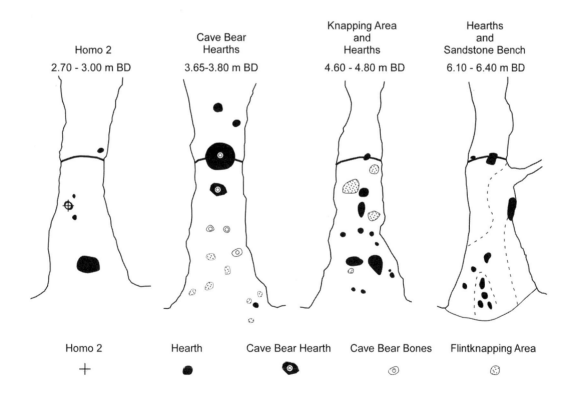

| Homo 2 | Hearth | Cave Bear Hearth | Cave Bear Bones | Flintknapping Area |

that these details be filled in so that its assemblages could be put into a modern framework. Second, as is the case with many sites excavated long ago, a number of questions had eventually arisen concerning the nature of the industries from Fontéchevade. Ever since the earliest definition of the Tayacian by Breuil (1932), there has been controversy about the industry, even to the point that some have suggested that it was the result of taphonomic rather than behavioral factors. Because Fontéchevade is one of the most important representatives of the Tayacian, particularly in terms of the size of the collection and the completeness of its publication, it was important to restudy the site with an eye toward site-formation processes in order to assess the impact such processes may have had on the creation of this industry.

In view of the site's importance to interpretations of both the European fossil record and the Tayacian industry, we designed the new research at Fontéchevade to accomplish the following goals:

- To evaluate the validity of Henri-Martin's stratigraphy and in general to evaluate the integrity of the deposits. Specifically, we wanted to evaluate the reliability of both chronological and behavioral inferences based on the stratigraphy of the site. Doing so involved investigating the sources of sediments in the cave and the means by which they were deposited.
- To evaluate the associations of lithics, fauna, and hominin remains. More specifically, we wanted to know to what extent human occupants of the site were responsible for the lithics and the faunal remains found there. We also wanted to test the integrity of those collections.
- To understand better the nature of the Tayacian, especially in reference to those characteristics that could be explained through taphonomic agencies.
- To apply modern dating techniques to the site, with particular emphasis on understanding the age and implications of the Fontéchevade I frontal bone.

In many ways, Fontéchevade was typical of archaeological sites excavated in the past. Although it was well excavated and indeed exceptionally well published by the standards of the time, the discipline has advanced enough in the intervening decades so that questions were raised that could not be answered on the basis of Henri-Martin's report. Because the implications of Fontéchevade in terms of our understanding of both human evolution and lithic industries are of greater importance than is the case for most sites, it was highly desirable to carry out new excavations there, on a smaller scale than those of Henri-Martin, with the purpose of answering some of those questions.

2

Introduction to the 1994–1998 Excavations

EXCAVATION METHODS

What follows is a description of the methods used in the current excavation of Fontéchevade and an overview of the work accomplished.
The methodology is based in part on French tradition for Paleolithic
excavations and in part on the methodologies that our team has
developed through the years at the sites of La Quina, Combe-Capelle
Bas, Cagny-l'Epinette, and Cagny-la-Garenne. Much of the methodology is based on the application of computerized recording techniques, which have been extensively described in previous publications (Dibble 1987b; Dibble et al. 1995; Dibble and McPherron 1989;
McPherron and Dibble 1987, 2002). Special emphasis was given to
standardizing the excavation techniques and recording methods at
Fontéchevade, both to optimize analysis of the site itself and to make
the data comparable with data collected at the previously listed sites.

The excavation grid

The site was excavated in 1-m units following the traditional French
system of labeling excavation units with a letter-number designation.
In this system, it is also traditional to place grid north directly into
the cave. We followed this tradition, despite the fact that true north is
almost exactly 180 degrees opposite. One of the principal advantages
of doing so is that all of our maps are thus oriented in relation to
the long axis of the cave, very much as we saw the cave each day.
The principal disadvantage to this system is that there can be some
confusion between, for instance, "west" and "grid west."

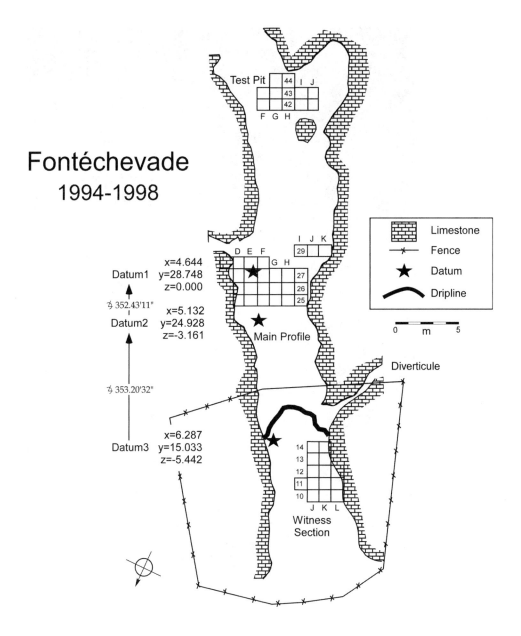

Fontéchevade
1994-1998

Test Pit

| 44 | I | J |
| 43 |
| 42 |

F G H

x=4.644
Datum1 y=28.748
z=0.000

352.43'11"

x=5.132
Datum2 y=24.928
z=-3.161

Main Profile

D E F
G H

I J K
29

27
26
25

353.20'32"

x=6.287
Datum3 y=15.033
z=-5.442

Diverticule

14
13
12
11
10

J K L

Witness
Section

| Limestone |
| Fence |
| Datum |
| Dripline |

0   m   5

Figure 2.1
Plan view of the cave,
showing excavation
grid, permanent datums
(with coordinates), and
horizontal reference
angles between them.

In the traditional French system, letters follow along the X axis and numbers follow along the Y axis. Thus, in our grid, squares along the Main Profile begin with C at the east (grid west) wall of the cave and progress to I at the grid east end of the profile (Fig. 2.1). In the Y axis, the Main Profile covers squares 26–29, moving into the excavation (grid north). The Witness Section in the front of the cave (Henri-Martin's "Témoin") covers squares 10–14, and the test excavations in the very back of the cave cover squares 42–44. Thus, square D26 necessarily refers to excavations on the Main Profile, F42

Figure 2.2
Topcon GTS-3B total
station connected to a
hand-held computer.

is a square in the back of the cave, and J12 is a square on the Witness
Section. In terms of the global coordinate system, the Y axis increases
toward grid north, the X axis increases toward grid east, and the Z
axis increases with height.

A number of datums were installed at the site for our own work,
though three remain as permanent site datums. These datums, as
well as all piece-provenience data discussed later, were recorded
using total stations with 5-second accuracy connected to handheld
computers running self-authored data collection software (Fig. 2.2).
Datum1 is a small bolt affixed to the cave ceiling, and Datum3 is a
nail sunk into a concrete block just outside the dripline. Datum2 is
a permanent pillar erected as a stand for the total station (Fig. 2.3).

Unfortunately, it was not possible to locate any datum points from Henri-Martin's excavation. In terms of X and Y, this is not surprising, but it was hoped that her Z elevation datum could be located so that it would be possible to correlate the new excavation depths with her published section drawings. That datum was not discovered, and so these correlations must be estimated. However, she did leave tagged wires along the cave walls indicating the boundaries between her beds (Fig. 2.4). Along with her published figures and text, these wires provided some help in making these estimates.

Point proveniencing

Piece proveniences were recorded with millimeter precision in the X, Y, and Z axes using the total station. The following kinds of objects were recorded:

- Any piece of flint or other allochthonous material (worked or unworked) more than 2.5 cm in one dimension

Figure 2.3
Datum2, which also served as a permanent stand for the total station. The coordinates of this datum correspond to the center of the metal platform on which the total station is installed.

Figure 2.4
Henri-Martin left wires
indicating the depths of
boundaries between her
beds.

- All retouched pieces, even those smaller than 2.5 cm
- Bones and bone fragments larger than 2.5 cm in one dimension
- Identifiable bones such as teeth or podials smaller than 2.5 cm
- Samples for dating or geological analysis
- Buckets of sediment (see next section)

Every point-provenienced object was assigned a unique identifier, based on a combination of the excavation unit and ID number or ID letter sequence. For artifacts and samples, the ID was a sequential ID number, which started at 1 in each unit and continued to be incremented from year to year until excavation of that unit came to an end. Thus, a typical UNIT-ID looks like D28–123, which would represent the 123rd object recorded from unit D28. For many other non-artifactual materials, the ID was a random five-character code (e.g., D28-XXHSX) generated by the computer program used for field recording. The random letters allowed us to give unique identifications to these points that did not interfere with the number sequence used for artifacts.

Objects that had a clear orientation were measured with two points, which gave not only the position of the piece relative to the site datum but also the orientation of the piece in three-dimensional space (McPherron 2005). In order to distinguish among multiple measurements of the same object, an additional number, SUFFIX, was

Table 2.1. Object codes and their meanings

Object Code	Meaning
ANTLER	Antler
BONE	Other faunal object
CERAMIC	Ceramic
CHARCOAL	Charcoal
COMPFLAKE	Complete flake
COMPTOOL	Complete tool
CORE	Core
COREFRAG	Core fragment
CORETOOL	Core tool (chopper, chopping-tool)
DATING SAMPLE	Possible dating sample
DISTFLAKE	Distal flake
DISTTOOL	Distal tool
FLAKE	Flake
FLINT NODULE	Unworked flint
HAMMERSTONE	Hammerstone
HUMAN	Human remain
JAW + TEETH	Faunal element consisting of a jaw or fragment of a jaw with teeth
LEVEL TOPO	Topographic point taken at base of level
MAG SUS SAMPLE	Magnetic susceptibility sample
MANGANESE	Manganese
MEDFLAKE	Medial flake fragment
MEDTOOL	Medial tool fragment
NEWID	New ID assigned to object
OTHER	Other
PHOTO	Point indicating photo target
PROXFLAKE	Proximal flake fragment
PROXTOOL	Proximal tool fragment
QUARTZ COBBLE	Other fragment of quartz
RECENT	Non-archaeological material
ROOT CAST	Root cast
SCREEN SAMPLE	"Bucket" shot
SEDIMENT SAMPLE	Sediment sample
SHATTER	Lithic shatter
TOOTH	Animal tooth or tooth fragment
TOPO	Topographic point
UNWORKED	Unworked flint material

appended to the object's UNIT-ID number. Suffix values began with 0 and were incremented. Thus, the UNIT-ID-SUFFIX combination represented the unique identifier for each measurement, while the UNIT-ID combination was unique for each object. Objects smaller than the minimum size for measurement were put in the bucket with the sediment and recovered during wet-screening.

In addition, as each point was recorded, a provisional Object Code (Table 2.1) was included, as well as the archaeological level from which the object was recovered, the name of the excavator, and the date. The object code assigned in the field was kept intentionally simple and then later expanded or corrected, as necessary, based on the analysis of the object.

The total stations were also used to make topographic maps, to define and locate excavation units, to record the boundaries between stratigraphic units, and so on. All of the same information listed in this section was recorded for these points.

Buckets as aggregated lots

All excavated sediment, as well as artifacts too small to be piece-provenienced, were placed into 7-liter buckets. Excavators were instructed to dig within an area regardless of unit boundaries, although the areas were usually limited to an extent of approximately 0.25 m². Once the bucket was filled or if a new level was begun, the bucket was ended, and the center of the area excavated was recorded with the total station. The bucket received a unique identification number (UNIT-ID) consisting of the unit at the center of the area excavated and a random letter code (e.g., D28-XXHSX), as described previously. The sediment was then wet-screened through 2-mm and 5-mm meshes into two fractions, and the artifactual material was bagged by material type (bone vs. stone) and by fraction with the UNIT-ID of the bucket.

This system was used in contrast to the traditional practice of bagging small finds by quarter meter square for two reasons. First, it facilitates excavation over an area because unit boundaries can be ignored. As artifacts are located, the total station automatically places them in the appropriate unit, and the data collection software assigns the next available ID number for that unit. Similarly, buckets are associated with the unit on which they are centered, even though the sediment they contain may come from several different units; all of this greatly simplifies the excavation process while at the same time retains the level of accuracy of the traditional methods. Second, using buckets of a specified, standard volume greatly simplifies a number of analytical calculations. For instance, it is very simple to calculate the volume of sediment from a layer by totaling the number of buckets. This in turn makes it quite easy to calculate artifact densities for a particular layer and to compare densities between layers. With the traditional system, in the case of sloping stratigraphic layers that may pinch out in one square or another, samples from a quarter square will not be of uniform volume. The same is true of squares along the cave wall or squares that include large limestone blocks.

The buckets also served as a single, aggregated unit for wet-screening. After screening, all objects of archaeological interest were removed and bagged under the UNIT-ID identifier associated with that bucket. In this way, the samples recovered from a bucket of sediment were also associated with the specific X, Y, and Z coordinates indicating the location from which they came. If artifacts that would normally have been assigned their own ID during excavation were found in the bucket, they were removed from the bucket sample and given a new, numeric ID number, and their coordinates were considered the same as the coordinates of the bucket. In these cases, the excavator field in the database was given a code of LAB, indicating that the position of these objects should be considered approximate.

The database and geographic information system

Data from the total station computer were transferred at the end of each day to a central computer and integrated with the rest of the site data in a single, relational database. The total station data themselves are stored in two related tables: CONTEXT and XYZ. The CONTEXT table contains only one entry for every recorded object and includes the kind of object or recorded point (Object Code), the date it was recorded, the associated level, and the initials or name of the excavator. The actual three-dimensional coordinates are stored in the related table XYZ, which contains one record for each measurement taken with the total station. The data are arranged this way because each object can have several points associated with it. As described previously, a counter in the field SUFFIX of the XYZ table distinguishes measured points for the same object. The CONTEXT and XYZ tables are related on the basis of two fields: UNIT and ID. The remaining tables in the database contain analysis and reference information.

One of the main tools used in the excavation of Fontéchevade was a geographic information system (GIS) to access and plot the relational database just described. In particular, the GIS helped maintain control over the stratigraphy and spatial integrity of the data day to day and year to year. For instance, at the end of each day, the points from that day were plotted and checked for provenience errors. There are primarily two sources of error. First, the total station can be improperly initialized or can lose its reference angle during the day. These errors, however, are typically caught very quickly because the total station data collector program compares the coordinates of each recorded point with the boundaries of open or valid excavation units. A loss of angle or an incorrect setup quickly results in points falling outside a valid excavation unit and thus alerts the operator to a problem.

The second source of error has to do with the poles on which prisms are mounted. Although we recorded most points with a "nail" prism (a small prism with a nail attached to it with a hose clamp), we used several poles of different heights because at times the view to the nail prism would be obstructed (Fig. 2.5). The height of this pole must be subtracted from the Z measurement (reflecting the location of the prism) to obtain the correct Z of the object located at the base of the pole. After each point is recorded, the total station operator must note which kind of pole was used. By far, the most common type of error we encountered in the provenience information occurred when the operator forgot to switch prism heights. Fortunately, by plotting the points after each day, these errors were easily identified and corrected. Had we waited until the end of the season, the outliers would have been much more difficult to identify.

The GIS was also essential for maintaining control over the stratigraphy. Though level designations were made on the basis of field observations as the excavation progressed, it was nevertheless necessary on many occasions to revise earlier stratigraphic distinctions and to correct the level designations in the CONTEXT table. These corrections were made entirely with the three-dimensional GIS. In addition, unless the stratigraphy was extremely clear when excavation resumed each year, the GIS was used to verify where stratigraphic units ended and where they were begun each year. Doing so ensured consistency from year to year.

Photographs

Photographs were taken with a film camera, and every one was numbered by year, roll, and shot (e.g., 1996, roll 3, shot 2). Paper records with information about each photo were kept for all rolls. To make it possible to locate in space photographs of stratigraphy, special photo targets were placed on a profile or on the floor of an excavation. Where possible, these targets were on the same plane

Figure 2.5
Excavator using a prism
mounted on a pole.

as the photograph and in diagonal corners of it. These photo targets were recorded with the total station, assigned an identification
number, and included in the database. The photographer recorded
the identification numbers of any targets appearing in the photograph on the photo sheet, along with the other information about the
photograph. Because the coordinates of each target are known, it is
possible to match each photograph to the excavation grid and to the
coordinates of level boundaries, samples, artifacts, and so on.

Samples

Sediment samples for sedimentological analysis, geophysical analysis, and dating were, in general, treated like artifacts; the coordinates of each were measured using the total station, and the sample was given an identification number (in the format of UNIT-ID, although the unit was not necessarily an actual excavation unit) and a field code identifying the purpose of the sample. The initials of the specialist for whom the sample was recorded were entered into the EXCAVATOR field. Magnetic susceptibility samples, which were taken using 1-cm^3 boxes in a continuous series with no gaps between them, were not shot in independently. Each received a unique identification number, but only the top and bottom of each series of samples were recorded with the total station; the coordinates of the rest were interpolated.

Bones needing consolidation

Whenever a consolidant, glue, or any other chemical was used on a bone or tooth, that information was recorded in the CHEMICALS table of the database. In the field, small tags with the identification number of the artifact and the product used were folded into the aluminum foil containing the artifact and were returned to the laboratory with it. Chemicals used in the laboratory were entered directly into the database.

Routine processing

As artifacts were excavated and their proveniences recorded, the computer connected to the total station printed a small paper tag that reproduced all of the information noted for that object. The excavator wrapped this tag in aluminum foil along with the artifact. The object was then transferred to the lab where it was washed, and the identifying number taken from the tag was written on the object with indelible ink (Fig. 2.6). In addition to identifying the object, the tag provided a backup in the event that the computerized data were lost before being transferred to the main database.

When a bucket was filled with sediments, it was wet-screened as a single lot through the two size fractions mentioned earlier. After drying, all of the lithic and faunal material were separated from the coarse fraction sediments and bagged with the UNIT-ID of the bucket.

Figure 2.6
Photo showing the let-
tering format used for
objects recovered during
the current excavation.

In addition, we recorded digital images of all excavated lithics.
These images are named with their UNIT and ID (e.g., D28–123) and
include a scale.

With the exception of digital photography, most of this routine
processing was performed in a temporary outdoor laboratory erected
next to the site (Fig. 2.7). The close proximity of the excavation and
lab facilitated communication between them.

Figure 2.7
The field lab where rou-
tine artifact processing
took place.

This section defines the observations taken of the lithic materials and explains how they were made. This information is important not only for understanding the results contained in this report but also for using the computerized data that are published independently. Each of these variables can be found in the computer data files, and the values defined here correspond to the values that will be found in them. Some of these observations were made on all of the excavated lithics, whereas others are relevant only to particular classes of material. Most of them adhere to standard lithic nomenclature used in Paleolithic research (see Bordes 1961; Debénath and Dibble 1994), though some clarifications are necessary. The same observations and measurements were taken for both the collection generated by the new excavation and the collection of Henri-Martin housed in the Musée d'Archéologie National in St. Germain-en-Laye.

Qualitative observations

Various qualitative observations were made on the lithics based on standardized menu options for each variable. All variables include a choice of "**N/A**," which essentially means that for whatever reason the observation could not be taken, and so these values should be treated as missing data. Variables or observations that were not relevant for particular pieces were left as blank in the database.

ALL LITHICS

The following observations were made of all lithics:

DATACLASS: This is the basic categorical observation. Flakes that exhibit no retouch are considered as **flakes,** even though they may have been assigned to one of Bordes' tool types (such as Levallois flakes or naturally backed knives), and retouched pieces are called **tools. Complete** (vs. **proximal, distal,** or **medial**) refers to the absence of any significant breakage, so that a retouched piece will be considered complete even though material was removed through retouching. To be **proximal,** the point of percussion must be present. **Shatter** is defined as a flint fragment that exhibits no identifiable flake characteristic or interior surface (Sullivan and

Rosen 1985). **Manuport** refers to any unworked, allochthonous material. **Cailloux** is the term used for limestone blocks, whereas **rognon** refers to flint nodules (which must be larger than 10 cm to be considered as such); **unworked** refers to other pieces (e.g., thermal fractured chert) that were inadvertently given artifact numbers by an excavator. In the course of later analyses, all complete and proximal portions of both tools and flakes are often combined and referred to as **blanks**.

CORTEX: Cortex was observed on all flakes and flake tools according to the following scale in percentages: **0, 1–10, 10–40, 40–60, 60–90, 90–99, 100**. This measure of cortex also includes all natural weathered surfaces on artifact exteriors.

TECHNIQUE: Basic flaking technique was recorded on all flakes, flake tools, and cores. Nine basic categories were recognized (see Debénath and Dibble 1994): **Levallois, disc, blade, biface retouch** (or thinning) **flake, retouch flake, undiagnostic, Clactonian, Kombewa**, and **other**. Blade technique was recognized on the basis of parallel flake scars on the exterior surface and was not based on the normal Bordian method of relative length to width (see FORM, this section). Retouch flakes are small flakes that appeared to be the result of retouching flake tools. It is important to keep in mind, however, that only objects larger than the 2.5-cm cutoff were analyzed in this detailed fashion and that most retouch flakes were recovered during screening, though they are not reported on here except in terms of their overall density (see Chapter 12).

ALTERATION: This observation refers to post-depositional alteration of the surface of the flint. Patination was recorded as four states: **light** (with light speckling on the surface), **heavy** (for which at least one entire surface was patinated **white** (at least one surface being completely white), and **double** (where a previously patinated surface had been subsequently retouched). **Burned** pieces show signs of thermal alteration, including crazing, pot-lid fracture, and color changes.

EDGE DAMAGE: For pieces that showed edge damage (presumably post-depositional), the surface on which damage occurred was noted: **exterior, interior, both** (as either alternate or alternating), or **rolled**. It should be noted that this observation did not record the extent or degree of this damage, but simply its presence or absence. Furthermore, the degree of damage required to characterize it as present was less than is normally required to assign an otherwise unretouched piece to Bordes' types 46–49, pieces with abrupt/alternating retouch.

PLATFORM SURFACE: Platform surface was recorded for each complete and proximal flake or flake tool. Nine categories were used: **cortical**, **punctiform, plain**, **dihedral, faceted, Chapeau de Gendarme, removed, other,** and **missing**. Removed platforms were identified when the platform was removed by retouch; missing platforms simply means that the proximal portion of the flake was broken off. This variable served to compute the standard faceting indices.

EXTERIOR PLATFORM: Exterior platform preparation (i.e., on the exterior surface of the flake adjacent to the platform) was noted on complete and proximal flakes and on flake tools with identifiable platforms. The categories for external preparation, when present, included **beveled**, **straight, center ridge, side ridge concave, convex**, and **cortical**.

FORM: The overall form of each flake and flake tool was recorded using the following categories: **normal, angular, point, blade, broad, burin, débordant, expanding, lame à crête, naturally backed, overshot,** and **other**. Angular pieces were defined as those with two exterior surfaces that met at an angle of less than 90 degrees. Points were flakes with margins that converged toward the distal end, whereas expanding pieces were those that diverged distally. Flake blades were elongated flakes (length greater than twice their width) without parallel flake scars on the exterior surface, and blades exhibited such flake scars on the exterior surface. A broad flake is one whose width is more than double its length. Débordants are flakes whose lateral margins intersected the core edge, and similarly, naturally backed pieces are those with an abrupt exterior surface along one of the margins. All other nondescript flake shapes were classified as normal.

SCAR MORPHOLOGY: Scar morphology was recorded only on blanks and cores as **unidirectional, bidirectional, subradial, radial**, or **plain** (cf. Baumler 1988). The category of plain was noted if virtually the entire surface was covered by a single previous flake scar. Uni- and bidirectional designate flakes and cores that exhibit exterior scars that, respectively, originate from either the distal or proximal end exclusively, or from both ends. Subradial is used when the flake scars originate from two or three directions, but at least one of these directions includes lateral scar removals. Both cores and flakes are considered to have a radial scar pattern when the scars originate from at least four different directions, including both lateral margins.

RAW MATERIAL: **Chert** refers to the material that comes from the limestone of the cave itself; **flint** refers to other materials brought into the site, in addition to **quartz, chalcedony,** and **jasper**.

RETOUCHED TOOLS

The following observations were made of retouched tools:

TYPE: All of the flake tools were typed according to the typology of Bordes (1961). Two minor modifications to this typology were that the types 46–49 (abrupt/alternating retouch) were grouped together as 48, and type number 64 was assigned to the truncated-faceted pieces (see Dibble 1984; Dibble and McPherron 2006, 2007; Nishiaki 1985; Solecki 1970). In the case of multiply retouched pieces (a burin and scraper on the same piece, for example), Bordes normally only assigned them to a single type category. However, secondary and tertiary types were noted in this material as TYPE2 and TYPE3, although this was normally not done for the unretouched "technological types" (Levallois flakes and points, pseudo-Levallois points, and pieces with abrupt/alternating retouch). It should also be noted that the assignment of pieces to the notched or denticulated types was done in a very conservative fashion. If a piece with shallow retouch of this sort exhibited signs of alternating or abrupt edge damage, it was assigned to type 48 (abrupt/alternating retouch).

NUMBER OF RETOUCHED EDGES: This variable was recorded for all retouched tools.

RETOUCH INTENSITY: This variable was observed on all scrapers. The categories of retouch intensity included **light, normal, heavy, Demi-Quina,** and **Quina**. Light retouch is shallow and sometimes discontinuous retouch with little alteration of the flake perimeter. Normal retouch is continuous and moderately invasive; heavy retouch is very steep or invasive. Demi-Quina and Quina retouch are heavy and stepped retouch.

TRUNCATED-FACETED: variables: Three variables were recorded for truncated-faceted pieces. T-F CHARACTER refers to the type of retouch that was applied, as **bifacial, core-like, burin-like,** or **normal** truncated-faceted character. T-F SURFACE referred to which surface had the flake removed from it: **exterior, interior,** or **multiple.** T-F LOCATION referred to the part of the flake that received the truncated-faceted retouch: **proximal, distal,** or **multiple.**

COMPLETE CORES

The following observations were made of complete cores:

TYPE: The core shapes included **Levallois, inform, globular** (multi-faced, rectangular or spherical forms), **chopping-tool** (including choppers), **Kombewa, prismatic, single surface** (one prepared surface), **diverse, tested,** and **other.** Inform cores were those without a clearly definable form and generally included all angular forms. The diverse category included cores with shapes that were neither regular nor patterned. Because the inform and diverse categories were difficult to separate, they were grouped together for the final analysis. Tested pieces were the least reduced, with evidence of one or two flake removals.

SUPPORT TYPE: This variable was used to record whether the core was made on a **block, cobble, nodule, gelifract,** or **flake.**

NUMBER OF PROXIMAL FLAKE REMOVALS: This is the number of flake scars whose proximal end intersected the core margin. To a large extent, the number of proximal flake removals represents the minimum number of removals from a core, and especially only the last removals from a particular platform edge.

NUMBER OF PREPARED PLATFORMS: Platforms on the core surface that were prepared prior to flaking were counted.

LENGTH OF THE LARGEST FLAKE REMOVAL: Flake removals were measured using the same technique used to measure flakes and tools (see next section), except that the landmarks were noted on the negative flake scar.

Measurements

All linear measurements were taken with digital calipers in millimeters to the nearest hundredth of a millimeter, and weights were taken with a digital scale in grams; if a particular measurement could not be taken, then a 0 was entered and should be treated as missing data.

LENGTH: Length was recorded for all complete flakes, tools, and cores. On flakes and tools, it was measured from the point of percussion on the platform to the farthest distal end of the blank. On cores, it represented the maximum dimension.

WIDTH: Width was recorded for all complete flakes and tools and was taken at the mid-point of the length axis and perpendicular to it.

MAXIMUM WIDTH: This was recorded for all complete flakes, tools, and cores, and represented the widest breadth of the piece perpendicular to the length axis.

THICKNESS: Thickness was recorded for all complete flakes, tools, and cores. It was measured at the mid-point of the long axis of blanks and as maximum thickness for the cores.

PLATFORM WIDTH: Platform width was recorded for all blanks with complete platforms, regardless of whether other extremities were broken. This measurement was taken along the platform from one lateral edge to the other.

PLATFORM THICKNESS: Platform thickness was measured from the interior to the exterior surface of the platform at the point of percussion and was similarly recorded for all intact platforms.

WEIGHT: All lithic material was weighed to the nearest gram.

Computed classes, indices, and ratios

Standard Bordian indices (see Debénath and Dibble 1994) are used throughout this report, though they are sometimes augmented by other ratios.

TYPOLOGICAL INDICES

The following typological indices (except the first) were computed on the basis of both the "real" count (types 1–64) and a modified "essential" count (eliminating types 1–3, 5, 38, and 45–50).

TYPOLOGICAL LEVALLOIS INDEX (Ilty): The number of types 1–4 divided by the total type count of types 1–64.

SCRAPER INDEX (IR): The percentage of types 9–29 relative to the total type count.

UNIFACIAL ACHEULIAN INDEX (IAu): The number of backed knives (types 36–37) relative to the total type count.

GROUP II (MOUSTERIAN GROUP): The percentage of types 5–29 relative to the total type count. It thus differs from the Scraper Index by the inclusion of pseudo-Levallois points, Mousterian points, and limaces.

GROUP III (UPPER PALEOLITHIC GROUP): The total of types 30–37 and 40 divided by the total type count.

GROUP IV (DENTICULATE GROUP): The number of denticulates divided by the total type count.

TECHNOLOGICAL INDICES

LEVALLOIS INDEX (IL): The number of Levallois flakes, blades, and points (retouched or not) divided by the total of the non-biface assemblage.

FACETING INDEX (IF): The percentage of faceted or dihedral platforms relative to the total number of recognizable platforms.

STRICT FACETING INDEX (IFs): The percentage of faceted platforms (excluding dihedrals) relative to the total number of platforms.

BLADE INDEX (Ilam): The number of blades (flakes whose length is at least twice their width) divided by the total number of complete flakes, blades, and points, regardless of technology (i.e., Levallois or not or true blade technique or not).

QUINA INDEX (IQ): The number of objects in types 6–29 that exhibit Quina or Demi-Quina retouch, relative to the total number of these types.

FAUNAL RECORDS IN THE DATABASE

The FAUNA table of the database was used for recording basic information about faunal remains. Each entry has a UNIT and an ID field that links it to an entry in the CONTEXT table. Each entry also has a SUFFIX field, but it should be noted that this is not the same thing as the SUFFIX in the XYZ table. Rather, every faunal specimen recovered received a SUFFIX of 0 (zero). In the case of a jaw (mandible or maxilla) with teeth, or of a jaw with tooth sockets, it was necessary to record information about the individual teeth, as well as about the jaw. This was done using a separate database record for each tooth but with a unique suffix beginning with 1. Thus, a mandible fragment with three teeth would have four entries. The first would have a SUFFIX of 0 and would contain information about the mandible fragment. Each of the teeth would have a record with a suffix of 1, 2, or 3 (mesial to distal).

Taxonomic identifications were recorded in the TAXON field. These identifications vary from EQUUS HYDRANTINUS to less specific identifications, such as UNGULATE, LARGE HERBIVORE, BIRD, SMALL MAMMAL, and so on. The field TENTATIVE contains "CF." (as in "cf. *Dama*") in the case of a tentative identification. This was done to permit the automatic combining of tentative and positive identifications in lists.

Each specimen was recorded using three fields, following (at least in part) the suggestion of Gifford and Crader (1977). The first field, PART, records the most precise identification of the skeletal element possible (e.g., LOWER 3RD PREMOLAR, PREMOLAR, CHEEK TOOTH, 7TH CERVICAL VERTEBRA, VERTEBRA, HUMERUS, LONG BONE). The second field, PORTION, records what portion of that element is present (e.g., COMPLETE, DISTAL, CROWN, FRAGMENT). The third field, SEGMENT, is used when further elaboration is desirable. For example, a fragment of the lateral shaft of a tibia would be recorded (using these three fields) as "TIBIA, SHAFT, LATERAL." SIDE (L or R) was recorded in a separate field. In addition, a field called BONE TYPE contained an entry of either ANTLER, BONE, TOOTH, JAW + TOOTH, or HUMAN. This was done primarily for convenience during analysis and for use by computer programs used in analysis.

OVERVIEW OF EXCAVATIONS

When we first encountered the Cave of Fontéchevade in 1994, it was in very good condition and apparently little changed from when Henri-Martin stopped her excavations decades earlier. As described in Chapter 1, Henri-Martin removed nearly all of the archaeological

Figure 2.8
Excavation in progress on
the Main Profile during
the 1994 season.

deposits outside the dripline and stopped some 9 m into the cave, leaving a section approximately 2.5 m high that traversed the cave from side to side. To prevent a collapse of the section, she left it with a significant slope. The only modification to her section was a series of large holes made when pollen samples were taken from the length of the section approximately in its center. In the back of the cave, her Test Pit 3 was still mostly intact though, as we learned later when we excavated it, a fair amount of material had fallen into the hole. In the mouth of the cave, her Witness Section appeared to be intact as well, though at the time we had only her map (which we could not precisely align with our grid – see Chapter 1) and the recollections of the landowner, who was present during the Henri-Martin excavations, as guides to its exact location.

YEAR-BY-YEAR SUMMARY

1994

In October 1994, a short, 2-week field season was directed at cleaning and straightening the Main Profile (Fig. 2.8) so that the stratigraphy could be seen more easily. At this time, the grid west half of the section was excavated first, and rather than straightening the whole 2.5-m high section at once, a step was left approximately halfway.

A provisional stratigraphy was created at this time and refined over the course of excavation (Figs. 2.9–2.11). The levels in the Main Profile use Arabic numbers (Levels 1–8), with smaller subdivisions indicated first with lowercase letters (e.g., Level 3d) and then with Arabic numbers (e.g., Level 3b1). However, although the sequence in the central part of the section followed a fairly straightforward stratigraphic progression, it was clear that on the margins, adjacent to the cave wall, the sequence had been heavily altered and reworked. These levels were called X and further subdivided into X0 and X1. Level distinctions were made in an attempt to follow lithostratigraphy, relying on visible changes in sediments, including color, texture, compaction, composition, and

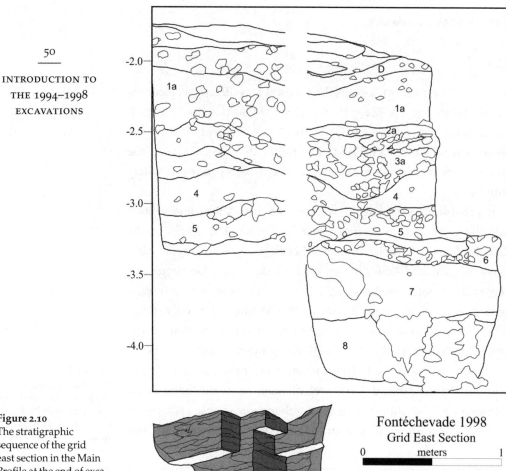

Figure 2.10
The stratigraphic
sequence of the grid
east section in the Main
Profile at the end of excavation in 1998.

Fontéchevade 1998
Grid East Section

the like. The differences between the larger units (e.g., between Level
2 and 3) are more clearly defined, whereas the subdivisions (e.g.,
Level 3a vs. 3b) represent more subtle changes within a given sedimentological unit. A geological description of these levels is provided
in Chapter 3.

Note that this stratigraphy is completely independent of Henri-
Martin's. Throughout the excavation, we made every effort to relo-
cate a vertical point of reference that would allow us to link our
stratigraphy to her published sequence, but we were unable to locate
her datum.

In addition to the excavation, topographic points were taken to
make a plan view of the cave, a longitudinal section through the cave,
and several lateral sections.

1995

The 1995 season took place in June and continued for slightly more than 3 weeks of excavation. The process of cleaning and straightening Henri-Martin's section was continued on the grid east portion of the Main Profile. By the end of this season, the entire profile had been cleaned, giving us our first clear view of Henri-Martin's stratigraphy (Fig. 2.12). Some excavation was also conducted in low benches along the cave walls above and behind (grid north) the Main Profile to assess whether these sediments were intact and would, therefore, give us samples from higher in the sequence. The results were equivocal.

In addition, a topographic map of the area around the cave was completed this season, and several electrical resistivity lines were recorded on the plateau above the cave to assess the possibility of additional caves and to better understand the structure of the limestone bedrock, particularly immediately above the cave. One of these

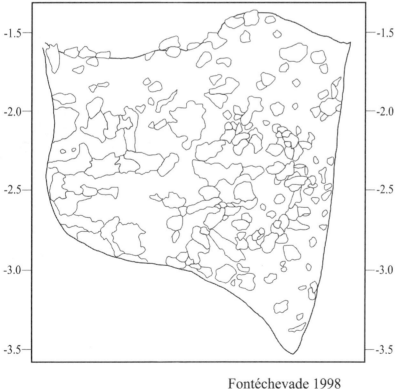

Fontéchevade 1998
Grid West Section
0   meters   1

Figure 2.11
The stratigraphic sequence of the west section in the Main Profile at the end of excavation in 1998, showing homogenous deposits of Level XI against the cave wall.

lines, along the east edge of the plateau, detected an anomaly that perhaps represented an additional cave entrance (see Chapter 5). A trench was excavated at this location along the edge of the plateau in an effort to evaluate this possibility. Unfortunately, the results were equivocal. It was determined that heavy machinery would be needed to resolve the question, and this was not attempted.

1996

A 6-week field season was conducted in 1996 from late June through July. At this point, we had to decide exactly how to sample the Main Profile. Rather than taking the whole section back 1 m, we decided instead to excavate only one half of it. Thus, the grid west portion of Henri-Martin's Main Profile, an area 3 m across, was excavated 1 m back (grid north). The step midway through the section that had been created in 1994 was retained (though now a meter farther into the section). By limiting excavation to one half of the original section, we were able to expose a small longitudinal section, something that was completely missing from sections left by Henri-Martin.

Excavations were also conducted in the same area above and behind the Main Profile in an attempt to further resolve whether those sediments were in situ. It was determined that they are likely

Figure 2.12
Photo of the Main Profile at the end of the 1995 season.

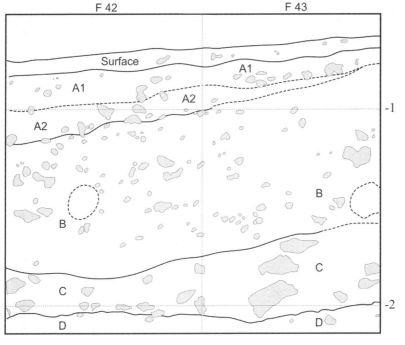

F 42   F 43

Surface

A1

A1

A2

A2

-1

B

B

C

C

-2

D   D

Fontéchevade 1998
West Section

0   meters   1

Figure 2.13
The stratigraphic
sequence in the eastward
extension of the Test Pit,
looking east (grid west).

not in situ or at a minimum are highly disturbed, and no further excavation was done in this area.

Excavation was also begun in the rear of the cave in and around Henri-Martin's Test Pit 3 (Figs. 2.13–2.17), which we redesignated as "Test Pit" in our sector definitions. The goals of this excavation were to sample these deposits and perhaps to link them to the stratigraphy visible in the main section. Here we defined a stratigraphy using letter designations (e.g., Level B), with sublevels defined using Arabic numerals (e.g., Level B1). This labeling was used to avoid confusion with the Main Profile, and here again these levels do not follow Henri-Martin's stratigraphy.

Last, a few more electro-resistivity lines were recorded on the plateau above the cave.

1997

In this 6-week field season, from late June through July, excavation was evenly divided between the Main Profile and the back of the

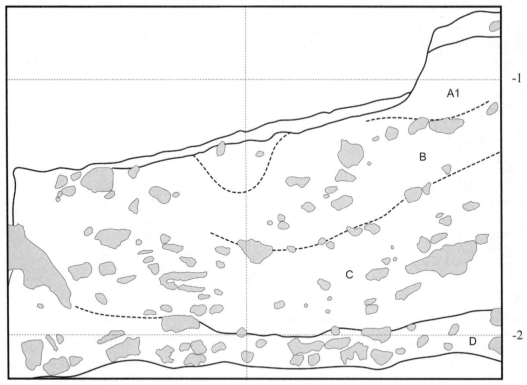

G 42   F 42

A1

B

-1

C

D

-2

Fontéchevade 1998
South Section

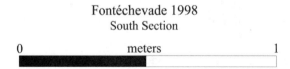

0   meters   1

Figure 2.14
The stratigraphic
sequence in the east-
ward extension of the
Test Pit, looking north
(grid south).

cave (Figs. 2.18 and 2.19). In the back, four units were open to the east (grid west) of Henri-Martin's Test Pit 3 and excavated to a depth of approximately 1 m. On the Main Profile, the main issue for the work was our low sample size in each level. The artifact density at Fontéchevade is extremely low (see Chapters 11 and 12 on lithics and site formation processes, respectively). Thus, we decided to remove one more meter from the grid west portion of the Main Profile. In 1997, this area was excavated nearly to the level of the step left from the previous year and finished in 1998. Additionally, to mitigate a crack that had developed near the center of the section and to remove traces of the pollen samples taken from the main section, a unit in the center of the section was opened and excavated to a depth of approximately 0.5 m.

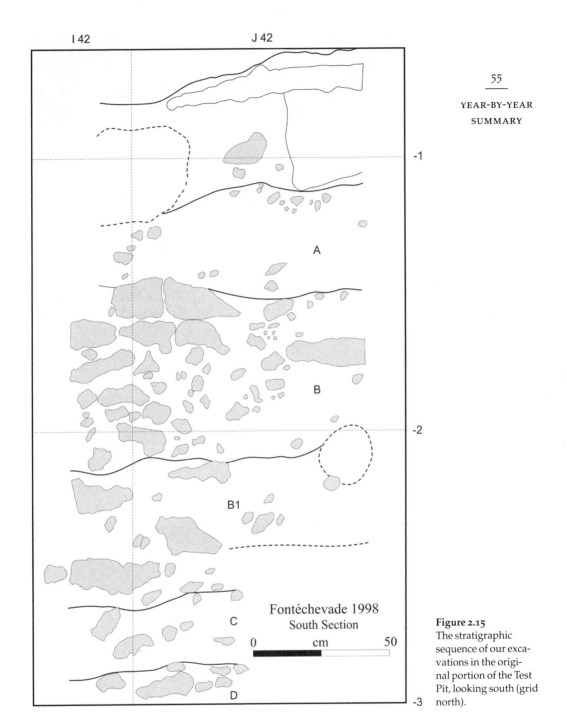

I 42   J 42

-1

A

B

-2

B1

Fontéchevade 1998
South Section

0   cm   50

C

D

-3

Figure 2.15
The stratigraphic
sequence of our exca-
vations in the origi-
nal portion of the Test
Pit, looking south (grid
north).

Figure 2.16
Excavation in progress
in the back of the cave
during the 1996 season.

1998

In the final season of excavation we finished work on the main section. We removed about 50 cm from squares D29, E29, and F29 to complete the upper portion of the step and about 120 cm from the squares E28 and F28 to complete the front portion of the step. Some additional work was also done on the grid east portion of the profile to regularize this area and to leave it in a good finished state. Additionally, work

Figure 2.17
View of the Test Pit.

Figure 2.18
Excavation in progress on the Main Profile during the 1997 season.

continued in the center of the profile to mitigate the crack that was discovered the year before. This resulted in approximately 200 cm of excavation. The end result is a multi-stepped profile (Fig. 2.20) as an alternative to the sloped profiles that Henri-Martin had left, presumably for the same reason of stabilizing the section.

By the final season of excavation, it was apparent that certain aspects of Henri-Martin's excavations and interpretations could not be evaluated because we found no equivalents. In particular, though by this time we suspected they were likely misinterpreted by Henri-Martin, we had not yet located anything that could

Figure 2.19
Recording stratigraphy during the 1997 season.

Figure 2.20
Two views of the Main
Profile at the end of the
1998 season.

Figure 2.21
View of the excavation
of the Witness Section
during the 1998 season.

be described as a hearth. Thus, we decided to open the Witness Section left by Henri-Martin (see Chapter 1) in the grid east portion of the cave entrance (outside the dripline). Here we excavated an area of approximately 2 m² (Fig. 2.21) and cleaned a section more than 3 m in length. Three levels were identified (T2, T3, and TX) in a depth of approximately 80 cm. Additionally, patches of darkly stained sediment were indeed encountered here, but the coloring comes from manganese and not from fire.

PART II

SPECIALIZED ANALYSES

3

Sedimentology and Stratigraphy at Fontéchevade

William R. Farrand

INTRODUCTION

The following discussion is based on 42 sediment samples collected in 1998 and processed at the University of Michigan; it also includes comparisons made with the sediment studies published by Henri-Martin (1957). Coordinates of the sample locations were determined in the field with a total station, except for the samples from the Witness Section and samples FCH 11 and FCH 12 in Henri-Martin's old Test Pit 3 (designated as "Test Pit" in recent excavations). Stratum designations were taken from tags on the section faces, where these still existed, and from information supplied by the excavators. Strata identified in the 1998 study are labeled "Levels" in this chapter, and the term "Beds" is retained for the strata in Henri-Martin's earlier study.

In attempting comparisons with the sections of Henri-Martin, it would have been useful to know the relation of the present datum to her *"ligne de repère"* (datum line), but it could not be located. Although Henri-Martin's sediment analysis, both physical and chemical, has been studied in some detail, the locations of her samples are quite indeterminate, being identified only to *"secteur"* (sector; see Fig. 1.8) and *"couche"* (bed), but she gives no depths, limiting close comparisons with the current data.

SAMPLE COLLECTION

Samples are labeled FCH 1–2, FCH 3–1, etc., where the first digit stands for the sample column and the second is the specific sample number from "1" at the top progressively downward in that column. Sample column FCH 2 begins at the top of the east side of the Main Profile as it existed in 1998, at a depth of 1.86 m below datum. (Geographic directions – east, west, north, and south – as used in this section are actual or natural directions, roughly 180° opposite the orientation of the site grid [i.e., the cave entrance faces roughly true north].) FCH 1 is the lower part of the Main Profile,

Table 3.1. The X-Y-Z coordinates based on the site grid for sediment sample series FCH 1, 2, 3, and 5, as determined by total station*

Sample Column	Sample ID	X	Y	Z	Level
FCH1	1A	5.63	29.03	−3.48	7 top
FCH1	1B	n.d.	n.d.	−3.55	7
FCH1	2	n.d.	n.d.	−3.63	7
FCH1	3	n.d.	n.d.	−3.77	7 lower
FCH1	4	n.d.	n.d.	−3.92	7 base
FCH1	5	5.266	29.052	−4.012	8 top
FCH1	6	5.533	28.991	−4.193	8 middle
FCH2	1	5.571	30.114	−1.86	1A upper
FCH2	2	5.553	30.068	−2.051	1A lower
FCH2	3	5.54	30.024	−2.386	2A base
FCH2	4	5.554	30.029	−2.528	3A mid
FCH2	5	5.009	30.01	−2.689	3A
FCH2	6	5.33	30.052	−2.774	3B/3C
FCH2	7	5.309	30.046	−2.873	3C mid
FCH2	8	5.535	30.02	−2.998	3C lower
FCH2	9	4.679	30.004	−3.227	5 mid
FCH2	10	5.236	29.949	−3.363	6 top
FCH3	1	5	42.914	−0.876	A1
FCH3	2	4.998	42.94	−1.021	A2
FCH3	3	4.977	42.942	−1.193	B top
FCH3	4	5.014	42.931	−1.417	B mid
FCH3	5	5.037	43.09	−1.729	B lower
FCH3	6	5.05	43.121	−2.013	B base
FCH3	7	6.334	42.023	−1.592	C top
FCH3	8	6.496	42.045	−1.739	C mid
FCH3	9	6.43	42.049	−2.035	C lower
FCH3	10	6.215	43.038	−2.463	D
FCH5	1	7.798	27.977	−2.233	2A
FCH5	2	7.628	27.996	−2.38	2A
FCH5	3	7.845	28.018	−2.571	3A
FCH5	4	7.751	28.024	−2.772	3A
FCH5	5	7.558	28.058	−2.989	3A/3C
FCH5	6	7.578	28.083	−3.103	4C/5
FCH5	7	6.889	28.031	−3.132	5
FCH5	8	6.881	28.001	−3.268	5/6

* Series FCH 4 was not done.

beginning at 3.48 m below datum. FCH 5 is from the west side of the Main Profile, about 2 to 2.5 m west of column FCH 2, from depths of −2.23 to −3.27 m. FCH 3–1 through 3–10 are from the east and south faces of the newly expanded Test Pit, and FCH 3–11 and 3–12 were collected in Henri-Martin's old pit. FCH 4 samples the lower part of the Witness Section. The exact coordinates of the samples except FCH 4 are given in Table 3.1, based on the site grid. The samples are described in Table 3.2, which includes information on stratum, depth, color, and calcium carbonate and organic matter ($CaCO_3$) content, along with a general description and notes on the rock fraction of each sample.

Samples were not collected continuously down each column but only wherever a perceptible change in sediment type or color was noted. Each sample was about 5–6 cm thick and weighed between 400 and 2000 g, the larger samples being taken of the coarser sediments. All sediment, including clasts up to 128 mm (−7 phi) in the longest dimension, was collected.

ANALYTICAL METHODS

Granulometry

The coarse fraction (128 to 8 mm) of each sample was measured by hand. The finer sediment was then separated by wet-sieving, and the finest material (silt and clay < 0.063 mm) was measured in a Spectrex™ laser counter. The results are displayed in Figure 3.1 through Figure 3.5 in terms of four fractions – pebbles and cobbles between 128 and 16 mm, granules from 16 to 2 mm, sand 2 to 0.063 mm, and silt + clay less than 0.063 mm. In addition, the division between sand and silt + clay in the fine fraction (total < 2 mm) is shown in Figures 3.6–3.8. The data on which these figures are based are given in Table 3.3 and Table 3.4.

$CaCO_3$ and organic matter

In the sedimentary fraction smaller than 2 mm, these values were determined by means of a muffle furnace in which the organic matter was combusted at 500°C and the carbonate at 1000°C. The carbonate values are straightforward and agree in general with those

Table 3.2. Comprehensive list of all samples arranged by levels, based on field observations and laboratory analyses

Level	Sample ID	Depth below datum	Color (Munsell dry)	Color (verbal)	Percent CaCO₃	Percent organic matter	General description	Rock fraction
MAIN PROFILE EAST								
1A Upper	2-1	1.86	10 YR 5/7	Yellow brown	10.96	11.2	Sandy clay loam with chalky rock fragments; horizontally bedded; lower contact wavy; some bone fragments	Large chert rognons, slab, and nodule; a Mn pebble; numerous small chert chips; two small bone scraps
1A lower	2-2	2.05	10 YR 5/8	Yellow brown	3.76	10.5	Very rocky loam with fewer bones and fewer chalky rock fragments (clear, wavy contact)	Very irregular chert fragments and rognons, some with spongy concretion
2A BASE	2-3	2.39	10 YR 6/4	Light yellow brown	1.45	11.4	Silty clay loam with large rognons; note color contrast with sample 2-2 (clear, wavy contact)	Five large chunks of chert, but mostly smaller chert fragments; some dolomite fragments
3A MID	2-4	2.53	10 YR 5/2.5	Grayish brown	1.34	10.5	Loamy sediment with dolomite pebbles and fragments, not as much chert (clear, wavy contact)	Dolomite dominant over chert, including one subrounded dolomite cobble; one well-rounded quartz pebble (30 mm)
3A	2-5	2.69	10 YR 6/5	Light yellow brown	0.98	10.9	Silty loam with small pebbles common; Level 3B not recognized here during excavation, but appears clearly now; slightly stratified; dips to the east where it disappears into coarse open-work of rognons and galets of Level X (described as a lens in 1994)	Some well-rounded chert cobbles and pebbles, and minor dolomite; a stalactite fragment, and a small hematite pebble
3B/3C	2-6	2.77	10 YR 6/4	Light yellow brown	0.76	10.7	5-cm thick layer of "ashy" loam with few rocks	Mostly small chert fragments; one yellow ochre pebble

Unconformity

3C MID	2-7	2.87	10 YR 6/7	Brownish yellow	1.06	11.6	Dry, porous or vesicular, slightly cemented silty loam with a blocky structure; quite different from Levels 3A and 3B; sharp upper contact with 3B; probably an unconformity	Rounded quartz pebbles in 8- to 32-mm fraction; several larger chert fragments
3C ower	2-8	3.00	10 YR 6/6	Brownish yellow	0.96	10.5	Similar to sample 2-7 above, with porous, cemented aggregates in 2- to 8-mm fraction.	Large chert fragments are rounded (but are not pebbles); three fragments of red ochre
5 MID	2-9	3.23	10 YR 5.5/3	Pale brown	2.02	11.3	Soft loam with rock fragments common	Lots of small chert chips; larger angular chert fragments with spongy siliceous coatings; one large silicified stalactite fragment, also with a spongy surface
6 top	2-10	3.36	10 YR 5/8	Yellow brown	3.01	10.3	Very rocky loam; very sharp upper contact with Levels 5; note also color contrast. (clear and slightly wavy lower contact)	Chert fragments only, including two large rognons and a subrounded cobble
7 top	1-1A	3.48	10 YR 6/6	Brownish yellow	0.96	10.5	Soft silt loam with streaks and blotches of white powdery phosphate, but very few rocks	One well-rounded quartz pebble, some red ochre, and cortex and chert fragments
7	1-1B	3.55	10 YR 7/4	Very pale brown	1.43	9.6	Silt loam, firmer than above, with phosphate nodules	Only one pebble-sized rock (dolomite?); mostly phosphate clumps; two angular chert fragments
7	1-2	3.63	10 YR 5/8	Yellow brown	1.24	10.4	Soft silt loam with rare rocks; some small round nodules; dips slightly to west passing below lighter silt mass with white streaks	One small chert fragment; one stalactite fragment; number of small dark brown cemented "tubes" (burrows?)

(continued)

Table 3.2 (continued)

Level	Sample ID	Depth below datum	Color (Munsell dry)	Color (verbal)	Percent CaCO$_3$	Percent organic matter	General description	Rock fraction
7 lower	1-3	3.77	10 YR 5/7	Dark yellow brown	1.24	10.7	Soft, moist clay loam with few rocks	A few weathered scraps and corroded crusts of chert; a small stalactite fragment
Unconformity								
7 base	1-4	3.92	10 YR 4/6	Yellow red	1.47	10.3	Clay loam with few rocks (lower contact clear and very slightly wavy)	Weathered, crusty chert fragments and rinds; a few, small fresh chert chips
8 top	1-5	4.01	5 YR 4/6	Yellow red	2.00	9.4	Redder smooth, firm clay; top 3–4 cm has blocky structure below a sharp contact with Level 7; contact rises to west	One chert fragment (32–64 mm) with cortex; otherwise almost no rock fraction
8 middle	1-6	4.19	5 YR 5/8	Yellow red	2.10	9.8	Massive clay, stiffer and redder than sample 1–5; rare small rock fragments; large, irregular rognons adjacent to sample	Some grains of red ochre; otherwise only a few granules
MAIN PROFILE WEST								
2A	5-1	2.23	10 YR 5/8	Yellow brown	2.10	9.6	Sandy loam with few rocks	One retouched flake (scraper); otherwise only medium to small chert fragments; a few Mn granules
2A	5-2	2.38	10 YR 6/3	Pale brown	1.28	8.6	Much grayer, porous silt loam with abundant small rock fragments	Mostly irregular chert fragments up to 64 mm; two crystalline quartz pebbles, one rounded and heavily stained red and the other irregular
3A	5-3	2.57	10 YR 6.5/3	Pale brown	1.34	15.1	Loam, clayier than above, with some small rocks	Angular chert fragments with silty coatings; some yellow ochre stain

3A	5-4	2.77	10 YR 6/2	Light brownish gray	1.16	12.7	Soft loam with rock fragments	Some large, very angular chert fragments without coatings (cf. sample 5-3); one large, hollow, silicified stalactite fragment
3A/3C	5-5	2.99	10 YR 6/3	Pale brown	2.29	20.0	Soft loam with few rocks	1 subrounded white quartz pebble with pink stain, and 1 very irregular chert fragment in 32–64-mm fraction
Unconformity?								
4C/5	5-6 (cf. 2-7)	3.10	10 YR 6/4	Light yellow brown	3.30	16.5	Abrupt change from above to bright "orange brown"(?) sandy layer with numerous rock fragments only 5 cm thick, undulating	Many cemented aggregates in 2–8-mm fraction, flecked with white phosphate; among larger fragments are 2 rounded quartz pebbles and very angular cherts, one degraded
5	5-7	3.13	10 YR 6/2	Light brownish gray	2.22	19.6	Duller silt loam with very few rocks	Mostly smallish angular chert fragments; 1 silicified dolomite fragment (32–64 mm) with yellow ochre stain
5/6	5-8	3.27	10 YR 6/2	Light brownish gray	2.30	17.5	Similar to sample 5-7 but more rocks	2 large rognons, 1 rounded, 1 angular; 1 silicified dolomite fragment with yellow ochre stain
TEST PIT								
A1	3-1	0.84	10 YR 5/8	Yellowish brown	6.73	12.4	Compact clay loam, hard to dig, with numerous 4- to 7-cm rocks (not included in sample); Mn stained	1 cemented aggregate; 1.4-g charcoal fragments; small Mn granules

(continued)

Table 3.2 *(continued)*

Level	Sample ID	Depth below datum	Color (Munsell dry)	Color (verbal)	Percent CaCO$_3$	Percent organic matter	General description	Rock fraction
A2	3-2	1.00	10 YR 4/6	Dark yellowish brown	7.38	12.8	Compact clay loam with 5- to 8-cm rocks, hard to extract; clear to sharp lower contact. Levels A1 & A2 dip toward cave mouth at 5–10°	1 large chert fragment with cemented sediment; smaller angular chert fragments, some stained with red ochre; a dolomite fragment; a least 3 bone fragments; numerous well-rounded granules
Unconformity?								
B top	3-3	1.19	10 YR 5/8	Yellowish brown	1.88	18.8	Siltier loam with small rock fragments and pebbles; few cobbles	4 rounded quartz pebbles (32–64 mm); numerous smaller chert fragments
B mid	3-4	1.43	10 YR 5.5/6	Brownish yellow	1.84	16.1	Rocky, pebbly loam, easy to dig	7 well-rounded quartz pebbles (16–32 mm); 1 rounded dolomite; larger angular chert fragments and rognons
B lower	3-5	1.69	10 YR 6/6	Brownish yellow	2.18	19.0	Similar to sample 3-4 above	8 well-rounded quartz pebbles; larger angular chert fragments; a large, porous, low density mass, enclosing quartz pebble
B base	3-6	2.08	10 YR 6/6	Brownish yellow	1.53	22.0	Moister, more clayey, and less rocky than above	4 quartz pebbles (8–16 mm); only 3 larger chert rognons and fragments
Erosional contact								
C top	3-7	1.57	10 YR 4/5	Dark yellowish brown	7.15	10.0	Mn-stained loam, sampled among large angular chert fragments, rognons, and rotten rocks, but few rocks in sample	8 quartz pebbles and a few dolomite fragments, stained or crusted with Mn

C mid	3-8	1.73	10 YR 6/6	Brownish yellow	8.27	6.9	Clay loam matrix amid decaying, broken dolomite rocks, angular chert fragments, and galets	2 rounded quartz pebbles and 1 quartz cobble with heavy Mn stain; some well rounded dolomite pebbles; fragments of weathering rinds
C lower	3-9	ca. 2.2	10 YR 5/8	Yellowish brown	7.39	8.2	Loam with rotten rocks and chert fragments; also crumbly yellow granules; a long bone fragment adjacent to sample location	2 bone splinters; several quartz pebbles; dolomite fragments with rinds; larger, somewhat rounded chert fragments
D	3-10	2.43	10 YR 7/3	Very pale brown	2.20	9.7	Silt with relatively few small rocks, but no Mn staining and no rotten rocks	2 well-rounded quartz and one red ochre pebbles; chert fragments coated with light gray silt; also conspicuous yellow ochre staining
"D" in pit	3-11	ca. 2.93	10 YR 7/3	Very pale brown	1.96	9.2	Pale silt with few rocks, similar to sample 3-10 above, although 50 cm deeper	2 quartz pebbles; cemented masses of silt enclosing rounded exotic pebbles and granules and some mica; a little yellow ochre
Below "D"	3-12	n.d.*	10 YR 6/6	Brownish yellow	2.73	12.2	Very compact loam with very few rocks	Most of "coarse" fraction is cemented aggregates enclosing exotic pebbles and some weathered dolomite fragments; 1 well-rounded quartz pebble
WITNESS SECTION								
T 1	4-1	25 cm below surface	7.5 YR 4/6	Strong brown	8.72	7.2	Heavy clay loam with few rocks; relatively fresh looking	1 fragment dolomite; a bone splinter; a few granules of exotic rocks; coarsest fragments are highly weathered chert fragments with porous interiors

(continued)

Table 3.2 *(continued)*

Level	Sample ID	Depth below datum	Color (Munsell dry)	Color (verbal)	Percent CaCO₃	Percent organic matter	General description	Rock fraction
T 2 top	4-2	n.d.*	7.5 YR 4/6	Strong brown	5.46	15.0	Crumbly clay loam with fragments and granules of Mn, below a mass of rognons at top of T2, which are heavily crusted with Mn; some rotten and empty rinds	Weathering rinds with hollow centers and heavy Mn coating; 1 fresh red chert; smaller chert fragments with white cortex; a broken quartz pebble
T 2	4-3	n.d.	7.5 YR 4/6	Strong brown	4.51	14.7	Crumbly clay loam matrix similar to above; less Mn stain on rock fragments, but Mn granules abundant. This sample lies above a jumble of rognons and rock fragments with heavy Mn stain	1 large, heavily weathered chert, pock marked with Mn spots; other chert fragments fresher looking than above; 6–7 bone splinters and a large tooth; many Mn granules in 2–4-mm fraction
T 2	4-4	n.d.	7.5 YR 6/4	Light brown	84.58	4.5	A soft pocket of silty matrix surrounded by large rognons; with numerous very soft dolomite "pebbles" that crumble when excavated. Mn not apparent; Note high CaCO₃ content	Small dolomite fragments with crust; a few chert chips; and a fair number of Mn granules (2–4 mm); 2 very small bones (micro pelvis)
T 3	4-5	n.d.; at the base of the coupe	7.5 YR 5/6	Strong brown	6.22	18.8	Smooth heavy clay with a few scattered, strongly decayed rocks; Mn cutans throughout the clay	Just a few, small weathered fragments

* n.d. = Not done

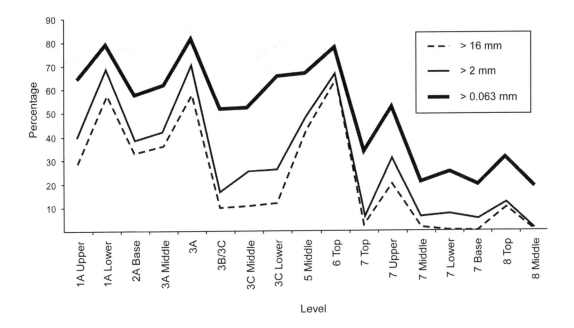

published in Henri-Martin (1957:89). However, the organic matter results appear to be too high overall – about 10 percent in FCH 1 and 2 and the lower part of FCH 3 and 15–20 percent in FCH 4 and 5 and the upper part of FCH 3. The higher values occur in levels that are rather rich in clay, and they probably, reflect dewatering of the clay minerals rather than the presence of organic matter. Nevertheless, the "organic matter" values are useful in illuminating shifts in sediment character within a given sample column, as we see in the following sections.

Figure 3.1
Cumulative granulometry of the eastern part of the Main Profile (sample series FCH 2 and 1) presented in four fractions: Cobble and pebbles 128–16 mm, small pebbles and granules 16–2 mm, sand 2–0.063 mm, and silt + clay < 0.063 mm. See also Table 3.3.

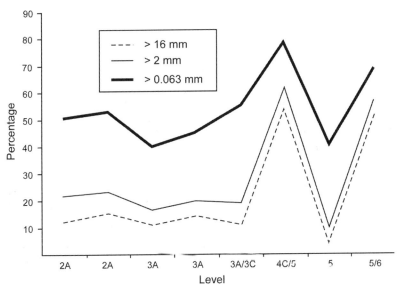

Figure 3.2
Cumulative granulometry of the western part of the Main Profile (sample series FCH 5), presented as in Figure 3.1 from data in Table 3.3.

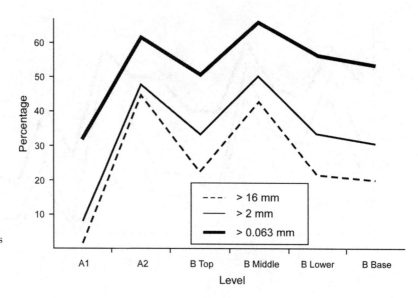

Figure 3.3
Cumulative granulom-
etry of the upper part of
the Test Pit (sample series
FCH 3-1 through 6), pre-
sented as in Figure 3.1
from data in Table 3.4.

Sediment color

To determine colors of the dry matrix, a Munsell Color Chart was
used under controlled lighting conditions in the laboratory.

Rock fraction

The sedimentary fraction larger than 2 mm was examined visually
to identify the lithology of the granules, pebbles, and cobbles; to
categorize the degree of roundness or angularity; to assess the state
of weathering; and to note the occurrence of any artifacts or faunal
remains. Those observations are noted in the right-hand column of
Table 3.2.

Figure 3.4
Cumulative granulome-
try of the lower and western part of the Test Pit
(samples series FCH 3-7
through 12), presented as
in Figure 3.1 from data in
Table 3.4.

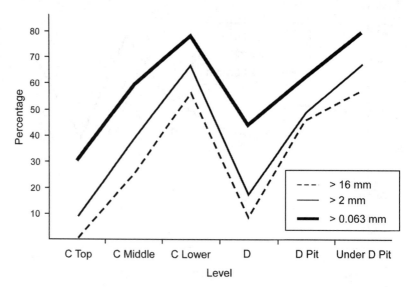

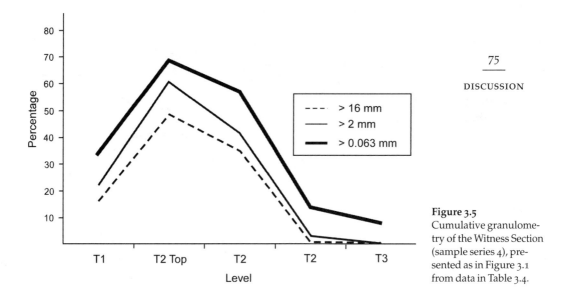

Figure 3.5
Cumulative granulome-
try of the Witness Section
(sample series 4), pre-
sented as in Figure 3.1
from data in Table 3.4.

DISCUSSION

Main profile

The following discussion is based on the information presented in
Table 3.2 and the granulometric data (shown in Tables 3.3 and 3.4
and Figs. 3.1–3.8, mentioned earlier). In general, in the fine fraction
(< 2 mm), silt + clay is dominant over the sand component, especially so in the FCH 3 series from the Test Pit, as well as at the base
of the Main Profile in Levels 7 (lower part) and 8. The one exception

Figure 3.6
Percentage of the sand
and the silt + clay frac-
tions in the total fine
fraction (< 2 mm) in the
eastern part of the Main
Profile (sample series 2
and 1).

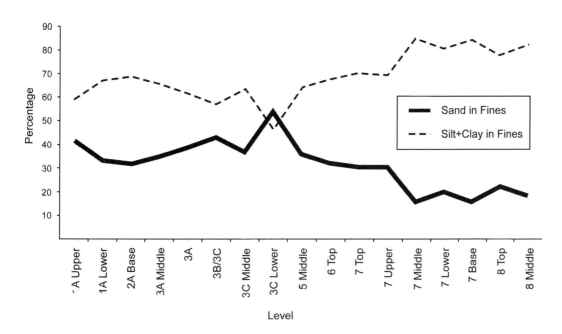

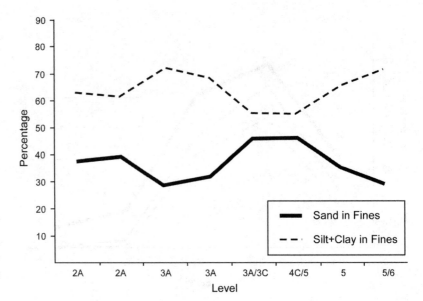

Figure 3.7
Percentage of the sand and the silt + clay fractions in the total fine fraction (< 2 mm) in the western part of the Main Profile (sample series 5).

is a sandy horizon in the Main Profile in the lower part of Level 3C (sample FCH 2–8 on the east side) and lower Level 3 or 4(?) (FCH 5–5 and 5–6 on the west), where the sand and silt + clay fractions are nearly equal. In addition, this sandy horizon is distinctly more yellow than the over- and underlying levels, and the sediment fraction smaller than 8 mm is lightly cemented into aggregates, which probably accounts for part of the apparent increase in "sand" because these aggregates of finer silt and/or clay grains act like sand-sized grains in sieving.

In any case, the color, grain size, and aggregation strongly suggest that an unconformity occurs at this horizon, and this horizon may

Figure 3.8
Percentage of the sand and the silt + clay fractions in the total fine fraction (< 2 mm) in the Test Pit (sample series FCH 3).

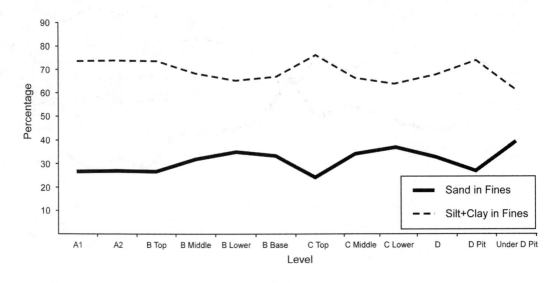

Table 3.3. Data for both total granulometry and the fine fraction separately for samples series 2, 1, and 5 of the Main Profile

Sample ID	Level	Depth below datum	Cumulative granulometry			Fine fraction only	
			Percent > 16 mm	Percent > 2 mm	Percent > 0.063 mm	Percent sand in fines	Percent silt + clay in fines
2-1	1A upper	1.86	28.8	39.4	64.6	41.6	58.4
2-2	1A lower	2.05	57.2	68.6	79.1	33.3	66.7
2-3	2A lower	2.39	33	38.3	57.9	31.7	68.3
2-4	3A	2.53	36.2	42	61.9	34.4	65.6
2-5	3B	2.69	57.4	70.1	81.7	38.9	61.1
2-6	3B base	2.77	9.7	16.2	52	42.7	57.3
2-7	3C top	2.87	10.6	24.8	52.3	36.6	63.4
2-8	3C lower	3	11.7	25.7	65.6	53.7	46.3
2-9	5 top	3.23	42.5	48.4	66.8	35.6	64.4
2-10	6 top	3.36	63.6	66.4	77.1	31.9	68.1
1-1A	7	3.48	2.2	5.8	33.9	29.8	70.2
1-1B	7	3.55	19.7	30.6	51.7	30.4	69.6
1-2	7	3.63	1.8	5.8	20.7	15.8	84.2
1-3	7	3.77	0	6.7	24.9	19.5	80.5
1-4	7 base	3.92	0	4.8	19.9	15.9	84.1
1-5	8 top	4.01	10.2	11.5	31.3	22.3	77.7
1-6	8 mid	4.19	0	0.7	18.7	18.1	81.9
5-1	1A ?	2.23	12.3	21.6	51	37.5	62.5
5-2	2 ?	2.38	15.5	23.4	53.4	39.1	60.9
5-3	2 ?	2.57	11	16.8	40.6	28.6	71.4
5-4	3 top	2.77	14.2	20	45.4	31.7	68.3
5-5	3 lower	2.99	11.2	18.7	55.4	45.1	54.9
5-6	3C or 4 ?	3.1	53.8	61.6	79.1	45.6	54.4
5-7	5	3.13	4	9.8	41.2	34.8	65.2
5-8	5	3.27	52.1	57	69.4	28.9	71.1

Table 3.4. Data for both total granulometry and the fine fraction separately for sample series 3 and 4, the Test Pit and Witness Section

Sample ID	Level	Depth below datum	Cumulative granulometry			Fine fraction only	
			Percent >16 mm	Percent > 2 mm	Percent > 0.063 mm	Percent sand in fines	Percent silt + clay in fines
3-1	A1	0.84	1.9	7.7	32.1	26.5	73.5
3-2	A2	1	44.7	47.6	61.5	26.5	73.5
3-3	B top	1.19	22.7	33.2	51	26.7	73.3
3-4	B mid	1.43	42.8	50.3	66.1	31.8	68.2
3-5	B lower	1.69	21.3	33.4	56.6	34.8	65.2
3-6	B base	2.08	19.7	30.7	53.8	33.3	66.7
3-7	C top	1.57	0.7	8.9	31	24.2	75.8
3-8	C mid	1.73	25.6	39.2	60	34.1	65.9
3-9	C lower	2.1	56.7	66.9	79	36.5	63.5
3-10	D	2.43	8.9	17.5	44.4	32.6	67.4
3-11	D pit	2.93	46.2	49.2	62.9	27	73
3-12	Under D pit	3.1	57.8	67.7	80.4	39.3	60.7
4-1	T1	n.d.*	16.3	22.3	33.5	14.4	85.6
4-2	T2 top	n.d.	48.8	60.7	69.2	21.6	78.4
4-3	T2	n.d.	34.8	41.6	57.4	27	73
4-4	T2	n.d.	0.5	3.1	14.1	11.4	88.6
4-5	T3	n.d.	0	0.2	8.2	8	92

* not done

well be an extension of Henri-Martin's *"Horizon à Ours"* (Cave Bear Horizon). According to Henri-Martin (1957), this horizon was rich in cave bear bones in the outer part of the cave, but this material faded away toward the interior. The Cave Bear Horizon is also marked by a ferruginous color, abundant phosphate, and a distinct reduction in certain heavy minerals (Henri-Martin 1957:77, 87), indicating in situ weathering compatible with an unconformity. The Cave Bear Horizon separates the Tayacian into two more or less equal parts vertically – Beds E1 and E2 of Henri-Martin (1957, Fig. 9). Although she does not give the specific depth of that horizon, it appears to be about 3 m deep in her section drawings. I believe, therefore, that the lower part of the present Level 3 at a depth of about 2.8 m below datum on the east side of the Main Profile and about 3.1 m on the west is the extension of Henri-Martin's Cave Bear Horizon and marks a hiatus of indeterminate but not insignificant duration.

Another unconformity in the Main Profile appears at about 3.9 m depth between Levels 7 and 8. Although my sample FCH 1–4 is labeled "Level 7 base" (Table 3.2) in accordance with labels in place when I sampled, I believe that it is really the top of Level 8 based on its clear similarity in color and grain size to the underlying sediments. Level 8 is yellowish red and is thus much redder than any other strata in the Main Profile or in the Witness Section. The top several centimeters of Level 8, as seen in sample FCH 1–5, have a conspicuously blocky structure underlying a sharp contact. In this area, there is almost no rock fraction and just a few granules, and according to Henri-Martin (1957:256) these sediments, called *"argiles de fond"* (basal clays), are archaeologically barren. Conceivably, Level 8 is much older than the immediately overlying Tayacian strata.

In addition, it appears that Level 7 should be divided into two strata on the basis of sedimentary characteristics. My samples – FCH 1–1A and 1–1B, and perhaps FCH 1–2 – are duller and contain noticeable white streaks and nodules of phosphate, but the rock fraction is moderately abundant and relatively fresh in appearance (Table 3.2). In contrast, the lower part of Level 7 (below about −3.7 m) is brighter in color, rich in silt + clay, and nearly lacking in rock fraction. Moreover, the chert fragments present are highly weathered crusts and rinds.

The rock fraction is particularly abundant in the upper strata exposed in the Main Profile. It consists of variable amounts of broken chert nodules, fragments and chips of chert, fragments of dolomitic bedrock, and exotic rocks, which are usually well-rounded cobbles, pebbles, or granules. In some strata, all these components exist together (see Table 3.2). Recall, however, that my samples are limited to clasts smaller than 128 mm; thus, larger chert nodules, which are abundant in many strata, are not included, but they generally appear in section drawings.

The occurrence of well-rounded exotic rocks is an important indicator of the source of the enclosing sediment. There is no evidence of fluvial deposits in the cave, at least in the remaining Tayacian levels, so these exotics must have entered through chimneys or fissures in the cave ceiling. Quartz pebbles, small cobbles, and even 2- to 4-mm granules occur more or less regularly, at least below −2.53 m, and the largest of them are commonly smaller than 30 mm or so, suggesting that they are integral parts of the natural sediment and not human manuports. The fact that these exotic pebbles appear regularly in my rather small sediment samples tends to confirm this opinion. They are even more abundant in the Test Pit, as shown in the following section.

The $CaCO_3$ and organic matter contents of the Main Profile (Table 3.2) are not particularly useful in characterizing individual strata. Organic matter values hover around 9.5 percent to 11.5 percent in columns FCH 1 and 2 and are a bit higher in FCH 5, namely 12.7 to 20 percent. As stated earlier, the "organic matter" analysis appears to be measuring more than just organic matter, which is scarce in these sediments, but most likely reflects dewatering of some minerals, especially clays. $CaCO_3$ values are consistently quite low, around 1 to 3 percent, with the exception of the top levels of the Main Profile. The very top sample, FCH 2–1, has a $CaCO_3$ value of around 11 percent, which approaches the high values of 41 to 49 percent found in the uppermost bed of the Tayacian (E1′) by Henri-Martin (1957:89), suggesting that the top of the present Main Profile is very near, but not at, the top of the Tayacian as excavated by Henri-Martin.

Test Pit

The excavation at the rear of the cave is a combination of Henri-Martin's original Test Pit and an extension to the east made during our excavations. Henri-Martin's pit was originally 3.5 m deep, exposing thin stalagmitic lenses near the top and uncemented boulders (*blocaille*) in its middle beds. She equated the latter with her Bed D in

the outer part of the cave (Henri-Martin 1957:57–59), which occurs at
a similar depth below the pre-excavation surface, if one allows for a
slight inclination of Bed D from the rear to the front of the cave. Like
Bed D in the outer part of the cave, she finds that this *blocaille* separates Aurignacian and Mousterian industries above it from Tayacian
beds below.

However, in the newly opened eastern sector of the Test Pit, the
situation is quite different. The topmost levels (A1 and A2, below the
disturbed material) are dark yellowish-brown, compact clay loams
with numerous rock fragments, charcoal, and bone fragments (see
Table 3.2). On the whole, they look quite young. Levels A1 and A2
slope toward the cave mouth at an angle of about 10 degrees. Next
below is Level B, which is less clayey than A1 and A2 (Fig. 3.8) but
still is quite rocky. The rock fraction contains numerous well-rounded
quartz pebbles and small cobbles, as well as granules (2–4 mm); as
many as four to eight pebbles and cobbles were included in each
of my relatively small samples. Given the small size of many of the
quartz pebbles (8–32 mm), it is unlikely that they were introduced
by humans.

Level B appears to be a mudflow or sludge sediment, most likely
introduced into the rear of the cave through an opening to the surface.
In fact, it appears that some very young sediment is still sliding into
the cave from the passage southeast of the Test Pit. The source of
this sediment is the surficial deposits that cover the Maurijo plateau
above the cave. In fact, much of the cave filling must owe its origin
to sediments that entered the cave from the plateau. Support for
this conclusion comes, in part, from the study of heavy minerals by
S. Duplaix (in Henri-Martin 1957:76–79), who finds that the heavy
mineral suites of all the cave sediments are quite similar and are
unlikely to have been derived from the cave bedrock, which contains
very few heavy minerals.

The upper contact of Level B below A2 is very sharp, suggesting
that an unconformity occurs there. Moreover, Level B clearly fills a
trough incised into Level C below. This trough cuts out Level C in
the entire eastern third of our recent Test Pit, specifically squares F42,
F43, and G43. (Note the overlap in depths-below-datum of samples from Levels B and C in Figs. 3.3, 3.4, and 3.8.) The contact
between Levels B and C is very clear, marking an erosional unconformity of unknown duration. Level B here contains Bronze Age artifacts (P. Chase, personal communication) and must be younger than

Henri-Martin's Bed C1 and/or C2, which she assigns to the Mousterian, in her Test Pit 3.

Level C presents a strong contrast to Level B. Although manganese stains or nodules were scarce in Level B, Level C is thoroughly impregnated with manganese coatings, stains, granules, and nodules. Moreover, the rock fragments, both chert and dolomite, are abundant, large, and highly weathered, with thick rinds and/or hollowed-out interiors. The matrix is a (dark) yellowish-brown, silty clay loam very similar to that of Level B. There is a marked decrease in organic matter from Level B to Level C, from values of 12 to 22 percent in B, as well as in Levels A1 and A2, to values consistently lower than 10 percent in Level C (Table 3.2). This decrease undoubtedly reflects the greater degree of weathering in Level C, reinforcing the conclusion of a major unconformity between B and C. Quartz pebbles continue to be abundant (Table 3.2). Note also that Level C has considerably more $CaCO_3$ than either Level B above or Level D below, specifically three to four times as much (Table 3.2). This certainly results from the residue of the decaying dolomite rocks in Level C.

Note that this Level C is not the same as Henri-Martin's Bed C, which overlies the *blocaille* (her Bed D) in Test Pit 3. In fact, Level C is more likely the equivalent of Henri-Martin's Bed D, given the abundance of large rocks. Unfortunately, because the upper parts of the old and new (i.e., western and eastern, respectively) sections of the combined Test Pit are now disconnected, one cannot trace Henri-Martin's beds physically into the newer part.

Level D of the new Test Pit is exposed at floor level, about 2.4 m below datum – corresponding to my sample FCH 3–10 (Table 3.2). It is silty and contrasts in color and rock content to the overlying levels, being very pale brown (or "gray") and containing less than 10 percent of rock fragments larger than 16 mm. There is no manganese staining, but quartz pebbles (8–32 mm) and a red ochre pebble were noted, along with conspicuous yellow ochre staining. The silty matrix is slightly cemented. This Level D may be the equivalent of Henri-Martin's Bed E, which she characterized as *"grisâtre"* or "light gray." Henri-Martin (1957:57) believed on sedimentological grounds that her Bed E, in which she found Tayacian artifacts, is the same as the uppermost Tayacian in the outer cave. If so, it is unlike any levels in the Main Profile as it exists at present, once again suggesting that the top of the Main Profile is not the very top of Henri-Martin's Tayacian (her E0 or E1').

Witness Section

The Witness Section left by Henri-Martin was sampled at coordinates of $X = 10-11$ and $Y = 11$, approximately, in the open-air portion of the cave entrance, beginning at a depth of about 25 cm below the surface of the Witness Section as it existed in 1998. The sediments here are mostly dark reddish-brown ("strong brown" in Munsell notation) heavy clay loam (Table 3.2), with the exception of my sample FCH 4–4 at the base of Level T2. The latter sample is from a pocket or lens that is light brown in color and silty in texture, including many dolomite fragments in an advanced state of decay and hardly any coarse fraction (Fig. 3.5) – nothing larger than 32 mm. The decaying dolomite "pebbles" contribute to a high value of $CaCO_3$ in the sediment matrix (about 85 percent, Table 3.2), and note also that the "organic matter" value drops conspicuously in this lens to about one-third of that in the over- and underlying, more clayey levels. Manganese granules are abundant, but manganese staining is not apparent. There are a few chert chips and some microfauna.

In contrast, the other samples, FCH 4–2 and 4–3, from the top and middle of Level T2 contain numerous rocks, in addition to chert nodules too large to sample. Many of the nodules are rotten and heavily manganese stained or exist only as weathering rinds. Overall, Level T2 resembles Level C of the Test Pit (see preceding section and Table 3.2) with its rotten cherts, decaying dolomite fragments, and manganese impregnation. No other exposed stratum in the cave has these characteristics. The sedimentological similarity of these strata suggests, but does not prove, that they are correlative. They differ by about 5 m in depth below datum. However, that difference is not necessarily an argument against their contemporaneity. In Henri-Martin's (1957:46) interpretation of site formation, the outer part of the cave fill slumped as result of erosion at the cave entrance, thereby producing the pronounced slope from her Secteur 1 outward. This slope had a height of about 5 m (Henri-Martin 1965, Figs. 2 and 4), dropping down from the outer (north) edge of Secteur 1 to the bedrock bench at the outer edge of Secteur 0, where the Witness Section is located (see also Coupe IX–X in Henri-Martin 1965). The *blocaille* D was disrupted by sliding down this slope and rests on top of the bedrock bench in Secteur 0. Presumably, the overlying Mousterian levels were translocated downward as well. Thus, it is possible that Level T2 of the Witness Section is a remnant of Henri-Martin's Mousterian Bed C. However, P. Chase (see Chapter 8) finds that the fauna in the Witness Section match that of the Tayacian beds.

FCH 4–5 from Level T3 at the base of the Witness Section has a similar clayey matrix, but essentially no rock fraction and just a few granules. It is also impregnated with manganese as coatings in cracks within the clay mass. Except for the manganese, this clay resembles the "basal clays" of Henri-Martin, which I sampled at the base of the Main Profile (Level 8, sample FCH 1–6). This resemblance may just be coincidental. Neither the excavation of Henri-Martin nor the present excavation reached bedrock in the area of the Witness Section (Henri-Martin's Secteur 0).

GENERAL CONCLUSIONS

The sedimentary filling of the Cave of Fontéchevade resulted from a combination of materials that were subsequently modified to a greater or lesser extent by weathering processes. Blocks of the dolomite bedrock were detached from the walls and ceiling, probably largely by solution processes, which also released numerous chert nodules that accumulated in the filling. Much or all of the dolomite has been subsequently dissolved from the cave sediments. Simultaneously, silty loam with greater or lesser amounts of clay and containing exotic rock types, largely quartz cobbles, pebbles, and granules, entered the cave from bedrock openings at its rear. These sedimentary components necessarily came from outside the cave because the enclosing bedrock contains none of these materials. Heavy-mineral studies by Duplaix (in Henri-Martin 1957) reinforce this conclusion. Henri-Martin also found little or no evidence of sediments entering the cave by fluvial or eolian processes, and, as far as the sediments still remaining in the cave are concerned, I concur with her conclusion. The basal deposit – the "*argiles de fond*" of Henri-Martin – found at the bottom of the Main Profile (Level 8) appears to be made up of residual karstic clays deposited before, perhaps long before, the cave was used by humans. It is a pure clay with no rocks and no exotics.

Relating the existing sediments to Henri-Martin's stratigraphy is somewhat problematic. The Main Profile corresponds to her Tayacian Bed E in part, but the uppermost Tayacian (Eo and E1′?) appears to be missing, judging from her observation that the top of the Tayacian just below the *blocaille* D is heavily charged with carbonate, whereas my analysis finds only a moderate increase in $CaCO_3$ at the top of the present Main Profile. Thus, Henri-Martin's Beds A, B, C, and D are completely missing at the current position of the Main Profile. Her Cave Bear Horizon appears to be represented by the lower part of our Level 3, which is more yellow and sandier than beds above and below and is slightly cemented.

Relating the existing sediments to the Test Pit at the rear of the cave is even more problematic. The sediments at the eastern and western extremes of the Test Pit are quite different from each another. The present Levels A1, A2, and B have no equivalents in the upper part of Henri-Martin's Test Pit 3, and the stalagmitic lenses and crusty silts of Henri-Martin's AB, C1, and C2 are absent in the east at the same depths. The present Level B fills a clear erosional channel cut in Level C, marking an unconformity. The present Level C is the likely equivalent of Henri-Martin's Bed D, with highly decayed, manganese-stained dolomite blocks and chert nodules. If these correlations are correct, then all beds in the eastern, newer part of the Test Pit should be Mousterian or younger. As mentioned in the preceding discussion, the bottom of Level T2 of the Witness Section is conceivably equivalent to our Test Pit Level C.

There are several gaps (unconformities) in the sediment infilling. As mentioned in the preceding paragraph, Level B in the Test Pit fills an erosional unconformity. Henri-Martin (1957:43) also noted an erosional channel in part of her Mousterian strata, which may be the equivalent of the channel now exposed in the Test Pit. There may be another minor unconformity above Level B where sloping Levels A1 and A2 appear to truncate the top of Level B.

Two unconformities were found in the Main Profile. The obvious one occurs between Levels 7 and 8. The heavy, bright-colored clay of Level 8 has developed a blocky structure (by desiccation), presumably as it lay exposed on the cave floor for an unknown duration, before being covered by Tayacian-bearing strata. Higher in the section, the sedimentary character of the lower part of Level 3 suggests another hiatus in sediment accumulation. This is the horizon that I have tentatively identified as the continuation of Henri-Martin's

Cave Bear Horizon. These sediments are oxidized to a brighter yellowish color, they are sandier than above or below, and they are slightly cemented, all of which suggests a period of incipient pedogenesis at this level.

In the Witness Section, it is possible that an unconformity occurs at the base of Level T2, between the odd, sandy stratum at the bottom of T2 and the clay-rich T3, which is perhaps a basal clay (*"argile de fond"* sensu Henri-Martin). This gap would have been produced by the slumping that occurred in the outer portion of the cave, as visualized by Henri-Martin.

It is not possible to make a quantitative estimate of the duration of any of these unconformities. In relative terms, the time gap between Levels B and C in the new Test Pit must be rather long, given the highly weathered nature of Level C and the rather fresh-looking Level B. The gap between Levels 7 and 8 in the lower part of the Main Profile may also be of considerable length, if the basal clays are indeed karstic deposits formed before the cave was exposed to the open air. In any case, the evidence of weathering associated with each of the unconformities (except in the Witness Section) means that they are not insignificant events.

4

Paleoclimate Delineation Using Magnetic Susceptibility Data

Brooks B. Ellwood

INTRODUCTION

This chapter reports on the use of the technique of magnetic susceptibility (MS) on sediments found in Fontéchevade Cave to describe the
paleoclimate of the region. It describes in detail the technique of MS
and its usefulness in detecting paleoclimatic trends from sediment
analysis.

It is well known that MS data from cave sediments found in
archaeological sites can be used as a high-resolution paleoclimate
proxy. MS is useful when other climate indicators and dates are
ambiguous or absent. Caves and perhaps deep rock shelters provide ideal environments for sediment deposition that is unaffected
by in-situ pedogenesis. Cave sediments are not as strongly affected by
iron variations produced within individual soils as are sediments at
open-air sites, nor are they strongly affected by bioturbation, which is
minimal in most caves and is usually easily recognized during excavation. From cave sediments, paleoclimatic trends and estimates of
duration of sediment deposition can be extracted. Because paleoclimate analyses of this type are performed on the entire data set from
which archaeological materials are extracted, we believe that MS data
provide a unique opportunity to evaluate the effect of climate on the
behavior of ancient peoples.

In recent years, MS measurements of sediments have been used
in paleoclimatic studies of loess and as a paleoclimate proxy in other
materials. (The MS work in loess has been summarized by Heller
and Evans [1995].) MS works as a proxy in many materials because
changing climate alters the magnetic properties of sediments during

pedogenesis (see Mullins 1977 for an early summary). Production of maghemite, hematite, or possibly greigite (Stanjek et al. 1994) during soil formation (with corresponding increases in MS) is high during periods when the climate is relatively warm (assuming that moisture is available for pedogenesis). For example, Tite and Linington (1975) showed that magnetic minerals, primarily maghemite, are formed as the result of alternating chemical reduction and oxidation during pedogenesis. Dehydration of soils has also been suggested as an explanation for the widespread occurrence of maghemite in warmer climates. The result is high production of maghemite and corresponding increases in MS when alternating weather patterns for part of the year, from wet to dry, cause soil oxidation and dehydration. Further work by Singer and Fine (1989) showed that both temperature and moisture can have a significant effect on MS and that, in general, warmer/wetter conditions enhanced the MS signature during pedogenesis. Much of the work concerning the production of ferrimagnetic minerals in soils has been summarized by Fassbinder, Stanjek, and Vali (1990).

The variations and trends in the observed magnitude of MS make it possible to make correlations among excavation units within or across sites. This has been demonstrated in several cases. For example, Ellwood, Harrold, and Marks (1994) showed excellent correlations among Upper Paleolithic sites in Portugal. The Riverbend site near Fort Worth, Texas, is another example of intrasite correlation using MS (Ellwood, Balsam and Schieber 1995). Other examples of such correlations were shown for excavation units within Konispol Cave, Albania (Ellwood, Petruso and Harrold 1996; Ellwood et al. 2004), and elsewhere (Ellwood et al. 1998). MS variations from different caves in Europe have been used for intersite correlation and the development of a standard MS zonation covering the last 46,000 years (Ellwood et al. 2001).

METHODS

The magnetic susceptibility method

All materials become magnetic when placed in a magnetic field. MS is an indicator of the strength of this magnetism. This "induced" magnetism is very different from natural remnant magnetism (NRM), which accounts for the magnetic polarity of materials. In a geoarchaeological context, MS is generally considered to be an indicator of iron mineral concentration. It can be measured quickly and easily using small samples of sediment. Essentially, all mineral grains, but especially those containing iron, such as maghemite or magnetite, are "susceptible" to becoming magnetized in the presence of a magnetic field. Generally, the greater the volume of iron-containing grains, the higher the MS. For paleoclimate studies, MS, independent of other measurements, has been shown to be sensitive to subtle changes in total iron concentration in sediments (Banerjee 1996). Thus, the addition of maghemite to sediments increases the MS. Maghemite produced by pedogenesis appears to be relatively stable chemically (Mullins 1977), resulting in a stable MS signature.

MS measurements are made by placing sediment samples in a low-intensity magnetic field and measuring the resulting induced magnetization. This procedure is different from the NRM measurements used to determine magnetic polarities. MS measurements require that an inducing magnetic field is present within the sample-measuring space. Conversely, NRM measurements are made in magnetic-field-free spaces and indicate the spontaneous magnetization carried by samples that is independent of external magnetic fields

PALEOCLIMATES: GENERAL COMMENTS

Verosub et al. (1993) have argued that future research involving MS data in sediments should focus on the role of climate in the development of soils. One problem with soils, however, is the removal of the iron from the A horizons and reprecipitation in the B horizons, which results in a removal of mobile surface iron. The mobility of iron in the generation of paleosols can result in large MS variations within single soils (Ellwood et al. 1995). As noted earlier, this problem is less severe in sediments found in caves.

For that reason, we have been examining protected sites, primarily sites from caves and deep rock shelters. We have used MS measurements of sediment samples from different excavation units within a cave near the town of Konispol in the Sarandë district of southwestern Albania to make intrasite correlations (Ellwood et al. 1996). In Konispol Cave, MS trends resulted from the production of maghemite by pedogenesis outside the cave. The soils had washed, been blown, or tracked into the cave, and maghemite had accumulated in varying amounts, depending on the climatic conditions during overall pedogenesis outside the cave. (In other environments, ferrimagnetic minerals such as magnetite or greigite may be produced during pedogenesis and in turn be deposited in caves or deep rock shelters.) ^{14}C dates indicated that, during the period from about 3500 to 9000 BP, Konispol Cave exhibited a unique record of essentially constant sedimentation. Ellwood et al. (1996, 1997) have developed a composite profile for the Konispol Cave site and have used the constant (near-linear) sedimentation rate at the site to assign ages to this profile.

Because warm climates should yield high MS values and cold climates should yield low MS values, Ellwood et al. (1997) have argued that the composite profile for Konispol Cave represents paleoclimatic trends in southeastern Europe (the region of the cave). The main data trend ranges from lower MS values in older sediments to higher values in younger sediments and indicates overall warming during the Holocene. This result is broadly consistent with paleoclimatic data published elsewhere for the northern hemisphere (e.g., Denton and Karlén 1973; Gradstein, Ogg, and Smith 2004; Ruddiman and Mix 1993), including regional pollen studies (Bonatti 1966; Bottema 1994).

It is clear from the work at Konispol Cave that the MS record exhibits quite a bit of short-term variability that can be correlated to major paleoclimatic events. To illustrate these climatic events, Ellwood et al. (1997) have correlated times of significant northern hemisphere glacial recessions/advances to MS data fluctuations, using data identified for the Holocene by Denton and Karlén (1973) and from a cold period reported for the Summit, Greenland, ice core by O'Brien et al. (1995).

More recently, the MS of samples from Halls Cave, Texas, shows clearly that the MS is a proxy for paleoclimate (Ellwood and Gose 2006). In the Halls Cave study, samples were recovered from a 3-m excavation at approximately 1-cm intervals, and the section was dated using calibrated ^{14}C data. Three major climatic events were represented in the MS data set: the H1 Heinrich Event, 17,500 to 17,000 BP, the end of full glaciation on the Edwards Plateau in Texas at 14,200 BP, and the 8200 BP climatic event from 8250 to 8050, which was also observed in the Konispol Cave data set (Ellwood et al. 1996). The data demonstrate an excellent correlation between independent climate indicators and the MS data set at Konispol Cave. We have been working to develop an extended paleoclimate curve for Europe from protected cave and shelter sites using MS data (Ellwood et al. 2001; Harrold et al. 2004). Toward this end, we have collected samples in Fontéchevade Cave.

FONTÉCHEVADE CAVE RESULTS

Paleoclimate and duration

In Fontéchevade Cave, the two main excavation areas are separated by approximately 14 m. The main excavation (Main Profile) is located toward the front of the cave, and a secondary excavation (the Test Pit) is located at the back of the cave. Both areas had been previously excavated and were reexcavated by the current team. Here, we report MS results from the Test Pit located at the back of the cave.

We collected 105 samples at approximately 3-cm intervals from the Test Pit and measured the MS using a susceptibility bridge. In addition, we measured the thermomagnetic susceptibility using a Kappa Bridge KLY3S to evaluate the magnetic mineralogy and identify any iron mineral alteration effects that might have affected the deposited sediments.

MS data from the Test Pit showed two types of sedimentation in three layers (see Fig. 4.1). In the upper zone (0.2 to approximately 1.3 m) and the lower zone (approximately 2.7 to 3.4 m) of the sampled section, there is relatively non-varying MS, indicating rapid, fluvial-type deposition. These segments are relatively free of lithic fragments and bone; again, typical of rapid sedimentation. In the middle zone (between 1.3 and 2.7 m), sediment is typical of very slow, non-fluvial accumulation. Within this zone there are lithic artifacts that do not exhibit typical fluvial-type depositional characteristics. However, the MS data from these sediments indicate typical paleoclimatic cyclicity, where the MS curves appear to correlate with the marine isotope stage (MIS) zonation. These data, along with age estimates for the cave, were used to infer a proposed climatic correlation to the standard MIS data. This correlation is based on interpretation of variations in the MS values in light of recently reported dates (see Chapter 7). Therefore, deposition in the middle zone appears to represent a fluctuating climate – from cold to warm, back to cold, and a return to warm – that is inferred to begin in MIS 6 and to continue through MIS 5 to MIS 4. The overall MS trend appears to represent part of one climate cycle that contains several shorter climate cycles (MIS 5e to 4).

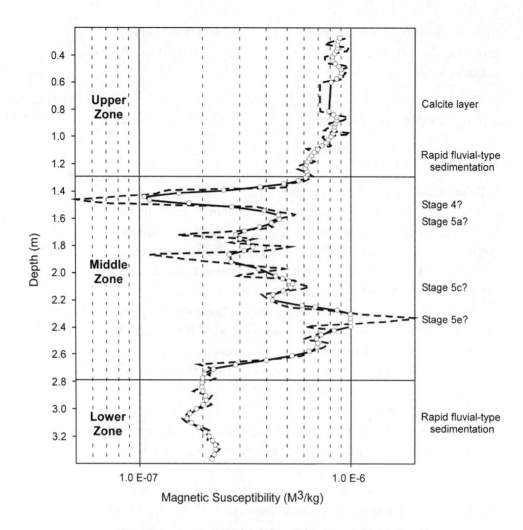

Figure 4.1
An MS profile for the Test Pit at the back of Fontéchevade Cave, southwest France. Ages are estimated from marine isotope stage (MIS) assignment and are based on the interpretation that slow sedimentation mainly occurred during MIS 6–4. These dates may not be correct, but are based on the best information available at this time.

These results suggest that deposition represented at the site occurred for approximately 100,000 years, from about 155,000 to < 60,000 BP. The data are interpreted to represent sedimentation beginning during the later part of Riss glacial time, continuing through much of Riss-Würm interglacial time and then into Würm glacial time. We recognize that diastems exist in the sedimentary record, but it is clear that a fairly well-defined sequence was recovered in this continuously sampled profile. This age and duration assessment is very preliminary and poorly constrained by independent dates but is consistent with the glacial–interglacial cyclicity we see elsewhere.

Thermomagnetic measurements: A test of sample alteration effects

We heated a number of samples from room temperature to 700°C and took measurements periodically during the heating process. Such

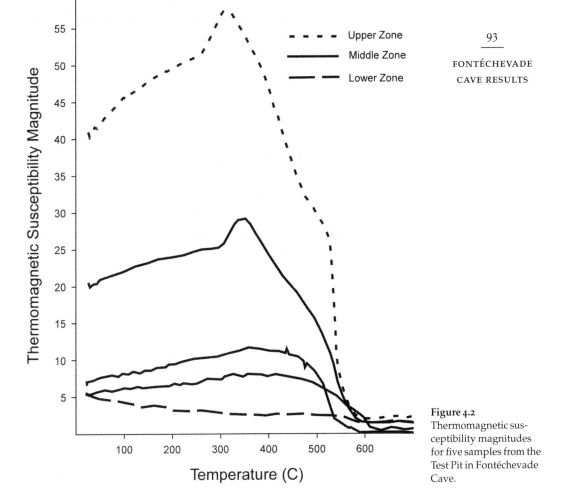

Legend:
- - - - Upper Zone
——— Middle Zone
— — Lower Zone

(Y-axis) Thermomagnetic Susceptibility Magnitude

(X-axis) Temperature (C)

Figure 4.2
Thermomagnetic susceptibility magnitudes for five samples from the Test Pit in Fontéchevade Cave.

measurements are useful for characterizing the magnetic mineralogy in samples and can be compared to those in standard samples with known magnetic components.

Figure 4.2 reports some of these results. A sample from the Test Pit upper zone (Fig. 4.1), interpreted to have been deposited in a rapid, fluvial-type environment, shows a typical magnetite Curie temperature (approximately 580°C) and ferrimagnetic curve shape (convex upward). This sample also exhibits the highest values, as is expected for younger samples where the magnetite is relatively pristine. A sample from the lower zone shows a paramagnetic curve shape (downward parabola), indicative of a much older age and/or some alteration of the original ferrimagnetic components. Middle zone samples exhibit unaltered ferrimagnetic shapes expected for samples that have not had significant alteration of their magnetic components. It is concluded from these data that the upper and middle zones contain ferrimagnetic components that have not been altered and therefore still reflect the climate trends responsible for producing these components

CONCLUDING REMARKS

The data presented in this chapter demonstrate that MS provides a useful tool for climate analysis. Using the results from Fontéchevade profiles, a composite MS profile has been developed that provides a proxy for climate at the time these sediments were deposited. A preliminary paleoclimate curve suggests that deposition probably started during the Riss glacial and included much of Riss-Würm interglacial time. Analysis of the MS data set indicates that deposition of the sediments recovered from the Fontéchevade Test Pit occurred over a period of about 100,000 years.

ACKNOWLEDGMENTS

Sue Ellwood is gratefully acknowledged for her help in sampling; James Marlatt, a McNair Research Fellow, is acknowledged for his help in sampling and laboratory measurement. Partial funding in support of this work was provided by the SOAR-McNair Scholars Program, the College of Science, and the Department of Earth and Environmental Sciences at the University of Texas at Arlington.

5

Electrical Resistivity Survey of Fontéchevade

Shannon P. McPherron and Brooks B. Ellwood

INTRODUCTION

It was clear that the geometry of the Fontéchevade Cave system was likely much more complex than it appeared initially. Other caves in this area, particularly La Chaise, demonstrate complexity with their multitude of subsidiary chambers, entrances, and connecting passageways. To some extent, the complexity of Fontéchevade is apparent in Henri-Martin's map of the site. Just inside the entrance of the cave there is a side branch, which she labeled the Diverticule. Just behind the main section, there is another side branch that is too full of sediment to enter, and likewise the very back of the cave ends with apparent passageways choked with sediment. In part to look for additional caves in the area and in part to look for alternative entrances to Fontéchevade, we conducted an electrical resistivity survey of the area immediately above and adjacent to the entrance to the cave.

METHODOLOGY

Electrical resistivity is a well-established remote sensing technique that has been applied to archaeological situations for some time, typically to map changes in lithology and to locate buried features (Ellwood and Harrold 1993; Ellwood et al. 1993, 1995). The usefulness of electrical resistivity is based on the fact that soils and rocks vary in the degree to which they are able to conduct electrical current. The ability of soils and rocks to conduct current is controlled by several factors, including moisture content, clay content, porosity, and the presence of free ions (Ellwood and Harrold 1993). Rock and air spaces (such as one can encounter in a cave) are poor conductors of electricity, whereas sediments are much better conductors.

In resistivity surveys, a current is usually applied to the ground via two electrodes, and the potential difference (voltage) is measured between a second set of electrodes (Fig. 5.1). These four electrodes can be arranged in a number of configurations, but in this study we used the Wenner array (even spacing between electrodes), which is the most common configuration employed in archaeological work (Weymouth 1986). Between measurements, the set of electrodes is moved along a straight line by a distance equal to the spacing between individual electrodes (Darwin et al. 1990).

The Williams resistivity meter used for this study operates by applying an alternating current at 145 Hz using four steel electrodes that are inserted in line about 4–5 cm into the ground (see Williams 1984 for a detailed description of the instrument). We chose this frequency to reduce the effect on surveys of the 50–60 Hz noise usually found in urban areas. The frequency is also relatively low and somewhat insensitive to slight changes in water ion content. As with many of these instruments, the Williams meter is designed so that the potentiometer and galvanometer are linked by the same circuit, making it unnecessary to measure current and voltage independently. Therefore, the potentiometer can be calibrated in ohms (Ω). A rotary switch on the Williams meter allows for the reconfiguration of the probes, so that only one electrode must be moved per measurement while profiling, thus increasing the speed of data acquisition.

The flow of current establishes an equipotential in the subsurface from which a potential drop (voltage) can be measured. The value of apparent resistivity depends in part on the distance between electrodes. For the Wenner array, the fundamental resistivity equation for apparent resistivity (ρ_a in Ωm [ohm meters]), where the term "apparent" is used because there are different electrical properties in different directions (anisotropy) in the subsurface and therefore measurement over the same area but in different directions will produce a slightly different resistivity value, reduces to

$$\rho_a = 2\pi \, \mathrm{DR}$$

where 2π is a geometric factor, D is the distance between electrodes, and R is the measured resistance (Keller and Frischknecht 1966); ρ_a values represent the weighted average of all ρ_a variations in the

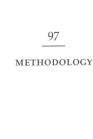

Figure 5.1
Acquiring electrical
resistivity data in the
field in front of the cave.

subsurface. Typical values of ρ_a for soils generally range from 5 to 100 Ωm and, for clays, from 5 to 150 Ωm (e.g., Palacky 1988).

We used several site survey methods to acquire resistivity data, including obtaining data in a rectangular grid pattern over the desired area, sounding, and profiling. The usual approach is to choose multiple electrode spacings and, using the Wenner configuration, have each profile follow the same traverse. In this manner, data from a series of profiles can be presented as an ρ_a pseudosection (Imai, Kanemori, and Sakayama 1987; Zohdy, Eaton, and Mabey 1974). The preparation of sections is fundamental for the interpretation of ρ_a data. Pseudosections are constructed by plotting the ρ_a values for each measurement beneath the geometric center for the electrode array at a vertical depth of penetration, which corresponds to the electrode separation used. The ρ_a values are then contoured in Ωm intervals to illustrate the broad vertical distribution of subsurface ρ_a variations. The result of this type of mapping is a geoelectric cross-section (pseudosection) of the subsurface.

Apparent resistivity pseudosections can be considered roughly analogous to "time-stratigraphic units" as used in seismic stratigraphy. Time-stratigraphic units are interpreted as depositional sequences consisting of various lithologies and grain sizes. In seismic stratigraphy, reflections usually indicate unconformities within strata so time surfaces may be identified without regard to lithologic contrast (Sheriff 1980). Geoelectric stratigraphy has some similarities to seismic stratigraphy in that it can be used to trace widespread marker horizons. Because electrical variations are

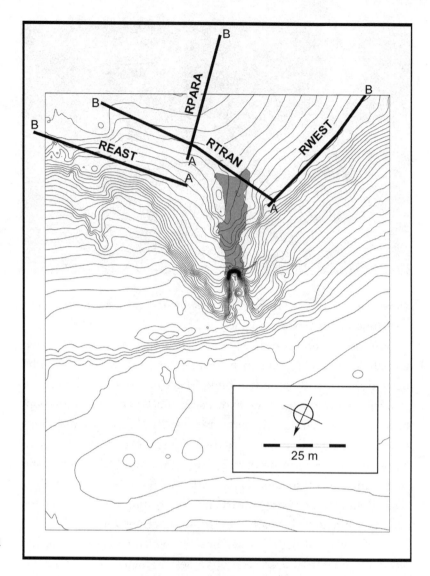

Figure 5.2
Location of the electrical
resistivity lines.

controlled more by lithologic contrasts than by unconformities, they have been shown to be especially useful in correlating facies surfaces between wells (Vail, Mitchum, and Thompson 1977). Because sudden physical events often control the patterns of sedimentation, it is often possible to map the resulting surfaces electrically as nearly synchronous deposits. This does not imply that an individual ρ_a contour is a time line but rather that the deposits bounded by particular ρ_a horizons are related genetically. With adequate sampling and subsurface control, lithologic boundaries that represent unconformities can be delineated by use of the resistivity method.

RESULTS

REast

This resistively line runs along the edge of the plateau to the east of Fontéchevade Cave (Fig. 5.2). Its placement was designed to address two questions. First, generally, we wanted to investigate the possibility of other cave openings at the interface between the plateau and the valley. Second, specifically, as a result of topographic mapping to the east of the Fontéchevade Cave entrance, we identified an anomaly along the slope of the valley edge that could be interpreted as a talus deposit resulting from a now-closed cave entrance (Fig. 5.2).

The results of resistivity profile REast showed a significant resistivity anomaly between 30 and 35 m that correlates well with the previously mentioned topographic feature (Fig. 5.3). Toward the cave mouth, particularly between 5 and 30 m along profile REast, the high resistivity contours are best interpreted as limestone bedrock close to the surface. One possibility for the subsequent low resistivity between 30 and 35 m could be a sediment-filled collapsed cave entrance. Thus, two lines of evidence, electrical resistivity and topography, indicate that this location could be worth archaeological investigation.

On inspection of this location, a large tree was discovered growing at the edge of the plateau. On the one hand, the root system of this

Figure 5.3
Electrical resistivity pseudosections for the lines shown in Figure 5.2.

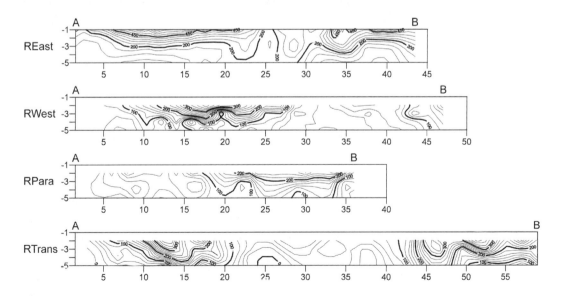

tree could be responsible for the anomaly observed in the resistivity data. On the other hand, the unusually large size and the placement of this tree may be yet another indicator of a buried cave entrance, in that the root system may be tapping into the deeper sediments and possibly water that this cave mouth would provide.

A test excavation was conducted at the edge of the plateau in an attempt to verify the cave entrance hypothesis. The excavation was conducted with pick and shovel, and the sediments were not screened. Unfortunately, progress was extremely slow because the tree's root system prevented us from removing enough sediment to get a good view of the bedrock. It was also difficult, with only a limited exposure, to distinguish between in-situ bedrock and large, collapsed blocks. No artifacts were recovered from the excavations or from a surface survey of the possible talus slope below the excavation. Thus, the interpretation of this location as a cave entrance remains equivocal.

RWest

RWest, like REast, was designed to investigate potential cave entrances to the west of Fontéchevade (see Fig. 5.2). The first 25 m of this line are best interpreted as representing limestone bedrock close to the surface (see Fig. 5.3). The next 5 to 7 m show a low resistivity anomaly that could indicate a pocket of sediment. This location is unremarkable on the topographic map, and an inspection of the actual location revealed no surface indications that would aid in the interpretation of this anomaly. The remainder of the line is best interpreted as bedrock close to the surface.

RPara

RPara runs parallel to the axis of the cave, begins approximately 10 m from the edge of the plateau, and extends into the plateau and away from its edges (see Fig. 5.2). Along with RTrans (see next section), these two lines give us an indication of the plateau's resistivity characteristics, of the bedrock's location (or depth below surface), and the presence of possible sinkholes or cave entrances. The first 15 to 17 m of this line show very low resistivity values and likely indicate the presence of pockets of deeper sediments, whereas the final 20 m show higher resistivity values and parallel contour lines indicative of bedrock or perhaps thinner soils (see Fig. 5.3). The low resistivity of the first portion of this line is confirmed by the intersecting RTrans line discussed next.

RTrans

This line, by far the longest at approximately 60 m (Fig. 5.2), is particularly interesting because it crosses the plateau above the back end of the accessible portion of Fontéchevade Cave. It begins at the edge of the plateau on the west side of the cave and extends eastward roughly parallel to REast, approximately 10 to 12 m farther into the plateau. Overall, the resistivity pattern in RTrans is similar to that of RPara, the other plateau line (Fig. 5.3). In both lines, resistivity values are generally low in comparison to the two lines along the edge of the plateau (REast and RWest). Of significance for interpretation of the formation of Fontéchevade Cave, however, are the particularly low resistivity values at 25 m. These values seem to indicate a deep pocket of sediment perhaps caused by a sinkhole or related feature. A later inspection of this location revealed a slight but clearly noticeable depression. Furthermore, in overlaying the profile of the cave on the contour map, it became clear that this location corresponds to the back limit of the cave where fairly loose sediment appears to be filling in from above. Because of the danger of a possible collapse, it was difficult to investigate this location from inside the cave. However, fresh roots were observed coming into the cave from above this location. Thus, several lines of evidence support the idea that the electrical resistivity survey located a sinkhole or, more properly, a chimney at the back of Fontéchevade Cave. This chimney, potentially one of many, could have been the source of sediments (see Chapter 3) and perhaps also the artifacts (see Chapter 12) in the Fontéchevade archaeological deposits.

After the 25-m point, the RTrans line shows low resistivity values for approximately the next 20 m, perhaps indicating a larger complex of sinkholes. After that, the resistivity contour lines become more parallel and show higher resistivities similar to the final portion of the RPara line.

CONCLUSIONS

Overall, the electrical resistivity survey of Fontéchevade confirmed our expectations that the area has a complex lithology. In the course of doing the survey, we learned from discussions with the property owner, M. Buffet, that tractors occasionally slip into previously unnoticed sinkholes, a point that the survey confirmed.

The most significant result of the survey was the identification of a feature on the plateau that may represent a sediment-filled chimney that connects with Fontéchevade Cave. The presence of a chimney has important implications for the taphonomy of the cave.

6

The Fossil Human Remains

Philip G. Chase and Virginie Teilhol

Probably the most dramatic events of Henri-Martin's excavations at Fontéchevade were the discoveries of two fragments of human skull. A bit of frontal bone lacking a supraorbital torus (Fontéchevade I) was found in apparent association with a more archaic-looking partial calotte (Fontéchevade II). (Henry-Martin [1957] referred to these as Homo I and Homo II, respectively.) Both came from the upper parts of her Bed E, which she dated to the last interglacial (OIS 5) or earlier. Because of this date, the modern appearance of Fontéchevade I has posed a problem for paleoanthropologists. Although these are the most famous of the Fontéchevade human remains, the site also contained Bronze Age burials, and during the 1994–1998 excavations more human remains were recovered. In this chapter, the various interpretations and descriptions of the Fontéchevade I and Fontéchevade II specimens are summarized, followed by descriptions of the other human remains from the cave.

THE "TAYACIAN" REMAINS

The fragment of frontal bone was discovered on August 13, 1947. A block of breccia coming from Henri-Martin's Bed E0 in her Sector 1, 2.40–2.60 m below her datum and some 6.5 m in front of the present dripline (Vallois 1958:7–8), was transported to her laboratory in Le Peyrat to permit methodical disengagement of the archaeological material. It was during the course of this work that the fragment of frontal bone appeared. Vallois (1958:7) noted that no trace of fire was observed at this bed. These specimens are housed in the Musée de l'Homme in Paris.

The calotte was found in place on August 16, 1947, "in a hearth of hardened red silt" (Henri-Martin 1957:51). It was located approximately 2 m behind Fontéchevade I and a little lower, in the zone corresponding to Sector 2 (see Fig. 1.8). It came from high in the 2.60–2.80 m horizon, which corresponds to Bed E1′, about 4.50 m in front of the present dripline, 1.40 m from the east wall, and 3.80 m from the west wall (Vallois 1958). It was located 0.70 m below the bottom of the stalagmitic floor. An isolated fragment of the parietal was found 15 cm from the calotte. The sediment in which the calotte was found constituted one of the "pockets" containing both a mixture of fauna and an industry "characteristic of the Tayacian beds of Fontéchevade" (Vallois 1958:7–8). Specifically, there were remains of boar and aurochs (or bison), as well as about 15 tools and flakes.

Henri-Martin rejected the hypotheses that these hominins might have been deliberately buried, because the Tayacian beds from the anterior part of the cave yielded no other human remains. Moreover, the frontal and the calotte were isolated and were mixed with other animal bones. However, she wrote that the calotte showed clear traces of burning and the mark of a violent blow. She also described traces of defleshing on Fontéchevade I. She interpreted these findings as evidence of ritual cannibalism (Henri-Martin 1957:242–243). Vallois reported that the exocranial face of Fontéchevade I had incisions above the left brow ridge (1958:17) and that Fontéchevade II had signs of burning and of tool-induced trauma (1958:31–33). A slight deformation and a slight retraction of part of the frontal bone that rendered its reconstruction difficult had probably been caused by burning. He also reported a 5-cm opening parallel to the lambdoid suture, which he considered to be the result of a blow struck downward on the upper left part. During a subsequent study, however, the authors of this chapter were unable to observe any traces of fire, defleshing, or trauma on either specimen. Although portions of the bone surface of Fontéchevade II are currently obscured by the mastic used in its reconstruction, the surface of Fontéchevade I is unobstructed.

The most thorough description of both specimens is that of Vallois (1958:17–85). It also formed the basis for his interpretation of the remains, an interpretation that, although often disputed, has provided the framework for subsequent analysis.

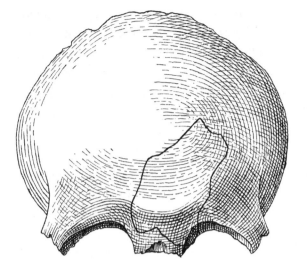

Figure 6.1
Vallois's (1958) figure 7,
showing the portion of
the skull represented
by the Fontéchevade I
fragment. (Reproduced
by permission of Elsevier
Masson.)

Fontéchevade I

Fontéchevade I consists of a fragment of frontal that includes the
glabella, the medial portion of the left superciliary arch, and a small
part of the squamous portion above these (Fig. 6.1). It measures
55 mm (maximum height in projections) by 35 mm (height of the
exocranial face in the medial line) by 45 mm (maximum width).

What is remarkable about this piece, given its apparent age, is
the complete absence of a frontal torus (Fig. 6.2). This feature, as

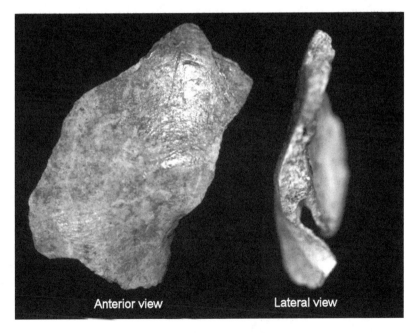

Anterior view   Lateral view

Figure 6.2
Frontal and lateral
photographs of the
Fontéchevade I frontal.
(Photograph by Erik
Trinkaus, reproduced
with his permission.)

well as the thinness of the squamous portion, gives it a very modern appearance. Two measurements, one on the medial line above the end of the internal frontal line and the other at the middle of the left frontal eminence, indicated that the frontal is a little less thick than those of Neanderthals, but thicker than those of modern humans. In its morphology, Vallois described the glabella as similar to those of modern European women. Although there is no frontal torus, the superciliary arch appears for about 2 cm as a slight swelling above the internal angle of the left orbit. It grades into the neighborhood of the glabella on one side and does not reach the superior border of the orbit on the other. No transverse groove is visible between it and the flat portion of the frontal bone.

Vallois interpreted its morphology as that of a modern human. The attenuation of the bony reliefs indicated to him that it was probably a female. He cited values obtained from other Neanderthals and from Knowles' (1911) study of modern humans to argue that the interorbital distance was as large as that of Neanderthals and larger than the mean for modern populations, though it fell within the modern range. Vallois noted that, if this were a young Neanderthal, it would explain why the thickness was less than that of other Neanderthals and why the bony reliefs were less pronounced than those of Neanderthals. However, he rejected this interpretation. The frontal sinus, which develops late in the course of growth, is well developed (Fig. 6.3), indicating that the individual had passed puberty, and the cavities are as voluminous as those of modern adults. Vallois believed they had reached their maximum development,

Figure 6.3
Vallois's cross sections of the Fontéchevade I sinus. (a) on the medial line, (b) 1 cm from the medial line, (c) 2 cm from the medial line. (Reproduced by permission of Elsevier Masson.)

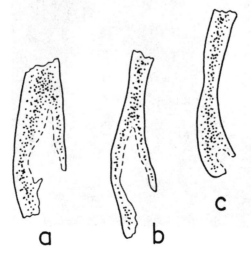

Figure 6.4
Superior view of
Fontéchevade II. (Pho-
tograph by Erik Trinkaus,
reproduced with his
permission.)

meaning that Fontéchevade I would not have developed a torus had
it lived longer. For Vallois, Fontéchevade I resembled not a juvenile
Neanderthal but rather a modern adult female.

Fontéchevade II

The specimen consists of almost the entire left parietal and the upper
portions of the right parietal and frontal (Fig. 6.4). The occipital is
missing, as well as the temporals. Four isolated pieces were found
nearby that do not fit with the calotte but that nevertheless come from
the missing portion of this bone: a fragment of the inferior border of
the right parietal and three smaller fragments. The great thickness of
the cranial walls, the clear reduction of the lateral frontal eminences,
and the advanced degree of fusion of the cranial sutures indicated to
Vallois that this was a male between 50 and 60 years old.

Several of Vallois's observations and inferences concerning the
Fontéchevade II calotte influenced his interpretation of the taxonomic
status of the Fontéchevade remains. He compared the thickness of
the calotte at nine different points with those of modern Europeans,

Neanderthals, and Swanscombe. The calotte surpassed moderns and Neanderthals in thickness, being comparable only to Swanscombe. In addition, the cross section of the parietal where it was beveled by the surface adjoining the temporal is short and thick, as in Swanscombe, rather than long and thin as in Neanderthals and fossil moderns (Fig. 6.5). When viewed in norma verticalis with bregma matching, Vallois argued that the Fontéchevade II specimen showed an absence of the post-orbital constriction found in Neanderthals (La Chapelle and Steinheim). Viewed in norma lateralis, the platycephaly of Fontéchevade II is even greater than that of the pre-Neanderthals (Steinheim and Saccopastore), and, in Vallois's opinion, it was equivalent to that of Swanscombe.

In spite of the fragmentation of the calotte, Vallois believed that the cranial diameters could be estimated, especially the lateral diameters. The posterior expansion and widening of the Fontéchevade II cranium, as measured by various indices, resemble that of Neanderthals, rather than of modern humans. The maximum breadth is lower and farther back than among Neanderthals. The skull is wider and lower than in that population, but the architecture is close to the Saccopastore I and Swanscombe skulls. He estimated the cranial capacity at 1470 cm³. Grimaud (1982) later calculated it at 1330 cm³ on the basis of the isolated parietal.

The lower portion of the frontal bone is missing from Fontéchevade II, and Vallois's analysis convinced him that the missing portion would have been large enough to have included the entire frontal torus, if one had been present. However, Fontéchevade II preserves a tiny portion of the upper end of the frontal sinus. Vallois

Figure 6.5
Vallois's drawing showing the cross section of the parietal where it articulates with the temporal (below the point marked with an x). (H) modern human, (Sw) Swanscombe, (F) Fontéchevade II, (Ch) female chimpanzee. (Reproduced by permission of Elsevier Masson.)

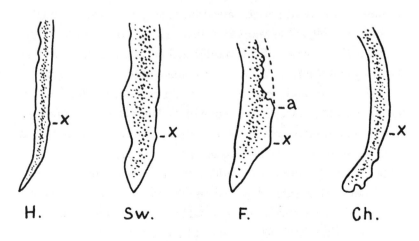

H.   Sw.   F.   Ch.

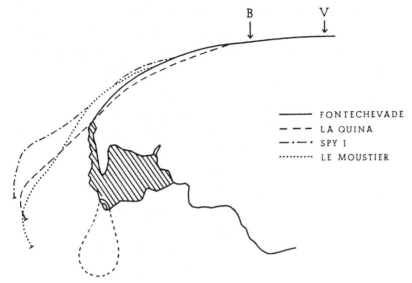

——— FONTÉCHEVADE
– – – LA QUINA
—·—· SPY I
·········· LE MOUSTIER

Figure 6.6
Vallois's drawing com-
paring the position of the
remaining bit of sinus
cavity in Fontéchevade II
with the location of
the toruses of the Spy,
Le Moustier, and La
Quina Neanderthals.
(B) bregma, (V) vertex.
(Reproduced by permis-
sion of Elsevier Masson.)

argued that the frontal sinus in Fontéchevade II would have been
far posterior to its position in Neanderthals (when the crania were
aligned by matching bregma and vertex; Fig. 6.6). In fact, it was
posterior to the position in Upper Paleolithic fossils (Cro-Magnon,
Predmost, and Roc de Combe Capelle). On this basis, he argued that
Fontéchevade II could not have had a supraorbital torus of the kind
found in Neanderthals. This analysis also led him to believe that the
location of the frontal sinus on Fontéchevade II would have been
consistent with both present-day humans and the Fontéchevade I
specimen.

Vallois's interpretation

Vallois observed that the two specimens, Fontéchevade I and
Fontéchevade II, belonged to different individuals. The two bones
look dissimilar and are of different thicknesses and, because they
include similar bones, would overlap if refitted. However, he also
inferred that they were members of a single taxonomic population
that differed significantly from both Neanderthals and anatomically
modern humans. There was, in fact, a patchwork of similarities and
differences between this Fontéchevade population and classic Neanderthals ("Neanderthals 'sensu stricto' of the European Würm I"),
Pre-Neanderthals (Saccopastore, Ehringsdorf, Steinheim), and the
"Neanderthaloids of Palestine" (Vallois 1949:88, 1958), and he also

found differences and similarities between Fontéchevade and fossil modern *Homo sapiens*. Table 6.1 is a translation of Vallois's (1958) table 14, in which he summarized a point-by-point comparison of the Fontéchevade population to these various populations.

It is clear that for him, the Fontéchevade specimens differed from all populations except Swanscombe. He rejected chronological differences as a basis for the differences between Fontéchevade (which he believed to be Riss-Würm in age) and classic Neanderthals, because the former also differed markedly from the pre-Neanderthals, which he took to be either contemporary or, in the case of Steinheim, even older (Vallois 1958:90, 91). Especially striking to him was the larger cranial capacity of Fontéchevade. He also rejected any inclusion of Fontéchevade with the "early Neanderthals" of Palestine (Tabun I, Skhul IV, V, IX) as proposed by Howell (1951).

Table 6.1. Translation of Vallois's (1958) table 14, summarizing the similarities and differences he found between the Fontéchevade "population" and other fossil populations

Observation	Fontéchevade	Swanscombe	Pre-Neanderthals	True Neanderthals	Fossil *H. sapiens*
Cranial dimensions and capacity	Large	Large	Small	Large	Large
Thickness of skull	Very thick	Very thick	Thick	Thick	Moderate
Frontal torus	Absent	(Absent?)	Very large	Large	Moderate or absent
Post-orbital constriction	Absent	(Absent?)	Very strong	Strong	Moderate or absent
Platycephaly	Present	Present	Present	Less pronounced	Weak or absent
Asteric widening and expansion beyond the cranial cavity	Present	Present	Present	Present	Absent
Superior border of the parietal longer than the inferior border	Yes	Yes	Yes	Yes (eventually, no)	Yes
Parietal foramina	Absent	Absent	Absent	Usually absent	Usually present
Temporal lines	Very obscured	Very obscured	Obscured	Obscured	Clear
Beveling of the inferior border of the parietal	Short and thick	Short and thick	?	Long and thin	Long and thin
Gutter of the lateral sinus on the parietal	Absent	Absent	?	Present	Almost always present

Vallois (1958:95) argued that, on the basis of those traits that could be compared, Fontéchevade resembled the Swanscombe calotte very closely. The modern traits of Fontéchevade, notably the lack of a supraorbital torus, and the similarities with Swanscombe led him to place these specimens on a single evolutionary line leading from Swanscombe in the Middle Pleistocene through Fontéchevade to Upper Pleistocene Europeans from the Roc de Combe Capelle and Grimaldi (Vallois 1958:144–156), a line that was separate from the pre-Neanderthal to Neanderthal evolutionary line. This formed the basis of what is known as the presapiens lineage of hominins, which was believed to represent the true ancestral lineage of moderns.

Subsequent interpretations

The presapiens interpretation of the Fontéchevade remains set the stage for subsequent studies, most of which have taken issue with this construal. The main exception was Heberer (1951), who accepted Vallois's reconstruction of Fontéchevade II, along with the evidence of Fontéchevade I, and placed them in a presapiens category along with Swanscombe and Piltdown. However, he also accepted an older, Mindel-Riss date for the Tayacian of Fontéchevade (1951:69).

Sergi (1967, 1953a,b) essentially concluded that both the Swanscombe and Fontéchevade specimens were too incomplete to make it possible to separate them from either the Phaneranthropi (modern humans) or Palaeanthropi. The main similarities between Fontéchevade and moderns was the lack of supraorbital torus; the main differences were the low skull vault, its great biasteric breadth, the low position of the diameter of maximum width, and the thickness of the bones of the cranial vault. Sergi concluded (1967:520) that "the present hominids must trace their origins and roots not to a single type or a common forerunner, but to more than one."

Howell (1951, 1957, 1958) objected to the presapiens interpretation on several grounds. First, he argued that the hypothesis would require two reproductively isolated populations to have occupied the same area at the same time: "These must have represented distinctive sympatric species which led to dissimilar ways of life and were characterized by habit and behavioral differences, so much so that interbreeding did not customarily occur" (Howell 1957:342). He did not find any satisfactory paleoanthropological evidence to support such a hypothesis. He rejected also Fontéchevade II as evidence for presapiens because it fell within the range of variation of early Neanderthals. That left Fontéchevade I as the only evidence for a modern affiliation for Fontéchevade.

Howell differed from others who have discussed the Fontéchevade remains in questioning the age of this specimen and the stratigraphic and chronological association of Fontéchevade I and Fontéchevade II. He cited both anatomical differences (lack of a torus and the thin vault bone in Fontéchevade I) and differences in mineralization and state of preservation between the two specimens (Howell 1958:194). In fact, Oakley and Hoskins (1951) had tested the fluorine content of Fontéchevade I and of mammal bones from the Tayacian and Upper Paleolithic of Fontéchevade and had found the content of Fontéchevade I matched that of the Tayacian fauna. However, Howell argued that at the time the technique was not sufficiently sophisticated to distinguish between last interglacial and early last glacial times. Howell concluded, "At present, . . . it would appear judicious to withhold judgment on this particular fragment (No. 1) and to resist basing a broad and far-reaching theory of human evolution on it alone" (1958:194).

As will be discussed in Chapter 7, Howell's argument against an early date for Fontéchevade I is most likely the best interpretation for the context of this find. New dates from associated faunal material indicate a much younger age (OIS 3) than was previously thought, which suggests that, rather than representing an anomalous individual necessitating its own lineage, Fontéchevade I probably represents a more or less typical member of very early modern *Homo sapiens* in Europe.

Drennan (1956) cited some of the same similarities between the Fontéchevade specimens and Neanderthals that Vallois had done: He pointed out that the saggital contour of the Homo II calvarium matched that of the Neanderthal juvenile from Le Moustier and argued that the Fontéchevade specimens represented a pedomorphic variant of Neanderthaloids, whereas Swanscombe represented a gerontomorphic variant.

Brace (1964:7–9) took vehement exception to Vallois's analysis of the Homo II specimen, questioning the evidence he presented that it could not have had a supraorbital torus. He argued that Vallois could not preclude the possibility that Homo I was a juvenile, given the lack of knowledge of development of frontal sinuses in Neanderthal populations. Finally, he reiterated Howell's warning that major conclusions should not be based on fragmentary pieces of evidence.

Weiner and Campbell (1964) included Homo II in a generalized (Mahalonobis') distance analysis of the Swanscombe skull with other cranial remains. They noted (1964:203), "If the frontal was in fact 'sapiens' in configuration our results for the parietal would make the specimen quite anomalous." However, their main conclusions were that both Fontéchevade and Swanscombe were too fragmentary to serve as the basis for any theory of hominid evolution and that Fontéchevade II was neither as sapiens in nature nor as similar to Swanscombe as Vallois believed.

Trinkaus (1973) took exception to Vallois's interpretation of the Fontéchevade specimens as indicative of a population without supraorbital tori. Where Vallois had argued that Fontéchevade I was an adult, based on the size of the frontal sinus and the large interorbital breadth, Trinkaus held that the same dimensions were equally consistent with a juvenile Neanderthal. Because sinus size is very variable in modern humans, and the size distribution is unknown for Neanderthals, he argued that, if the specimen were in fact a Neanderthal, it would imply anything from a half-grown to a fully grown individual. The thickness of the squamous portion of the frontal could imply either an adult modern or a Neanderthal child of 8 to 12 years of age. In sum, it was impossible to reject an interpretation of Fontéchevade I as either a Neanderthal juvenile or a modern human, and Fontéchevade II could be reconstructed either with or without a supraorbital torus.

Based on a principal components analysis of Fontéchevade II with modern skulls, and fossil skulls from Upper Paleolithic humans, and classic, "conservative," and "progressive" Neanderthals, Corruccini (1975) argued, "It may be unnecessary to speculate on supraorbital torus form in the Fontéchevade fossils. The calotte shape is sufficient to demonstrate its archaic character, suggesting special affinity with the slightly earlier preneandertal from Steinheim" (1975:97).

MORE RECENT HUMAN REMAINS FROM PREVIOUS EXCAVATIONS

Several fragments of human bone were subsequently discovered during various excavations in the deposits overlying the stalagmitic floor (Vallois 1958:157). Some were associated with a Mousterian industry; others, with an Upper Paleolithic industry. However, their

stratigraphic position remains imprecisely documented. The following comprises the inventory of osteological remains, which were
described by Vallois (1958:157–164):

- An incomplete adult parietal, a fragment of a child's mandible,
  and an isolated molar discovered by Durousseau-Dugontier and
  his son between 1902 and 1912, and associated with an Aurignacian industry
- A fragment of radius discovered in 1932 by David and dated to
  the Aurignacian
- A metatarsal discovered in April 1948 by Henri-Martin in a Mousterian of Acheulian Tradition (her Bed C2), but whose dating to
  this period is unproven

During the summer of 1965, Joussaume discovered and excavated
a collective burial from the Middle Bronze Age. He wrote that it "was
found in a very disturbed Mousterian layer; no trace of a pit
was observed" (Joussaume et al. 1975:61–63). The human material
was studied by J. L. Heim (in Joussaume et al. 1975). There were three
fragmented skeletons: an adult male younger than 21 years old, an
adult male aged between 25 and 30, and a young female of about 20.
He described them as representing an "atlanto-mediterranian population of the Aquitaine type." The human remains were found in
association with several fragments of rather atypical pottery and
three bronze objects, among them an open bracelet in massive bronze
decorated with geometric motifs.

HUMAN REMAINS FROM THE 1994–1998 EXCAVATIONS

The 1994–1998 excavations produced two teeth (a right upper canine
and a left upper first premolar) and a fragment of parietal. These
pieces came from the Small Test in the uppermost part of the cave
just behind the Main Profile and are therefore of unknown age and
context. These sediments were severely disturbed and may have
been backdirt from Henri-Martin's excavations. The sedimentary,
cultural, and chronological associations of the specimens are therefore unknown.

Right upper canine

This tooth has a mesio-distal diameter of 5.5 mm at the neck, the
crown being completely worn in this axis. With a bucco-lingual

diameter of 8 mm, its dimensions are entirely comparable to those of present-day modern humans (Marseiller 1937; Olivier 1960).

The apex of the root is closed. The crown is completely worn – degree 4 in Olivier's (1960) system – with the wear reaching the upper border of the root. The pulp cavity is visible. These two observations indicate a subject of considerable age or one whose dental activity was especially pronounced. In addition, there is an unusual wear of the bucco-distal quadrant of the occlusal surface. This wear has an oblique orientation toward the buccal face of the root, extending to 2 mm below the neck. The wear is rounded in form, with several juxtaposed facets. Its interesting morphology does not appear to result from contact between teeth and may be behavioral in origin.

A brown coloring covers the enamel and more than a third of the root on the buccal half of the tooth. Because the surface is irregular and in places covered with cracking, it may indicate burning. Nevertheless, the possibility of a manganese deposit cannot be excluded.

Left upper first premolar

The mesio-distal diameter of this tooth (6.5 mm) is slightly smaller than the means of 7 mm reported by Marseiller (1937) and of 7.2 mm reported by Olivier (1960). It must be noted, however, that these measures were taken between the mesial and distal wear surfaces. As for the bucco-lingual diameter (10 mm), it is barely above the mean (9 mm). Again, this tooth thus falls perfectly within the range of modern teeth.

The apex of the root is closed. This root is extremely small, only 9 mm long compared with a mean of 14 mm (Marseiller 1937). The crown is worn, affecting the surface of the enamel and in places the dentine (Olivier's degree 2). The contact surfaces show different kinds of wear. Although the distal wear is perfectly smooth, the mesial wear shows deep, vertical, subparallel striations.

These two teeth are similar in their dimensions to those observed in modern individuals. Some traces of wear and coloration are interesting, but their isolation in the archaeological context does not permit us to draw any inferences.

The parietal fragment

This fragment of bone probably represents a portion of a human parietal, although the orientation of the fragment is difficult to determine.

It is small (25 × 35 mm) and triangular in form. Its circumference is broken so that the preserved area of the internal surface is smaller than that of the external surface.

The fragment of bone has a slight, regular curve that is identical in both the longitudinal and transverse axes. Vascular grooves are scattered about the external surface of the bone. The endocranial surface shows two divergent vascular grooves. The first is 2 mm wide and extends for 13 mm. The second is visible for only 5 mm, is less deep, and is 1 mm wide.

The bone is very thick, and in this respect it is similar to the Fontéchevade II specimens. However, no direct correspondence could be established between them.

7

Radiometric Dates

Philip G. Chase, Henry P. Schwarcz,
and Thomas W. Stafford, Jr.

Since its discovery in 1947, the dating of Fontéchevade I, a fragment
of human frontal bone (lacking a supraorbital torus), has posed a
problem for paleoanthropologists. In spite of its apparently modern
appearance, it has been considered to date from the last interglacial
or even earlier. Such a date would be much earlier than any other
convincing evidence of anatomically modern peoples in Europe. One
goal of the excavations reported in this monograph was to clarify the
chronological position of the Fontéchevade I specimen.

Fontéchevade I was recovered approximately 6.5 m in front of the
present-day dripline of the cave, in Henri-Martin's Bed E0 – that is
to say, 2.40 to 2.60 m below her datum (Henri-Martin 1957). About
2 m farther toward the cave, in Bed E1' (2.60–2.80 m below datum), a
more archaic-looking calotte (Fontéchevade II) was discovered.

Fontéchevade I consists of a fragment of frontal that includes
glabella, the medial portion of the left superciliary arch, and a small
part of the squamous portion above these. What is remarkable about
this piece, given its apparent age, is the complete absence of a frontal
torus. This feature, as well as the thinness of the squamous portion, gives it a very modern appearance. Fontéchevade II consists
of the upper part of the frontal bone and portions of the left and
right parietals. The specimen, much more archaic in appearance, is
distinguished by the thickness of the cranial walls.

Henri-Martin and others believed, on the basis of her excavations and of material from those excavations, that Bed E dated to the
last interglacial (OIS 5a) or earlier. The taxonomic problems posed
by these specimens and past efforts to solve them are discussed in

greater detail in Chapter 6. However, the radiometric dates reported here suggest that both Fontéchevade I and Fontéchevade II date to OIS 3, which is compatible with other evidence concerning the arrival of anatomically modern *Homo sapiens* in Europe.

PREVIOUS AGE ESTIMATES

Henri-Martin (1957:264–269) believed that the entirety of the "Tayacian" (that is to say, all of her Bed E) dated to the last interglacial – to the early part of OIS 5 or, in the terminology of the time, to the Riss-Würm. She based this conclusion on both sedimentology and fauna. The sediments at the base of her excavations contained pollen of oak (*Quercus*) and linden (*Tilia*), and bones of Merck's rhinoceros and of tortoise (*Testudo*) were found in clay sediments, indicating a humid and temperate environment. Throughout the rest of Bed E, the sediments showed no sign of frost action. The fauna, too, remained temperate throughout.

She also cited the presence of a Mousterian of Acheulian Tradition in her Bed C2, a bed with no signs of cold climate and with a fauna that, although poor in number, indicated a temperate climate. She did not interpret the layer of large éboulis (Bed D) that sealed the top of the "Tayacian" as thermoclastic in origin and therefore as representing a cold interval. Rather, she accepted Alimen's (1958 – then in press) explanation that it represented tectonic activity on the Orgedeuil fault.

She rejected a date earlier than the Riss-Würm, based on the fact that all the fauna recovered belonged to extant species. (She rejected the notion that *Dama clactoniana* identified in Bed E dated to the earlier "Mindel-Riss" interglacial, citing Arambourg's (1958) analysis of the fauna.) Alimen (1958) also argued for a date immediately following the Riss. He based this argument on correlations of the bedrock terraces and overlying sediments of the Tardoire Valley with valleys in the Massif Central, which in turn he correlated with those of the Pyrenees, which in their turn he correlated with the classic Alpine terrace sequence.

Henri-Martin did provide two qualifications to the uniformly temperate nature of the Bed E sediments. In the Cave Bear Horizon (between 4.70 and 4.50 m below her datum), there was an éboulis composed of subangular elements, but these were apparently not produced by frost action. Because the fauna indicated a humid environment, she doubted but did not entirely exclude the possibility that this horizon represented a colder interval.

The second qualification is more relevant to the radiometric dates reported here. Above E1″, the silts became coarser, more clasts had fallen from the cave roof, and there was evidence of increased erosion by running water. Thus, the top of Bed E was marked by the beginnings of a climatic deterioration.

It should also be noted that Henri-Martin assigned some significance to the relationship between the Tayacian industry of Bed E and the Mousterian of Acheulian Tradition in Bed C2: "The primary interest of the C2 horizon is stratigraphic; it confirms the presence of the Tayacian under a level with bifaces of the late Acheulian" [L'intérêt primordial de l'horizon C2 est stratigraphique; il confirme la présence du Tayacien sous un niveau à bifaces de l'Acheuléen tardif] (Henri-Martin 1957:190). In other words, the stratigraphic position of the Tayacian at Fontéchevade was, in terms of the industries, compatible with a Riss-Würm date.

In the years that followed, others suggested that Bed E might be even older than OIS 5e. Chaline noted that these sediments contained a mixed fauna, consisting not only of temperate species but also of species indicating a more continental regime: arctic fox (*Alopex lagopus*), steppe lemming (*Lagurus lagurus*), alpine marmot (*Marmota marmota*), European hamster (*Cricetus cricetus*), and root vole (*Microtus ratticeps*). This mixture "seems to correspond to a mixing of two levels of fauna apparently indiscernible in the course of excavation" [Elle corresponde, semble-t-il, à un mélange de deux niveaux de faunes apparemment indiscernables lors de la fouille] (Chaline 1972:108). Although he noted that the absence of micromammals known from Rissian deposits argued for a post-Riss age, he maintained that the presence of *Lagurus lagurus*, which was known to have migrated to Europe at the end of the Riss, argued for a date of terminal Riss (late OIS 6).

Bourdier (1967:202–204) had already mentioned Chaline's discovery of arctic fox and alpine marmot. Unlike Henri-Martin, he interpreted the presence of *Dama clactoniana* as evidence that Bed E was older than the Riss-Würm interglacial, and along the same lines, he cited the archaic appearance of horse teeth and of rhinoceros remains (perhaps *Rhinoceros etruscus*). He concluded that E belonged to the Riss glaciation, with Fontéchevade II probably coming from late in the "Riss II-III" and Fontéchevade I from the beginning of "Riss III."

Debénath (1974:338–344) came to a similar conclusion. He cited Chaline's report of cold species within Bed E. He also noted that both fallow deer (*Dama*) and Greek tortoise (*Testudo graeca*), although generally considered to belong to a temperate environment, had in other French sites been found in association with cold fauna. Finally, he pointed out that, given the depth of Bed E, if it dated to the last interglacial, one would expect to find similar significant interglacial deposits at the nearby site of La Chaise, but this was not the case. By the same token, episodes of breccification at Fontéchevade were without parallel indications elsewhere. He suggested, pending new data, that Bed E should be dated to a relatively late phase of the Riss.

In 1972, Bastin took and analyzed pollen samples from Bed E2. These corresponded well enough with the few known spectra from the Riss but differed from interglacial spectra from Amersfoort, Odderade, and Grand Pile. Birch (*Betula*), which was the principal deciduous tree at these three locations, made up only 3 percent of the Fontéchevade sample. Likewise, elm (*Ulmus*) made up less than 1 percent of the Fontéchevade sample but varied from 5 percent to more than 10 percent at the other sites. On this basis, and citing Chaline's faunal analyses, he argued that Bed E2 belonged to a Riss interstadial (Bastin, 1976).

It should be noted that Oakley and Hoskins (1951) reported the results of a fluorine test comparing Fontéchevade I and Fontéchevade II to bones from Levels E1 and E2 and to bones from an Upper Paleolithic context. The fluorine content of the hominin samples (0.4 and 0.5 percent, respectively) were very close to the fauna from E1 (0.5, 0.6 percent) and close to those from E2 (0.7, 0.9 percent). Human and non-human mammal remains from the cave fill above Level E or from the "Aurignacian breccia" all had much lower levels (< 0.1 percent). The provenience of one of the Upper Paleolithic specimens is suspect; it came from the excavations of Durousseau-Dugontier (Henri-Martin 1951; see Chapter 1). Nevertheless, the results were consistent and implied that Fontéchevade I and Fontéchevade II were both in situ rather than being redeposited from above the consolidated breccia that overlay Level E.

THE RADIOMETRIC DATES

Although one of our goals was to date the Fontéchevade I specimen, it became apparent that material from our 1994–1998 excavations could not be used for this purpose. Henri-Martin excavated the front half of the cave to several meters below where Fontéchevade I was found. Our excavations began at the profile she left, 9 m behind where Fontéchevade I was found. We uncovered a very complex stratigraphy, although she distinguished no natural layering within Bed E and excavated in arbitrary levels (see Chapter 1). This made any correlation between our levels and the exact provenience of the fossils problematic. Moreover, we were unable to date the sediments we excavated, because no heated flints or faunal remains were recovered in the area where we worked. Thus, we could date the hominin remains only by using material from Henri-Martin's excavations.

To this end, we selected five bovine teeth from upper Bed E for electron spin resonance (ESR) dating. Their depth varied from 2.60–2.85 m below Henri-Martin's datum. (Henri-Martin did not record horizontal provenience.) Fontéchevade I was found at a depth of 2.40 to 2.60 m; Fontéchevade II, at 2.60 to 2.80 m. When these specimens produced ESR dates within the time range of radiocarbon dating, we then selected five fragments of unidentifiable mammal bone and a fragment of a rib from a box marked as containing material from the vicinity of Fontéchevade II. Amino acid analysis of the sample showed that the six bones were highly suitable for accelerator mass spectrometer (AMS) radiocarbon dating. However, mineral staining indicated that they came from two different series.

ESR dates

The age of a fossil tooth can be determined from the intensity of a characteristic ESR signal in tooth enamel; this intensity is proportional to radiation received from surrounding sediment and from uranium (U) incorporated into the tooth (Rink 1997). Depending on the U content of the teeth, it may be necessary to model the U uptake history of the teeth to arrive at a possible range of ages. Ideally, we would measure the environmental dose rate in situ by inserting radiation dosimeters in the surrounding sediments. This was obviously impossible in the present case, but we were able to estimate the dose rate from the chemical composition – U, thorium (Th), and potassium (K) content – of samples of sediment that were associated with the teeth at their burial site.

Part of the enamel of the five teeth plus one replicate pair (99FCH5A,B) were powdered, and aliquots were irradiated with

Table 7.1. Summary of data for ESR dating (teeth)

Sample	U (ppm) Enamel	U (ppm) Dentine	Enamel stripped (μm) Outside	Enamel stripped (μm) Inside	Equivalent Dose (Gy)
99FCH1A	0.15	9.93	99	51	46.7 ± 1.7
99FCH2A	0.09	18.1	71	54	62.7 ± 0.9
99FCH3A	0.08	16.1	74	62	50.0 ± 1.5
99FCH4A	0.01	0.13	126	118	53.8 ± 2.0
99FCH5A	0	0.2	72	48	37.5 ± 0.7
99FCH5B	0	0.12	77	108	41.8 ± 0.8

γ rays from a ^{60}Co source, with doses ranging up to 500 Gy (Table 7.1). The g = 2.0018 signal was measured on a JEOL JES-FA100 ESR spectrometer. The dose–response curves were constructed using the ESR signal intensities, fitted with a single saturating exponential function using VFIT software. U, Th, and K concentrations of sediment, and U concentrations in dental tissues, were obtained by neutron activation at the McMaster Nuclear Reactor. Cosmic ray dose was estimated on the basis of depth (vertical provenience). We assumed average values of water content of the sediment and teeth for cave sites in this region.

Because of the low U content of the teeth, the uptake history of U has little effect on their ages. Therefore, the calculated ages of the teeth depend largely on the composition of the surrounding sediment and the resultant β and γ dose rates. Sediment attached to two of the bovid tooth samples and a sample of sediment from Layer E from Henri-Martin's excavations yield similar values for U, Th, and K (Table 7.2). Ages calculated assuming early and linear uptake (EU, LU) overlap at 1σ (Table 7.3). The ages for all teeth (plus the subsamples) are remarkably uniform and suggest that the sediment in which they were buried was quite homogeneous and not very stony ("lumpy," Brennan, Schwarcz, and Rink 1997).

Table 7.2. Summary of data for ESR dating (sediments)

	U (ppm)	Th (ppm)	K (%)
Sediment attached to teeth			
Sample a	3.16	8.3 ± 0.6	0.62 ± 0.02
Sample b	4.62	11.7 ± 0.8	0.91 ± 0.02
Sediment from Henri-Martin's excavations			
	5.08	10.0 ± 1.7	1.02 ± 0.15

Table 7.3. ESR ages

| | Sediment from museum | | Sediment attached to teeth (average) | |
Sample	EU	LU	EU	LU
99FCH1A	34.6 ± 2.9	37.1 ± 3.3	38.0 ± 3.5	41.2 ± 4.2
99FCH2A	40.3 ± 3.1	43.8 ± 3.7	44.5 ± 3.9	48.9 ± 4.7
99FCH3A	35.8 ± 2.9	38.0 ± 3.3	39.7 ± 3.7	42.4 ± 4.2
99FCH4A	39.4 ± 4.0	39.5 ± 4.0	44.6 ± 5.1	44.6 ± 5.1
99FCH5A	30.8 ± 2.7	30.8 ± 2.7	34.5 ± 3.6	34.6 ± 3.6
99FCH5B	33.9 ± 3.1	33.9 ± 3.1	38.0 ± 4.0	38.1 ± 4.0
Averages	35.8 ± 3.2	37.1 ± 4.1	39.8 ± 3.6	41.6 ± 4.5

The best estimate of the age of deposition of the teeth at this site is taken to be the average of the ages obtained using the two dose-rate estimates: 39 ± 2 ka.

Radiocarbon dates

The bone fragments used for radiocarbon dating ranged from white to yellowish brown and were coated with varying amounts of iron and manganese oxides. The preliminary hypothesis was that per-mineralization was related to geologic age and stratigraphic position. Data collected during chemical purification of the bone augmented the physical descriptions. Six cortical bone samples were tested chemically; three were AMS ^{14}C dated using XAD-purified collagen (Stafford et al. 1991), yielding these values: 33,720 ± 410 (UCIAMS-11216), 33,360 ± 380 (UCIAMS-11217), and >51,700 (UCIAMS-11218) (δ^{13}C-corrected, uncalibrated dates; see Table 7.4). Cortical

Table 7.4. Radiocarbon dating samples

| | | | Collagen | | | |
SR-	Type of bone	Radiocarbon age RC yr. BP ± 1 SD	Percent pseudomorph in HCl	Percent Pepseudomorph in KOH	Wt (%) protein	Color
SR-6717	Cortical bone	33,720 ± 410	99	98	5.30	Pale yellowish brown
SR-6718	Cortical bone	33,360 ± 380	97	96	6.20	Dark yellowish brown
SR-6719	Cortical bone	Not dated	5	0		Extremely pale yellow
SR-6720	Cortical bone	Not dated	98	98		White (opaque)
SR-6721	Cortical bone	>51,700	97	97	7.40	Extremely pale yellow
SR-6722	Rib	Not dated	85	85		White (opaque)

bone fragments and decalcified collagen were either significantly discolored with iron and manganese oxide mineralization or the bones and collagen had minimal mineralization. Brown to yellow-brown collagen samples dated 33 ka; the unstained specimen dated >51 ka. Protein yield, compared to 20–22 percent in modern bone, varied from 5.3 percent to 6.2 percent for 33 ka specimens to 7.4 percent for the specimen >51 ka. All dated specimens yielded 96 to 98 percent pseudomorphs of collagen, and two bones had 85 percent and 0 percent pseudomorphs (Table 7.4). These data are similar to those from Grotte XVI, France (Stafford et al. 1991), where collagen preservation initially increased with increasing geologic age because older bones experienced less environmental variation than more shallow fossils. The Fontéchevade data are an indication that (a) two populations (ca. 33 ka and >51 ka) of bones are present, (b) collagen preservation and mineralization are age related, and (c) greater mineralization in younger bones may be related to downward moving waters.

FAUNAL EVIDENCE

As reported in Chapter 8, the faunal material from Bed E includes *Equus aff germanicus* NEHRING (horse), *Equus hydruntinus* REGALIA (ass), *Dicerorhinus merckii*, JAGER (Merck's rhinoceros), *Sus scrofa* L. (pig), Bovinae (*Bos* and *Bison*), *Cervus elaphus* L. (red deer), *Capreolus capreolus* L. (roe deer), *Dama dama* L. (fallow deer), *Crocuta crocuta spelaea* GOLDFUSS (cave hyena), *Canis lupus* L. (wolf), *Cuon alpinus* PALLAS (dhole), *Panthera spelaea* GOLDFUSS (cave lion), *Ursus spelaeus* ROS. and HEINROTH (cave bear), and *Vulpes vulpes* L. (fox). This temperate fauna is typical of the early Upper Pleistocene. However, Bed E also contained species indicative of colder environments, as Chaline (1972) had reported (but without vertical provenience). Paletta (2005) also reported that the upper parts of E (E0 and E1) contained species typical of cold, open environments: *Rangifer tarandus* (reindeer), *Marmota marmota* (marmot), *Cricetus cricetus* (hamster), *Lagurus lagurus* (lemming), *Prunella collaris* (alpine accentor), and *Plectrophenax nivali* (snow bunting). She considered these specimens to be intrusive, but they are compatible with the radiometric dates reported here. Thus the "mixed" character of the fauna is apparently due to vertical differences and may indicate that the bulk of Bed E is older than the upper part, which is quite possible given Henri-Martin's failure to recognize geological stratigraphy within Bed E.

CONCLUSIONS

In sum, materials of three different ages underlie the brecciated roof-fall that isolated Henri-Martin's Bed E from later Mousterian and Upper Paleolithic deposits. Material dated by ^{14}C AMS to approximately 33 ka was in very close association with Fontéchevade II. Material vertically associated with Fontéchevade II and under Fontéchevade I was dated by ESR to about 39 ka. The discrepancy between the two sets of dates may be attributable to a dramatic increase in atmospheric ^{14}C at about 41–40 ka (Giaccio et al. 2006). Finally, one ^{14}C date of >51 ka indicates some mixing.

Our own excavations revealed reworked beds along the cave walls that Henri-Martin did not recognize. However, these beds contained obviously out-of-place archaeological material. No such material was found in her collections, indicating that what she excavated was for the most part in situ. Moreover, all but one of the ^{14}C and ESR measurements indicate that the upper part of Bed E dates to OIS 3. It would run against the odds to argue, therefore, that the association of Fontéchevade I and Fontéchevade II with OIS 3 dates was due entirely to mixing.

Although it cannot be absolutely excluded that either Fonté-chevade I or Fontéchevade II may have been redeposited, this date would be unsurprising for in situ remains. If Fontéchevade II was in situ, and, in accordance with the majority view, a Neanderthal, then it would date to the late Middle Paleolithic. The more modern-looking Fontéchevade I, if it was in situ, must be somewhat later and likely overlaps in time with the directly dated modern remains from Peștera cu Oase (Romania) (Trinkaus et al. 2003). In either case, there are no chronological grounds for interpreting Fontéchevade I as a Middle Pleistocene presapiens, and it is clear that the upper part of Bed E at Fontéchevade dates to OIS 3.

However, it must also be noted that there are no grounds for extending these radiometric dates to the lower parts of Henri-Martin's Bed E. The fauna from the upper part of Bed E – in other words, those from about the same depth as the hominin remains – is indicative of a colder climate than the fauna from deeper in Bed E. In addition, some experts believe that some of the fauna indicate an older, pre-OIS 5 age. Bed E was very thick. Our excavations at the Main Profile indicated that Henri-Martin did not recognize a very complex stratigraphy within this set of deposits. It is entirely possible, therefore, that the upper part of E, where Fontéchevade I and II were found, dates to OIS 3, while the lower part of E may be much older. Chaline himself (1972) suggested that the cold and warm faunas probably came from two different strata that had not been recognized in the course of Henri-Martin's excavations.

8

Faunal Taphonomy

Philip G. Chase

INTRODUCTION

The fauna recovered in the course of our excavations were grouped into six sectors:

1. Main Profile: from the upper levels of the main profile left by Henri-Martin's excavations
2. X Levels: from the disturbed deposits at the sides of the main profile, against the cave walls
3. Test Pit: from our expansion of Henri-Martin's Test Pit 3 near the back of the cave, with the exception of the Bronze Age levels
4. Bronze Age: from our expansion of Henri-Martin's Test Pit 3 near the back of the cave
5. Small Test: from our small test just behind and above the main profile; the sediments in this level had been severely disturbed and may have consisted of backdirt from Henri-Martin's excavations
6. Witness Section: the bench of sediments left as a "Témoin" by Henri-Martin; one level, TX, was a disturbed deposit analogous to or perhaps continuous with the X Levels

Fauna were generally not preserved in the Main Profile. There were faunal remains in Level 1A, but this level was seriously disturbed and its contents therefore suspect. Consequently, we have no material there corresponding to the majority of Henri-Martin's Bed E. Because she had removed all sediments above her Bed E, we also lack any material comparable to her Beds A–D.

The identified fauna consisted of rhinoceros, horses, bovines (*Bos* and/or *Bison*), cervids, carnivores, lagomorphs, birds, and turtle or tortoise (Table 8.1).

ORIGIN OF THE FAUNAL REMAINS AT FONTÉCHEVADE

Data from the 1994–1998 excavations

There are three fairly obvious hypotheses regarding how the faunal remains at Fontéchevade got into the site. First, because there are traces of human activity at the site, the fauna may have been brought into the cave by hominins. Second, the presence of carnivore remains in the cave, including hyenas, may indicate that these animals were responsible for the collection of herbivore and other bones in the site. Finally, both the lithic evidence and the abundance of quartz gravel and cobbles in the deposits indicate that the sediments in the cave entered by gravity and/or mudflow from the sediments on the plateau above the cave (see Chapters 3 and 12). This raises the possibility that faunal remains may have entered the cave with the sediments.

These hypotheses are by no means mutually exclusive. In fact, as is seen in this chapter, it is almost certain that different parts of the collection had different origins. It is probable, for example, that the carnivores and probably at least some of the lagomorphs entered the cave on their own and died there naturally. The main question to be answered in the context of these excavations is whether hominins can be considered responsible for the accumulation of the bulk of the herbivore remains so the site can be interpreted as a human occupation or whether human activity was only a very minor phenomenon in the cave's history.

The zooarchaeological evidence for human activity turns out to be rather slim. It consists of traces left on bones by stones and of fractures of the kind made in fresh bone by percussion or pressure. Because the sample of any one species recovered from any one level was extremely small, statistical analyses that are often of considerable usefulness in answering taphonomic questions could not be applied at Fontéchevade.

Of 467 specimens on which it was possible to observe the presence or absence of stone tool marks, only 7 bore marks that were clearly made by contact of sharp stone edges on the surface of the bone.

Table 8.1. Fauna recovered (number of identifiable specimens), by sector and level

Bed	Bos/Bison	Cervus	Dama	Capreolus	Rangifer	Capra	Ovis	Sus	Equus	Coelodonta	Canis	Vulpes	Large feline	Panthera	Crocuta	Ursus	Meles	Lagomorph	Erinaceus	Anatid	Anser	Colombid	Large corvid	Corvus	Pyrrhocorax	Galliform	Gallus	Turtle/Tortoise	Total
Main profile																													
Surf.	5	0	0	0	1	0	0	0	3	0	1	0	0	0	1	0	0	0	0	0	0	0	0	0	0	0	0	0	11
1A	25	2	0	1	2	0	0	0	12	0	1	3	0	1	10	0	0	0	0	0	0	0	0	0	0	0	0	0	56
2A	2	0	0	0	0	0	0	0	1	1	0	0	0	0	0	0	0	0	0	0	0	0	0	0	0	0	0	0	4
2D	0	0	0	0	0	0	0	0	0	0	0	0	0	0	1	0	0	0	0	0	0	0	0	0	0	0	0	0	1
3A	0	0	0	0	0	0	0	0	0	0	0	1	0	0	0	0	0	0	0	0	0	0	0	0	0	0	0	0	1
Bronze Age																													
A1	0	0	0	0	0	1	2	0	1	0	2	3	0	0	0	0	0	1	0	1	1	0	0	1	0	1	0	0	14
A2	0	0	0	0	0	0	0	0	0	0	0	2	0	0	0	0	0	3	0	0	1	0	0	0	0	1	1	0	8
B	0	0	0	0	0	0	0	0	0	0	0	0	0	0	0	0	0	4	0	0	0	0	0	0	0	0	1	0	5
Witness Section																													
T1	0	0	0	0	0	0	0	0	0	0	0	0	0	0	0	0	0	0	0	0	0	0	0	0	0	0	0	0	0
T2	4	13	13	2	0	0	0	1	0	0	3	2	1	0	13	0	0	2	0	0	0	0	0	0	0	0	0	4	58
T3	0	0	1	0	0	0	0	1	0	0	0	0	0	0	1	0	0	0	0	0	0	0	0	0	0	0	0	0	3
Small Test																													
A	2	0	0	0	1	0	0	0	1	0	1	0	0	0	1	0	0	0	0	0	0	0	0	0	0	0	0	0	6
B	5	0	0	0	2	0	0	0	4	0	0	1	0	0	2	0	0	1	0	0	0	0	0	0	0	0	0	0	15
Test Pit																													
A	2	0	0	0	1	0	0	0	5	0	0	1	0	0	1	0	0	0	0	0	0	0	0	0	0	0	2	0	12
B	15	0	0	0	1	0	0	0	19	0	0	1	0	0	1	0	0	0	0	0	0	0	0	0	0	0	0	0	36
B1	0	0	0	0	0	0	0	0	2	0	0	0	0	0	0	1	0	0	0	0	0	0	0	0	0	0	0	0	3
C	1	0	0	0	0	0	0	0	2	0	0	0	0	0	0	0	0	0	1	0	0	0	0	0	0	0	0	0	4
X Levels																													
X	0	0	0	0	0	0	0	0	0	0	0	0	0	0	1	0	0	0	0	0	0	0	0	0	0	0	0	0	1
X0	18	6	0	0	2	0	0	1	6	0	16	10	0	1	14	0	0	1	0	1	0	1	2	0	1	0	0	0	80
X1	4	0	0	0	2	0	0	0	2	0	0	1	0	0	1	0	0	0	0	0	0	0	0	0	0	0	0	0	10
TX	0	1	7	3	0	0	0	0	3	0	0	4	0	0	0	0	2	4	0	0	0	0	0	0	0	0	0	0	24
Total	85	22	22	6	12	1	2	3	62	1	24	29	1	2	47	1	2	16	1	2	2	1	2	1	1	2	4	4	358

Table 8.2. Marks made by stone on bones from different sectors of Fontéchevade

	No marks	Possible tool marks	Questionable marks
Bronze Age	48	0	0
Main Profile	101	2	
Small Test	44	1	3
Test Pit	59	2	6
Witness Section	93	2	2
X Levels	104	0	0

Eleven more bore marks that may or may not have been made in this way (Table 8.2).

Of the seven bones with such marks, one was almost certainly made by humans using a stone as a tool. The rest were ambiguous. In sediments or on surfaces where considerable quantities of broken flint occur naturally, there is a real likelihood of cuts, scratches, and scrapes occurring naturally. Thus, isolated marks of this nature, especially light ones, short ones, or light wavering scrapes, are somewhat ambiguous evidence for butchering. At Fontéchevade, there was no pattern of either deep or repeated marks appearing where butchering marks are usually found (e.g., adjacent to joints). Thus, although it is impossible to reject a human origin for the marks made by stone on the 7 bones or the marks that may have been made this way on the other 11 bones, it seems unlikely that they can all be attributed to human activity. These data are consistent with a sporadic use of the cave by hominins but do not support a major hominin presence in the site.

The second line of evidence consists of the kind of fractures caused by either percussion or pressure. The percentages of bones with such breaks are much higher than the percentages of bones with cut marks (Table 8.3), but the cause of these breaks is not self-evident. Humans often use percussion to break long bones to extract marrow.

Table 8.3. Specimens with and without green-bone breaks

	Without	With	Indeterminate	Total
Bronze Age	37	0	2	39
Main Profile	23	30	23	76
Small Test	16	13	6	35
Test Pit	17	36	38	91
Witness Section	51	32	8	91
X Levels	50	35	17	102

Table 8.4. Specimens with and without tooth marks

	Without	With	Indeterminate	Total
Bronze Age	47	0	1	48
Main Profile	93	11	7	111
Small Test	39	6	4	49
Test Pit	67	8	11	86
Witness Section	87	5	6	98
X Levels	101	8	23	132

Carnivores often use pressure to accomplish the same aim, and it is difficult to tell the two apart. However, at sites where there are large enough samples of long bone fragments from a single species, there are typically statistical indications of either animal or human use. Carnivores tend to leave behind, in addition to many long bone shaft fragments, long bones in which the epiphyseal ends have been destroyed but the entire shaft or at least the entire perimeter of the diaphysis ("complete tubes") at some point along the shaft has been preserved (e.g., Bunn 1983; Cruz-Uribe 1991; Pickering 2002). In contrast, humans tend to leave the opposite pattern, destroying the shafts of the long bones but leaving the ends intact. However, it is impossible at Fontéchevade to recognize such patterns, because the samples are too small for statistical analysis.

The collections from Henri-Martin's excavations include a large number of complete long bone shafts and of complete tubes. However, because it is not at all clear that she saved all bone fragments and much of the fragmentary material in the collections has never been analyzed, the statistical validity of this observation is questionable (see the following section).

What is clear is that there is more evidence for carnivore activity in the form of carnivore tooth marks than there is for human activity in the form of stone tool marks (Tables 8.4 and 8.5). (It should be noted

Table 8.5. Ratio of tool-marked to tooth-marked bones by sector

	Tool marks	Tooth marks	Ratio
Bronze Age	2	11	0.18
Main Profile	1	6	0.17
Small Test	2	8	0.25
Test Pit		8	0
Witness Section	2	5	0.4
X Levels	0	0	–

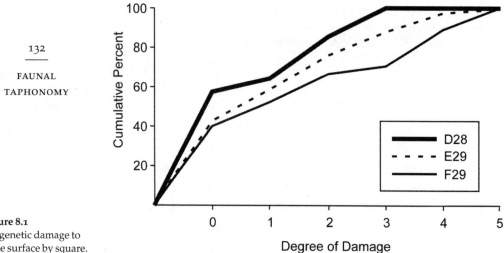

Figure 8.1
Diagenetic damage to
bone surface by square.

that Table 8.5 includes "tool" marks that may have a natural origin. Moreover, data on both "tool" and tooth marks undoubtedly include specimens that probably owe their presence in the cave to neither carnivores nor hominins.) This ratio is consistent with the presence of carnivores in the cave. There is no question that carnivores played a role in the accumulation of bones in the cave, and there seems little doubt that their role was more important than that of humans. The actual percentage of the assemblage that can be attributed to carnivore activity is, however, impossible to determine accurately.

Part of the problem in determining the relative levels of human and carnivore activity is the condition of the bones, which in many cases, makes observation of the surface or even of the broken margins very difficult. Diagenetic chemical processes have caused damage to or destruction of the surfaces of bones at Fontéchevade. As is to be expected in a cave environment, the nature and degree of this damage are not evenly distributed horizontally (Figs. 8.1 and 8.2). To a greater or lesser extent, this damage has obscured evidence of tooth marks, tool marks, and breakage. Analysis of diagenetic alteration can provide some slight clues to the origin of the faunal assemblage.

In Level A in the Test Pit, diagenetic alteration has in some cases been extreme. Bones are often severely pitted, and in some cases so much material has been removed that the shape of the specimen has in fact been altered. So much dentine has been removed from some teeth that they can best be described as "ghosts" (Fig. 8.3). However, alongside these specimens were found two bones whose surfaces are

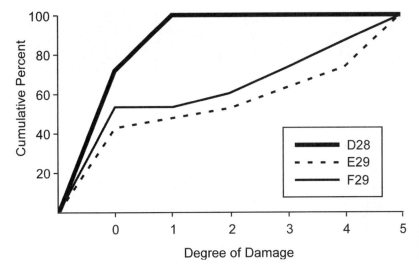

Figure 8.2
Diagenetic damage to
teeth by square.

completely unaltered because the bones themselves are fossilized. These bones also differ from the others recovered from this sector in that they are considerably rounded, probably due to abrasion in a stream bed (Fig. 8.4). Because the sedimentological analysis shows no evidence of stream action, these bones apparently entered the cave from the overlying plateau, along with the sediments and were rounded in the same pre-Pleistocene stream that rounded the quartz cobbles in the site, which also entered the site from the overlying sediments.

Overall, the faunal evidence for regular human occupation at Fontéchevade is weak. It would appear that hominins visited the site

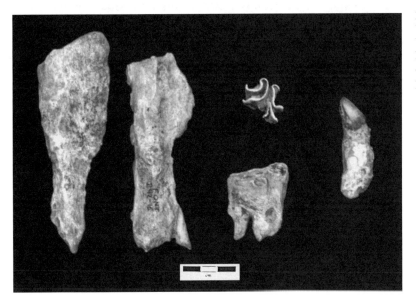

Figure 8.3
Bones and teeth from
Levels A and B of the Test
Pit showing diagenetic
damage ranging from
pitting to severe attrition.

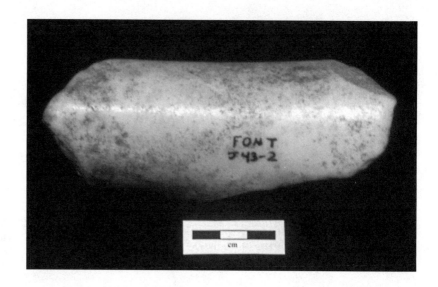

Figure 8.4
Fully fossilized bone
from Level A of the
Test Pit, showing fresh
surface.

sporadically, but that the faunal assemblage has several origins and that anthropogenic factors were of rather minor overall importance.

Significance of these findings for Henri-Martin's excavations

The collections from Henri-Martin's excavations are stored at the Musée d'Archéologie Nationale at Saint-Germain-en-Laye. At the time of our excavations and analysis, much of this material was still stored in boxes marked as unidentified, unidentified diaphyses, cooking debris, and the like, and these usually contained clearly identifiable specimens. It was also clear from looking at the material that she and her excavators did not save all faunal remains. Even by comparison with modern hyena dens, for example, teeth, complete bones, complete tubes, and epiphyses were overrepresented, and shaft fragments and other fragmentary remains were seriously underrepresented. It is also almost certain that large specimens were more likely to be kept than small ones. This means that most of the statistical analyses that would normally be of use to zooarchaeological or taphonomic analysis cannot be carried out.

Nevertheless, some conclusions can be drawn concerning the relationship between our excavations and those of Henri-Martin. According to her counts (in Vallois 1958:241–251; see Tables 8.6 and 8.7), the fauna she recovered from her Bed E indicate a temperate environment rather than the colder grassland environment. The sample from our Witness Section, although small, is quite similar. The Witness Section corresponds to the lower part of Henri-Martin's Bed E.

Table 8.6. Fauna from Henri-Martin's excavations, by bed

	E0	E1'	E1''	E2'	E2''	E2'''
Dicerorhinus	3	4	2	3	9	13
Equus	17	24	58	68	56	33
Bos/Bison	6	20	50	59	56	106
Sus	1	5	10	8	38	62
Capreolus		3	7	7	20	3
Cervus	3	17	17	9	34	15
Dama	7	39	143	129	399	224
Canis		4	5	6	1	
Crocuta	12	14	15	30	41	65
Ursus	1	80	28	14		
Felis	1	4	6	4	1	5
Total	51	214	341	337	655	526

By contrast, our excavations in the upper part of the Main Profile and Test Pit produced remains of species indicative of a much colder climate (although the samples were quite small). This probably does not indicate a lack of correspondence between our levels and the upper part of her Bed E. There is some indication, even in her counts, that her Bed E0 appears somewhat more similar to ours, with more *Equus* and *Coelodonta* remains and fewer *Sus, Capreolus, Dama,* and *Cervus* than the underlying beds. This impression is confirmed by Paletta's (2005) recent study of the fauna from Henri-Martin's Bed E. She reported that the upper parts of E (E0 and E1) contained species typical of cold, open environments: *Rangifer tarandus* (reindeer), *Marmota marmota* (marmot), *Cricetus cricetus* (hamster), *Lagurus lagurus* (lemming), *Prunella collaris* (alpine accentor), and *Plectrophenax nivali* (snow bunting). This report is in line with Chaline's (1972) observation that the fauna from Bed E included arctic fox (*Alopex lagopus*), steppe lemming (*Lagurus lagurus*), alpine marmot (*Marmota marmota*),

Table 8.7. Percentages of herbivore remains from Henri-Martin's excavations, by bed

	E0	E1'	E1''	E2'	E2''	E2'''
Dicerorhinus	8	4	1	1	1	3
Equus	46	21	20	24	9	7
Bos/Bison	16	18	17	21	9	23
Sus	3	4	3	3	6	14
Capreolus	0	3	2	2	3	1
Cervus	8	15	6	3	6	3
Dama	19	35	50	46	65	49

European hamster (*Cricetus cricetus*), and root vole (*Microtus ratticeps*). However, Chaline did not recognize that the faunas from the upper and lower parts of Bed E were different, probably because he apparently lumped the entire Bed E sample together for his analysis.

Thus, the differences between the fauna from our excavations in the Witness Section and those from the Main Profile (and presumably from the Test Pit) appear to parallel the differences described by Paletta. Although Paletta considered the colder fauna to be intrusive, radiometric dates from the upper part of Henri-Martin's Bed E indicate that these sediments date to OIS 3 (see Chapter 7), so there is no reason to believe that they are intrusive.

In order to study similarities and differences in the relative roles of carnivore and human activity in her collections, it was necessary to find a way to sidestepp the statistical problems posed by incomplete recovery and identification. This was done by observing a sample of herbivore limb bones in her collections. It is probable that the sample is still somewhat biased, but we assumed that limb bones and limb bone fragments were not collected on the basis of whether they bore tooth or tool marks. There were differences in the frequencies of carnivore tooth marks and green-bone fractures in the samples from various levels (Figs. 8.5 and 8.6). Bones from the upper levels of Henri-Martin's collection and bones from our excavations, including the Witness Section, showed similar frequencies of tooth marks. Such marks were considerably more common on bones from her lower levels, including those she designated as belonging to the Diverticule, which she recognized as a hyena den. It should be noted, however, that the Witness Section corresponds to her lowest bed, E2'''.

By contrast, there were fewer specimens with green-bone fractures in her collection than in ours. This finding may be interpreted in

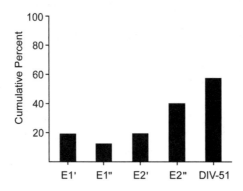

Figure 8.5
Carnivore tooth marks
on bones by bed (Henri-
Martin excavations).

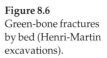

Figure 8.6
Green-bone fractures
by bed (Henri-Martin
excavations).

one of two ways. It may be that the difference is real and attributable to relatively greater human activity at the back of the cave, or it may be due to the relatively high percentage of complete long bones and long bone shafts in the sample from Henri-Martin's excavation. The latter interpretation is supported by the fact that the data from the Witness Section are in line with those from the rest of our excavations.

There were 4 bones with probable cut marks from the sample of 539 studied. There were 15 bones or bone fragments with a large number of light scratches scattered over the surface of the bone, which probably indicate trampling or sediment movement, rather than human activity. In addition, there were 10 specimens with questionable marks. These data indicate that hominin activity played a role in the formation of the faunal assemblage, but that this role was less important that that played by carnivores.

CONCLUSIONS

The faunal samples from Fontéchevade are far from ideal for understanding the taphonomy, much less the zooarchaeology, of the site. For Henri-Martin's collection, the relationship between what has been curated and what was actually in the ground is hard to assess. For our collections, the samples were very small and the amount of diagenetic damage high. This means that statistical methods are of minimal value for analyzing either collection.

What is clear is that both hominins and carnivores played a role in the creation of both assemblages. The evidence from both collections indicates that the role of hominins was significantly less than that of carnivores. What is less clear is the role played by other factors. There may have been some mixing of newer material with older *in situ* material, either through sediment movement or burrowing.

Certainly, there is every reason to believe that the X Levels are a mixture of materials of different ages caused by water action. To the extent that the faunal material from other sectors resemble this sample, they too may reflect mixture. A significant portion of the fauna may have died naturally in the site. This is probably true of most of the carnivores but probably not true of most of the ungulates that would have served as game for any hominins at the site. It would also appear that a portion of the faunal material at the back of the cave was allochthonous, entering the site with much older stream sediments from the overlying plateau. However, the condition of most of the bones indicates that they did not move this far.

In all, as far as can be determined with the material at hand, Fontéchevade would appear to be a rather heterogeneous assemblage, the product of a number of different factors, of which hominin activity was only one. Quantifying the role of humans is impossible, but they appear to have played a relatively minor part. Their occupations were probably more sporadic and less intense than those of large carnivores, notably hyenas.

Finally, the presence of chicken (*Gallus*) remains in the Bronze Age levels of Fontéchevade is to be expected. However, their presence in Level A of the Test Pit (see Table 8.1) indicates either that this level was entirely out of place or, more likely, badly disturbed. The level consisted of a large éboulis in a fine, very loose matrix. There were abundant indications of burrowing, although the loose matrix made it difficult to identify the limits of such burrows. Data from this level should be regarded with caution.

ACKNOWLEDGMENTS

The majority of the identifications reported here were made in Angoulême by J.-F. Tournepiche. Others, primarily of small fauna and of material from screens, were made by P. Chase using the comparative collection at the Institut de Préhistoire et de Géologie du Quaternaire at the Université de Bordeaux I. I would like to thank that Institute for permission to use the collection and Mlle. Dominique Armand for her help.

9

The Fauna from Henri-Martin's Excavation of Bed E

Jean-François Tournepiche

Almost 50 years after its publication by Arambourg (1958), the large mammal fauna of the "Tayacian" bed of Fontéchevade merits reanalysis in light of our current knowledge. Even though it was collected with minimal data concerning provenience, the collection remains a precious source of information concerning paleoenvironment, paleontology, taphonomy, and, above all, biostratigraphy.

This chapter presents only the essential results that permitted taxonomic attribution of certain large mammals from Bed E; it discusses as well the chronological position of the Fontéchevade fauna in the French Pleistocene.

HISTORY OF RESEARCH: THE EARLY EXCAVATIONS

From the earliest research, the fauna from the early beds of Fontéchevade took on a particular importance because they indicated the existence of an ancient temperate period rarely encountered in French Pleistocene deposits. The Abbé Breuil said to Henri-Martin in 1939, "Be aware that it is very old: [rhinoceros] Mercki, fallow deer, tortoise" (Henri-Martin 1957:6).

When the excavations were complete, Arambourg (1958:225) made a succinct study of this fauna and attributed it to a temperate period earlier then the Würm. He showed, however, a certain prudence in reaching this conclusion:

Chronologically, it is at least as old as the last interglacial, to which it may belong, but although it is thus possible to fix an upper limit to its age, no paleontological argument permits us to go further in the deductions we would like to draw from the fauna [chronologiquement, c'est donc au moins au dernier interglaciaire qu'elle peut correspondre mais, s'il est possible de fixer ainsi une limite supérieure à son ancienneté, aucun argument paléontologique ne permet, par contre, d'aller plus avant dans les précisions que l'on souhaiterait pouvoir en déduire].

This chronological attribution to the Riss-Würm, which was not demonstrated, has since been challenged. Chaline in 1972, Debénath in 1974, and Bastin in 1976 independently proposed (based respectively on micromammals, geology, and palynology) the hypothesis that the deposits had been formed during an interstadial of the Riss.

Because the fauna of the "Tayacian" bed remains one of the few means of assessing the chronology of this assemblage, it is of critical importance to revise its analysis in the light of new information concerning the evolution of mammalian species in southwestern France during the Middle and Upper Pleistocene.

DATA FROM THE 1994–1998 EXCAVATIONS

The excavations reported in this volume produced a small number of bones in three sectors.

Test Pit

The following species were found in the Test Pit:

- Bovinae
- *Equus caballus* (Linnaeus, 1758)
- Cervidae
- *Crocuta crocuta spelaea* (Goldfuss, 1823)

The species present give little indication of the age or environment of this fauna. Horses predominate, followed by bovines. Hyena remains are quite common. The remains are too few to attempt to correlate them to other animal populations of known age or to evaluate their degree of evolution.

Main Profile

In the Main Profile, these species were found:

- Bovinae, including *Bison* sp.
- *Equus caballus* (Linnaeus, 1758)

- *Equus hydruntinus* (Regalia, 1904)
- *Coelodonta antiquitatis* (Blumenbach, 1799)
- *Rangifer tarandus* (Linnaeus, 1758)
- *Cervus elaphus* (Linnaeus, 1758)
- *Crocuta crocuta spelaea* (Goldfuss, 1823)
- *Panthera leo spelaea* (Goldfuss, 1810)
- *Vulpes vulpes* (Linnaeus, 1758)
- *Canis lupus* (Linnaeus, 1758)

In addition to the bovines, horses, and red deer, the reindeer and wooly rhinoceros appear in squares C29, D29, E29, and F29. The climatic significance of the latter two species is clear: They indicate a cold, steppic environment.

It is difficult to attribute a precise biostratigraphic age to this fauna, whose homogeneity must be questioned. The elements recovered are too fragmentary and too few for a paleontological study and a chronobiological attribution.

Witness Section

Excavations in the Witness Section yielded these species:

- *Crocuta crocuta spelaea* (Goldfuss, 1823)
- *Equus hydruntinus* (Regalia, 1904)
- *Bos primigenius* (Bojanus, 1827)
- *Cervus elaphus* (Linnaeus, 1758)
- *Dama dama* (Linnaeus, 1758)
- *Capreolus capreolus* (Linnaeus, 1758)
- *Sus scrofa* (Linnaeus, 1758)

The species coming from this sector correspond to those found in Bed E by Henri-Martin. They form a homogeneous whole.

From the perspective of a paleontological study, because of the small sample size, the faunal material from the 1994–1998 excavations cannot provide definitive answers.

REVISON OF CERTAIN GENERA

The examination of certain species represented in Bed E leads to new taxonomic attributions.

Crocuta crocuta spelaea (Goldfuss, 1823)

The cave hyena is represented by 352 remains, of which 212 are cranial fragments (teeth and bone fragments). Their identification, which is based on cranial and dental morphology and which was done by Arambourg, poses no problem.

The biometry of the cheek teeth of hyenas from the Fontéchevade population, compared to those from other sites in the southwest of France, has several implications. Measurements of the teeth of present-day African *Crocuta crocuta* provide a reference and were given by Ballesio (1979). The choice of fossil material was limited to series coming from sites in the southwest of France that have been dated with relative certainty and that are numerous enough to permit statistical analysis.

GROTTE DU MAS DES CAVES (HÉRAULT)
These deposits date to the Mindel-Riss interglacial, that is, to about 350,000 years ago (Bonifay in Fosse 1997). Considered by Bonifay as an archaic species of cave hyena, the Lunel hyena is named *Crocuta spelaea intermedia* (Bonifay 1971).

GROTTE DE ROCHELOT (CHARENTE)
The species present in this very characteristic hyena den, which are highly diversified, reflect a temperate environment attributed to the beginning of OIS 5 (Tournepiche 1996).

GROTTE D'ARTENAC, C. 10 (CHARENTE)
Bed 10 of this site is characterized by the existence of a rich cave hyena den. This level is dated to a phase at the beginning of OIS 5 (Delagnes et al. 1999).

PAIR NON PAIR (GIRONDE)
The numerous hyena remains are dated to OIS 3. Their measurements are given by Clot (1980).

JAURENS (CORRÈZE)
The population of cave hyenas from the Jaurens Cave is homogeneous and well dated to OIS 3, about 30 ky (Ballesio 1979).

CHÂTILLON-SAINT-JEAN (DRÔME)
Chauviré, in 1962, attributed the remains of hyenas from the alluvial terrace of Châtillon to an archaic form of *Crocuta crocuta spelaea* (in

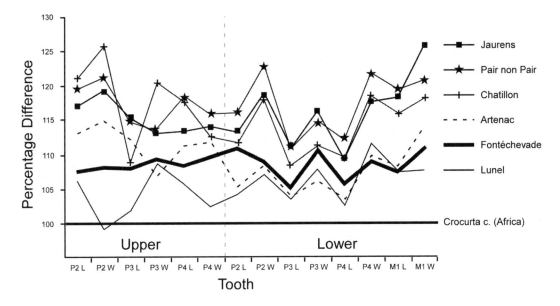

Figure 9.1
Dental series of fossil
Crocuta. Differences
in size expressed as a
percentage of those of
present-day African *C.
Crocuta*.

Clot 1980). These evolved in a cold, open environment dated to the
beginning of the Riss (OIS 9?).

SUMMARY OF CAVE HYENA FINDINGS

The teeth of fossil *Crocuta* populations are shown in Figure 9.1, in
which the Y axis shows the size expressed as a percentage of present-
day *C. crocuta*, which serves as a reference.

Fossil *Crocuta* teeth are larger than those of the present-day
African *Crocuta*. The lower cheek teeth demonstrate particularly well
the greater width of *C. c. spelaea* teeth compared with those of present-
day *C. crocuta*. Based on the size and proportions of its cheek teeth,
C. c. spelaea does not appear to be simply a present-day *C. crocuta* of
larger size.

The hyenas of Fontéchevade have lower teeth whose size variations fall within the range of those of other cave hyenas. By contrast,
the upper teeth are narrow and larger than those of present-day hyenas; however, their L/l (length/width) ratios are closer to those of
present-day species than are the L/l ratios of the lower teeth.

The cave hyena is not a rare element in Middle and Upper Pleistocene faunas. Nevertheless, a careful examination shows an unpre-
dictable distribution, ranging from total absence to abundance during
certain periods.

C. c. spelaea, which is present but rare in the middle part of
the Middle Pleistocene (the *C. c. prespelaea* of the "Mindel"), does
not develop fully until the Mindel-Riss (Holstein) Two sites have
produced abundant material dated to this period: the cave of Mas

des Caves at Lunel-Viel and the cave of Rameaux at Saint-Antonin-Noble-Val.

The hyena became rare at the end of the Middle Pleistocene, and only the terrace of Châtillon-Saint-Jean (Riss II) produced abundant remains.

One must wait for the beginning of OIS 5 to see the reappearance of hyena dens in karstic cavities. Rare and even absent in OIS 4, the hyena proliferates from stage 3 to the beginning of stage 2 of OIS 5 (Fosse 1997), disappearing for good shortly thereafter. Several hundred sites frequented by cave hyenas during the latter period have been found in western Europe. In particular, the sites of the Charente register this reappearance of cave occupations (Tournepiche 1996).

The length of M_1 compared with that of P_4 in Figure 9.2 shows a population distribution of different ages that falls into two groups based on size. Independent of the chronological period, size is correlated with climatic environment – hyenas with large teeth lived in a cold environment (Pair-non-Pair, Jaurens, Châtillon-Saint-Jean), whereas those with small teeth lived in a temperate environment (Rochelot, Artenac, Lunel, Fontéchevade). The small size of the Fontéchevade hyenas seems to reflect a temperate climate, but one cannot attribute to this a chronological significance. Several French authors (Bonifay 1971; Clot 1980) have argued that, like that of *Canis lupus*, the evolution of the genus *Crocuta* was characterized by a unidirectional increase in size from the Middle to the Upper Pleistocene.

A correlation between size variations and fluctuations in climatic factors in accord with Bergmann's rule is now well established (Klien 1986; Klein and Scott 1989; Kurtén 1957). Therefore, the small size of the Fontéchevade cave hyena population has no chronological significance, but is a result of environmental pressure resulting from a temperate period.

Ursus spelaeus (Rosenmüller and Heinroth, 1794)

Arambourg (1958) identified numerous and very fragmented remains of bears, which he attributed to *Ursus spelaeus*. Several observations made on the dental remains (25 cheek teeth) provide insights into the evolutionary status of this bear. Biometry provides only limited information because of the small number of specimens – they fall within the variation of both *U. deningeri* and *U. spelaeus*. By contrast,

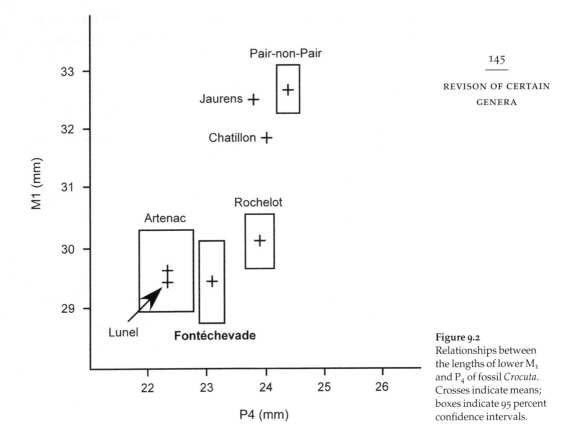

Figure 9.2
Relationships between
the lengths of lower M_1
and P_4 of fossil *Crocuta*.
Crosses indicate means;
boxes indicate 95 percent
confidence intervals.

the dental morphology of certain cheek teeth give indications of the place of the Fontéchevade bear along the *U. deningeri–U. spelaeus* lineage.

The two upper P⁴s show an alignment of peaks distal to the paracone and mesial to the metacone in one case, and in the other forming a slight angle. The deuterocone is separated from the metacone by a depression that shows no relief. These primitive characters are found in *U. deningeri*.

The reliefs of the three lower P_4s are poorly developed, and their distal portion has no relief. This modest development is an archaic characteristic. The crown is relatively low, which is also the case with the lower M_1s. The latter have a metaconid that is divided into two small bumps of equal size, a morphology that is typical of cave bear (Fig. 9.3). The crest linking the protoconid and metaconid is simple and sharp.

The transition from *U. deningeri* to *U. spelaeus* took place at the end of the Middle Pleistocene (Quiles 2003). The bears of Fontéchevade, whose teeth have a *spelaeus*-like morphology but show a certain number of primitive characters are probably a primitive form of *Ursus spelaeus* that arose at the beginning of the Upper Pleistocene.

Equus cf. *germanicus* (Nehring, 1884)

Since Arambourg's 1958 study, our knowledge of French Pleistocene equids has advanced greatly (Prat 1968). To place the Fontéchevade horses in the chronology of these different species, it was necessary to determine precisely their specific nature. To this end, we referred to well-documented horse populations from the southwest of France.

Several species replaced one another in the region during the Middle and Upper Pleistocene:

- *Equus mosbachensis* (V. Reichenau, 1915) is a large horse of which different subspecies are found in the Middle Pleistocene and disappear before OIS 6. We use as a reference the population of Artenac (Charente), dated to OIS 7 (Delagnes et al. 1999).
- *Equus pivetaui* (David and Prat 1962) comes from the final Pleistocene levels of the Abri Suard at La Chaise (Charente), dated to OIS 6 (Debénath 1976; Prat 1968). It is called *E. taubachensis* (Freudenberg 1911) by Eisenmann (1991).
- *Equus germanicus* (Nehring, 1884) is common in levels of the early Würm of southwest France (stages 5, 4, and part of 3). The site of Rochelot (Charente) yielded populations of archaic *E. germanicus* (Tournepiche 1996). The population of Pair non Pair (Gironde) dates to stages 4 and 3 (Guadelli 1987).
- *Equus gallicus* (Prat, 1968) appears at the end of OIS 3 and disappears during the first half of stage 2. The population collected at

Figure 9.3
Lower M$_1$ of *Ursus spelaeus* from Fontéchevade (lingual surface).

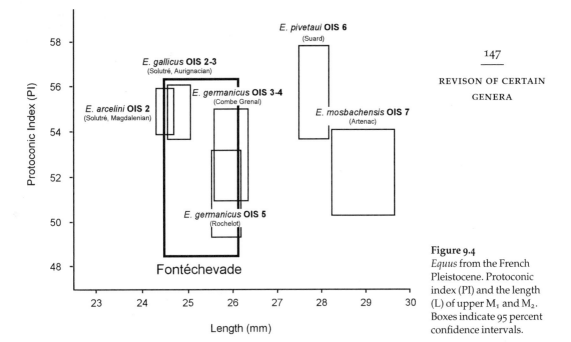

Figure 9.4
Equus from the French
Pleistocene. Protoconic
index (PI) and the length
(L) of upper M_1 and M_2.
Boxes indicate 95 percent
confidence intervals.

Solutré in the levels dating to the beginning of the Upper Paleolithic (Guadelli 1987) is used for reference.

- *Equus arcelini* (Guadelli, 1987) is known at the end of the Würm
  in Magdalenian levels. The site of Quéroy (Charente) and the
  Magdalenian of Solutré are used (Guadelli 1987; Tournepiche
  1996).

The upper teeth and metapodials are the most diagnostic elements for the taxonomic definition of the Pleistocene equines, so
only these are used in analyzing the horses of Fontéchevade. In
spite of the uncertainties that remain concerning the evolution of
Pleistocene horses, it is possible to distinguish populations of the
Middle Pleistocene from those of the Upper Pleistocene (Eisenmann
1991).

The mean lengths of lower P_3, P_4, M_1, and M_2 measured at the
occlusal level are greater than 28.5 mm in horses from the Middle
Pleistocene and shorter than this in Upper Pleistocene horses. The
Fontéchevade horses have a mean cheek tooth length of 28.4 mm.

It is possible to express the mean length of upper M^1 and M^2
as a function of their protocone index (PI). Populations of Middle
Pleistocene horses are clearly distinguished from the E. *germanicus*–
E. *arcelini* lineage of the Upper Pleistocene. The 95 percent confidence

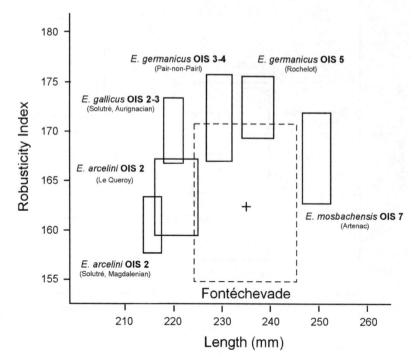

Figure 9.5
Equus from the French
Pleistocene. Length (L)
and robusticity index
(RI) of third metacarpals.
Boxes indicate 95 percent
confidence intervals;
crosses, means.

intervals of the Fontéchevade teeth are large, due to the small sample recovered, but they cover the Würm group (Fig. 9.4).

The mean lengths of the third metacarpals and the third metatarsals are greater than 235 mm and 280 mm, respectively, for Middle Pleistocene horses. The dimensions of the metapodials at Fontéchevade average 235.16 mm for the third metacarpals. Fourth metacarpals measure 270, 280, and 264 mm. The width of the distal articulation of the third metacarpals is 51.3 mm, narrower than that of Middle Pleistocene horses, which are greater than 53.5 mm. Figure 9.5, which graphs the mean length of third metacarpals relative to their robusticity index (IR), shows that the third metacarpals from Fontéchevade are close to those of Upper Pleistocene horses.

In terms of its dimensions, the horse of Fontéchevade is close to the horses of the Upper Pleistocene. It differs markedly from those of OIS 6 (*E. pivetaui*) and OIS 7 (*E. mosbachensis*).

Dama dama (Linnaeus, 1758)

The fallow deer is the most abundant species in Bed E of Fontéchevade. Arambourg (1958) designated it *D. clactoniana* Falconer, associating it with the Middle Pleistocene fallow deer of England. *Dama clactoniana* seems to disappear at the end of the Middle Pleistocene, and therefore, the fallow deer of the beginning of the Upper Pleistocene are assigned to *Dama dama* Linnaeus.

Although antlers are very numerous, the tines, which are useful for discriminating species, are not preserved. The lower teeth provide more information. The lower P_3s of fallow deer from Fontéchevade show a low frequency of fusion between the entoconid and the metaconid, as is the case in present-day *Dama*, but in *D. clactoniana* fusion is frequent. If this criterion has an evolutionary value, the Fontéchevade fallow deer show an evolved morphology.

Although the biometric variations in the teeth of fossil fallow deer are moderate, the size of their post-cranial skeleton varies greatly. The fallow deer of the Middle Pleistocene are much larger than both present-day fallow deer and those of Sclayn and Fontéchevade (Fig. 9.6).

Finally, the fallow deer of Sclayn and Fontéchevade differ very little from each other, either in dentition or in post-cranial skeleton. Simonet (1991) considers that the fallow deer of Sclayn and Fontéchevade are closer to those of the Upper Pleistocene than to those of the Middle Pleistocene, rejecting their attribution to *D. clactoniana*. Consequently, this excludes a date earlier than the beginning of the Upper Pleistocene for the site of Fontéchevade.

Figure 9.6
Fallow deer – evolution of proportions of post-cranial bones (after Simonet 1991).

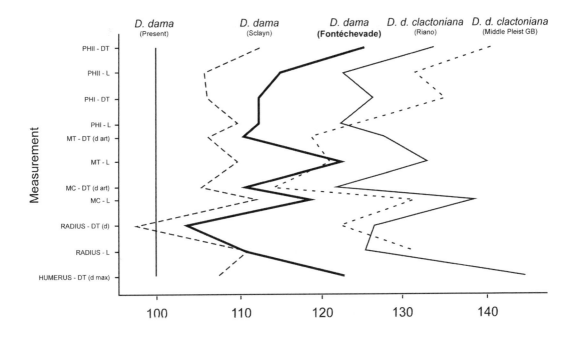

The revision of large mammals recovered from the whole of Bed E permits us to establish the following list of species:

Carnivores

- *Panthera (Leo) spelaea* (Goldfuss, 1810)
- *Lynx* sp.
- *Canis lupus* (Linnaeus, 1758)
- *Cuon alpinus europaeus* (Bourguignat, 1868)
- *Vulpes vulpes* (Linnaeus, 1758)
- *Crocuta crocuta spelaea* (Goldfuss 1823)
- *Ursus arctos* (Linnaeus, 1758)
- *Ursus spelaeus* (Rosenmüller and Heinroth, 1794)
- *Martes martes* (Linnaeus, 1758)
- *Meles meles* (Linnaeus,1758)

Herbivores

- *Dicerorhinus mercki* (Jäger, Kaup, 1839–1842)
- *Equus* cf. *germanicus* (Nehring, 1884)
- *Equus hydruntinus* (Regalia, 1904)
- *Bos primigenius* (Bojanus, 1827)
- *Megaloceros giganteus* (Blumenbach, 1803)
- *Cervus elaphus* (Linnaeus, 1758)
- *Dama dama* (Linnaeus, 1758)
- *Capreolus capreolus* (Linnaeus, 1758)
- *Sus scrofa* (Linnaeus, 1758)

Rodents and lagomorphs

- *Castor fiber* (Linnaeus, 1758)
- *Hystrix* sp.
- *Lepus europaeus*
- *Oryctolagus cuniculus*

The Greek tortoise (*Testudo graeca* Linnaeus, 1758) was in the past identified at Fontéchevade and held to be characteristic of the interglacial. Hervet (2000), who revised the tortoises of France, attributed that of Fontéchevade to Hermann's tortoise (*Testudo hermanni* Gmelin, 1789).

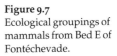

Open, non-arctic
(11%)

Wooded
(89%)

Figure 9.7
Ecological groupings of
mammals from Bed E of
Fontéchevade.

Three new species of mammals have been identified: *Hystrix,*
Megaloceros, and *Lynx* (Paletta 2005). The presence of brown bear is
attested by two teeth. The bison are absent from the faunal assemblage, and only aurochs are represented (J.-Ph. Brugal, personal communication). The fallow deer can be assimilated into *Dama dama,* and
more precise statements can be made concerning the horses, which
are close to *Equus germanicus.*

Bed E forms a body of sediments that reaches 7 m in its greatest
thickness and whose stratigraphy appears more complex than was
described by Henri-Martin (1957). A question thus arises concerning
the homogeneity of the fauna recovered in this bed.

The distribution of species from Bed E shows a uniform presence of taxa in the entire sequence, with only the number of remains
varying from one level to another (Paletta 2005:89). Only 40 percent
of the remains could be identified to species or genus, and of these
only those whose provenience (either bed or depth) was marked
were included in the analysis. Moreover, the volume of the different
sub-beds excavated is very variable, which affects the quantities of
bones collected. The quantitative variations observed can also correspond to the utilization of the cave, which was simultaneously or
successively occupied by humans and carnivores (Dibble et al. 2006).

For all these reasons, it is not reasonable to interpret these quantitative variations in the faunal remains in terms of environmental
variations.

This fauna present a paleoenvironmental unity. The majority of
large mammals belonged to a wooded environment, and the assemblage includes a smaller proportion of species from an open, non-
arctic, environment (Fig. 9.7).

The presence of reindeer in the upper portion of Bed E and a specimen of arctic fox, which are in ecological contradiction with the rest of the fauna, must be considered as an intrusion of more recent remains into the ensemble of Bed E (Chase et al. 2007).

We can find no arguments for splitting the fauna from Bed E into several assemblages, and we consider it as a biochronological whole.

None of the large mammal species in Bed E of Fontéchevade is entirely limited to the Middle Pleistocene. *Dicerorhinus mercki*, a marker species of the Middle Pleistocene (Guérin 1980), which is present at Fontéchevade, is quite rare in the southwest of France, where it seems to disappear only after the beginning of the Upper Pleistocene. The horse, *Equus* cf. *germanicus*, is linked to the species of horse from the Upper Pleistocene of southwestern France, whose lineage is well known. The bear from Bed E can be attributed to the species *Ursus spelaeus*, but it has archaic deningerian characters.

Knowing that the emergence of cave bears was completed at the extreme end of the Middle Pleistocene (OIS 6), the bears from Fontéchevade are probably later than this period. The fallow deer cannot be significantly different from the species *Dama dama* of the Upper Pleistocene.

All the evidence is consistent with a chronological attribution of the association of large mammals from Bed E to the beginning of the Upper Pleistocene. The very temperate character of this association with the abundance of fallow deer indicates an interglacial period that can be assimilated with the Eemian (OIS 5e).

If faunas dating from this period are well represented in northern Europe, such is not the case in the southwest of France.

CONCLUSIONS

The assemblage of large mammals from Bed E of the Cave of Fontéchevade forms a biochronological and paleoecologically homogeneous whole. This fauna lived in a temperate and wooded environment, as attested by the presence of species limited to this milieu (fallow deer, red deer, roe deer, boar, aurochs) and by the morphology (reduced size) of the hyenas.

The biochronological age of this bed can be determined from the fauna with relative certainty. The evolutionary stage of the horses,

cave bears, and fallow deer, as well as the specific association of the
large mammals, makes it possible to put this fauna chronologically
into the beginning of the Upper Pleistocene, and more particularly
into the Eemian interglacial (OIS 5e).

10

The Upper Paleolithic of Fontéchevade

Laurent Chiotti

HISTORICAL BACKGROUND

This chapter describes some of the Upper Paleolithic lithic material recovered from Fontéchevade during the early part of the twentieth century. Upper Paleolithic remains, in varying amounts and from both inside and outside the cave, had been noted by several excavators. The first to uncover these industries was L. Durousseau-Dugontier, between 1902 and 1910, but unfortunately his results were never published and his excavation notes have been lost (Henri-Martin 1957). In 1913 and 1914, M. Vallade undertook more systematic excavations, uncovering three beds of Upper Paleolithic. G. Henri-Martin used Vallade's unpublished results when she published her own excavations (1957). In 1921, M. and Mme. de Saint-Périer opened a trench at the opening of the cave, which yielded some Upper Paleolithic elements (1957). In 1933, P. David (1933) carried out several tests that also produced some Aurignacian artifacts. Although the most significant excavations were carried out starting in 1937 by Henri-Martin, the Upper Paleolithic had already been almost entirely removed, with only two remnants of the Aurignacian bed found (Henri-Martin 1957). In the course of the 1994–1998 excavations, no Upper Paleolithic was found in situ, though several indisputably Upper Paleolithic elements were uncovered in disturbed contexts.

DATA FROM THE OLD EXCAVATIONS

The first excavations by Durousseau-Dugontier produced pottery sherds as well as Typical Aurignacian and Châtelperronian lithics, although it is impossible to know if the excavator recognized any stratigraphy. Vallade's excavations produced the most information about the upper part of the cave fill, according to Henri-Martin (1957), who was able to reconstruct the stratigraphy on the basis of Vallade's excavation notebooks. This record recognized three distinct beds, from bottom to top:

- Bed 1: Châtelperronian
- Bed 2: Typical Aurignacian
- Bed 3: Probable Upper Perigordian (Gravettian)

These three beds, which according to Vallade contained numerous hearths, represented a thickness of 1.30 m. They were excavated from the level area in front of the cave to a meter inside the cave. According to Vallade, the Châtelperronian bed lay on "fine diluvial gravels that formed the bed of the cave." Later, the de Saint-Périers wrote that the Aurignacian bed (the only one they found) overlay a bed of éboulis agglomerated by a stalactite deposit. Still later, David (1933) recognized two horizons in the course of his test: a lower horizon with Middle Aurignacian and an upper bed that he considered to be Upper Aurignacian in Breuil's sense (the Upper Perigordian of Peyrony). He apparently believed that his lower bed corresponded to Vallade's Beds 1 and 2.

In the course of her excavations, Henri-Martin reported finding only two remnants of the Aurignacian bed in place, which corresponded to a typical Middle Aurignacian in the western part of the cave, as well as remnants of breccia adhering to the cave wall that corresponded to the same bed. The two remnants lay on a brecciated bed. This bed probably corresponds to the gravel that Vallade considered to be the base of the cave, likely because of its induration.

Different authors disagree on the attribution of the industry in the archaeological bed on top of the indurated bed. For Vallade, it was Châtelperronian, whereas for the de Saint-Périers, David, and Henri-Martin, it was Aurignacian. To explain these differing attributions, Henri-Martin argued that the Châtelperronian must have had a more limited distribution in the cave interior than did the Aurignacian. The latter must have been present in the entire cave, whereas the Châtelperronian was present only in the middle. It is also possible, however, that this difference was due to a disturbance of the deposits, perhaps even to their deposition, which would provide a basis for questioning the validity of the Upper Paleolithic beds described by Vallade (see the following section).

THE UPPER PALEOLITHIC MATERIAL FROM FONTÉCHEVADE

Material studied

The collection from the first excavation (by Durousseau-Dugontier) was given by the excavator's family to Henri-Martin and was supposedly conserved at the laboratory of La Quina. This collection could not be found. However, according to Henri-Martin (1957:203), the objects in it bore no indications of stratigraphic provenience, and there were no excavation notes. The material from Vallade's excavations was grouped into two series. The larger was a private collection, which, according to Henri-Martin, belonged to M. Lugol, an Inspector General of the Navy. This collection, sold at auction, could not be found. The second collection, composed of some representative pieces from the three beds defined by Vallade, was deposited at the Musée d'Angoulême but also could not be found.

The collection from Henri-Martin's excavations is currently housed at the Musée d'Archéologie Nationale at Saint-Germain-en-Laye. In this collection, three lots of material were attributable to the Upper Paleolithic.

The first lot came from the two remnants of Bed B, dated to 1939. It comprised 63 pieces without tickets or labels but bearing the following: "Font. B 1939." This lot appears to correspond to the material studied for the 1957 publication. However, the pieces drawn by J. Bouissonie and published (Henri-Martin 1957) there could not be found. They were probably removed by the artist and never reintegrated with the collection from Bed B.

A second lot came from the Test Pit in the east talus, excavated in April 1948. The ticket associated with these pieces read "Aurignacian hearth on the broken-up – Tayacian infiltration – [stalagmite] floor D, selection of flints." Most probably, this material represents Upper Paleolithic pieces selected by Henri-Martin from a mixture of Tayacian and Upper Paleolithic material. These 125 pieces are, without question, attributable to the Upper Paleolithic. They are not mentioned in the 1957 publication.

An undated lot of material was marked "comes from T.V. and the Aurignacian B, sensu lato – mixed: beds C, A, B." Among this material, we were able to select 52 pieces that were attributable to the Upper Paleolithic. They, too, were not mentioned in the 1957 publication.

The collection from the 1994–1998 excavations includes 68 pieces attributable to the Upper Paleolithic. These pieces come from all the disturbed levels of the Main Profile (Surface, Levels 1a, 1b, 2a, and X0) and from Levels A and B of the Test Pit (Henri-Martin's Test Pit 3 in the main gallery of the cave).

STUDY OF THE MATERIAL RECOVERED

Henri-Martin excavations (remnants of Bed B)

The material from the excavation of two remnants of Henri-Martin's Bed B consists of 63 pieces, of which 20 are debitage and 43 are tools. The relative proportion between these two categories indicates that the complete collection was not recovered during excavation. Only unusual or large pieces are present; among the 20 specimens there are 10 blades; 7 cores; 1 whole, untested block of flint; and only 2 flakes. One of these flakes is characteristic of the reworking of a carinated scraper (Chiotti 2000). Among the cores, 6 are prismatic, and of these, 4 have a single striking platform and 2 have two platforms. Of the cores with two platforms, only 1 is truly bipolar; the other has striking platforms associated with different surfaces. The last core is a Levallois core.

The tools coming from the two remnants of Bed B include a large proportion of endscrapers, with 15 specimens, of which 3 are Aurignacian scrapers (one carinated endscraper and 2 are thick-nosed endscrapers (Fig. 10.1g). There are four composite tools

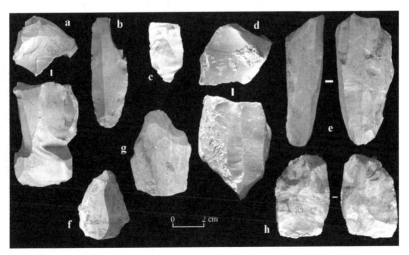

Figure 10.1
Pieces from Henri-Martin's excavations (Musée d'Archéologie Nationale): a: prismatic core; b: angled burin on a break; c: splinter from a splintered piece; d: prismatic core; e: prismatic core; f,g: nosed endscrapers; h: splintered piece. (Photos by L. Chiotti.)

Table 10.1. Inventory of tools from Henri-Martin's excavations (remnants of Bed B)*

Type	Number	
	Found	Drawn
1 Endscraper on a blade	2	1
3 Double endscraper	2	4
4 Ogival endscraper	1	
5 Endscraper on a retouched flake or blade	5	
6 Endscraper on an Aurignacian blade	1	
8 Endscraper on a flake	1	1
11 Carenated endscraper	1	1
13 Thick-nosed endscraper	2	
17 Endscraper-burin	2	1
18 Endscraper – truncated blade	1	
22 Borer-burin	1	
23 Borer (+ point)	1	
27 Right angle dihedral burin	3	
30 Burin on a break or a natural surface	1	
31 Multiple dihedral burin	1	
32 Busked burin		2
46 Châtelperron point	1	1
47 Atypical Châtelperron point	1	
59 Backed blade	1	
61 Obliquely truncated piece	1	
62 Piece with concave truncation	1	
65 Piece with continuous retouch on one edge	3	1
74 Notched piece	5	
Total typed objects	38	12
Pieces with discontinuous or partial retouch	5	
Overall total	43	12

and five burins (Table 10.1). Other relatively well-represented tools are pieces retouched on one edge (three specimens) and notched pieces (five specimens). The industry also includes one Châtelperron point and one atypical Châtelperron point.

As indicated previously, the pieces illustrated by Bouyssonie in Henri-Martin's (1957) publication were not found. We therefore add these to our breakdown. According to the drawings, these consist of one simple endscraper, four double endscrapers, one endscraper on a flake, one carinated endscraper, one endscraper/burin, two busked burins, one Châtelperron point, and one notched blade with continuous retouch on one edge. Among the pieces illustrated but not found there is also a small bladelet core.

According to Henri-Martin, "The industry recovered . . . in the breccia and the in situ remnant of Bed B seem to correspond to

Vallade's second bed and to the middle bed of the Typical Aurignacian, that is to say, to Breuil's Aurignacian 2." We agree that the majority of this industry does appear to correspond to an Aurignacian, although it is more likely an Evolved Aurignacian, identified essentially by the presence of busked burins (Fig. 10.2c,d). Nevertheless, it cannot be doubted that the industry we have here is the product of mixing. Such mixing is indicated by the presence of older pieces, such as the Châtelperron points and a typically Levallois core. In the description of her material, Henri-Martin indicated the presence of a Mousterian-type sidescraper. There are also pieces that are manifestly more recent, corresponding perhaps to a Gravettian: a composite tool (burin on an oblique truncation – point) on a very fine curved blade, a double dihedral burin (dihedral angle burin and straight angle burin, both polyhedral), and a backed blade. This last piece (Fig. 10.2a), which was considered by Henri-Martin (1957:207) to be a Gravette point, is definitely elongated and narrow, but it has a curved back resembling Châtelperron points and is considered as such here.

Henri-Martin's excavations (sorted material)

The sorted Upper Paleolithic material from Henri-Martin's excavations consists of 177 specimens: 126 pieces of raw debitage and 51 tools. The relationship between these two categories indicates a selection of the material that seems to have been somewhat less severe than in the preceding series. Unretouched flakes were notably better collected. There are 50 specimens, including a core rejuvenation tablet. Among these flakes are 7 Levallois flakes, which come from

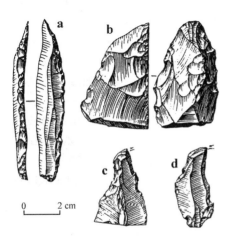

0   2 cm

Figure 10.2
Pieces from Henri-Martin's excavations: a: Châtelperronian point; b: carinated endscraper; c,d: busked burins. (Drawings by J. Bouyssonie in Henri-Martin [1957], reproduced by permission of Elsevier.)

the 1948 test and represent her original sorting of the material. There are also 48 unretouched blades (among them 3 crested blades and 1 neo-crested blade), 5 unretouched bladelets, 5 burin spalls, and 18 cores and core fragments. The material from the Test Pit in the east talus (Aurignacian hearth on the degraded stalagmite floor D) and that coming from the mixture of Beds A, B, and C (see previous section) have been grouped together here.

Of the 16 complete cores, most were blade cores (Fig. 10.1a,d,e): 6 prismatic blade cores with a single striking platform, 3 prismatic blade cores with two opposite striking platforms, and 4 prismatic cores with two striking platforms on separate (opposed or crossed) surfaces. The remaining three cores were flake cores: an amorphous core, a discoid core, and one core with prismatic tendencies. This last core has the same organization as a classic prismatic blade core, but its removal surface, being very short, could produce only flakes (Chiotti 2006).

The tools in this collection include as many endscrapers as burins (nine of each). Aurignacian endscrapers are represented by one atypical carinated scraper and one thick-nosed scraper (Fig. 10.1f). The burins also include two Aurignacian pieces (busked burins). There is a high proportion of retouched pieces, with 12 retouched on one edge and 3 on both edges. Aurignacian tools are also represented by a Font-Yves bladelet and a Dufour bladelet. There is a Mousterian limace in the category of "divers" [miscellaneous] pieces (Table 10.2).

Like that from the remnants of Henri-Martin's Bed B, this material includes a majority of elements attributable to the Aurignacian, in particular to the Evolved Aurignacian. Nevertheless, it also includes incongruous elements that indicate an indisputable mixing. There is mixing with the underlying Mousterian beds, given the presence of the Levallois flakes, one limace, and one discoid core. It is true that discoid cores, which produce a type of debitage characteristic of the Mousterian, are sometimes present in the Aurignacian but usually in an irregular form. Given the very characteristic form of the piece in question, it is very probably Mousterian. In addition, pieces that are more recent than the Aurignacian (probably Gravettian) can also be identified, such as a polyhedral right angle burin and a jasper-like flint core with two striking platforms with bipolar flaking (Fig. 10.1e).

Table 10.2. Inventory of tools from Henri-Martin's excavations (sorted material)*

Type	Number
1 Endscraper on a blade	1
2 Atypical endscraper	3
5 Endscraper on a retouched flake or blade	2
8 Endscraper on a flake	1
12 Atypical carenated endscraper	1
13 Thick-nosed endscraper	1
17 Endscraper-burin	1
19 Burin-truncated blade	1
23 Borer (+ point)	1
27 Right-angle dihedral burin	1
30 Burin on a break or a natural surface	2
31 Multiple dihedral burin	1
32 Busked burin	2
37 Burin on a retouched convex truncation	1
52 Font-Yves bladelet	1
61 Obliquely truncated piece	1
65 Piece with continuous retouch on one edge	12
66 Piece with continuous retouch on two edges	3
74 Notched piece	8
76 Splintered piece	1
90 Dufour bladelet	1
92 Miscellaneous	1
Type list total	47
Pieces with discontinuous or partial retouch	4
Overall total	51

* Types are those of de Sonneville-Bordes and Perrot (1954; 1955; 1956a,b).

The 1994–1998 excavations

The Upper Paleolithic material from the 1994–1998 excavations consists of 68 specimens: 50 pieces of debitage and 18 tools. In the course of this excavation, all lithics were collected, but it must be remembered that the material came from disturbed levels. In effect, therefore, it is a question of a posteriori selection. Given the difficulty of distinguishing unretouched flakes from the Middle Paleolithic from those of the Upper Paleolithic, the latter are relatively underrepresented in this selection. In addition, among the flakes collected, some could be from the Upper Paleolithic, but we cannot be certain of this attribution.

The debitage consists of 10 flakes (including 1 core tablet and 1 piece of shatter from a *pièce esquillée*); 26 blades, including 1 crested blade (see Fig. 10.3d); 10 bladelets, of which 4 come from carinated scrapers (Fig. 10.3g,h); and 2 burin spalls. There are also two cores: a bipolar bladelet core with two striking platforms and a core tending to the prismatic. The tools coming from the new excavations are a mixture of pieces with different origins, with some Aurignacian tools such as Dufour bladelets (Fig. 10.3a,e,f) and probably Gravettian pieces such as a backed bladelet (Fig. 10.3i), an endscraper on a retouched blade, and a probable base of a Gravette point (Fig. 10.3b; Table 10.3).

AURIGNACIAN BLADELET PRODUCTION

There were only a few bladelets that we could study: 5 unmodified and 2 modified bladelets from Henri-Martin's excavations and 10 unmodified and 4 modified bladelets from the 1994–1998 excavations. Nevertheless, we were able to identify two series of curved and twisted bladelets, one set (N = 6) removed from carinated scrapers or busked burins (Fig. 10.3g,h), and one set (N = 12), generally of large size, that was removed from prismatic cores.

The Aurignacian tools on bladelets consist of a Font-Yves bladelet and four Dufour bladelets (Fig. 10.3a,e). The latter are all large bladelets of the Dufour subtype (Demars and Laurent 1989). Such large bladelets, whose production is generally an extension of blade

Figure 10.3
Pieces from the 1994–1998 excavations (Musée d'Angoulême): a: Dufour bladelet; b: base of a Gravette point (?); c: retouched blade; d: crested blade; e, f : Dufour bladelets; g,h: bladelets from carinated endscrapers; i: backed bladelet. (Drawings by L. Chiotti). g and h are large bladelets from carinated scrapers. They are actually subproducts of the maintenance and shaping of the flaking surface/front edge of the endscraper to produce small curved and twisted bladelets (Bon and Bodu 2002; Chiotti 2003).

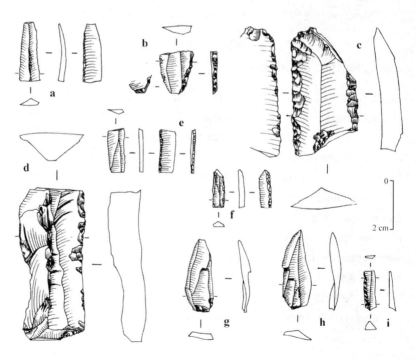

Table 10.3. Inventory of tools from the 1994–1998 excavations*

Type	Number
5 Endscraper on a retouched flake	1
21 Borer-endscraper (point-endscraper)	1
65 Piece with continuous retouch on one edge	2
66 Piece with continuous retouch on two edges	2
74 Notched piece	3
85 Backed bladelet	1
90 Dufour bladelet	3
Type list total	13
Piece with partial or discontinuous retouch	5
Overall total	18

* Types are those of de Sonneville-Bordes and Perrot (1954, 1955, 1956a,b).

production, characterize a facies considered as the oldest expression of the Aurignacian in France, called Protoaurignacian or Archaic Aurignacian by various authors. The extent of this industry, known from the margins of the Mediterranean, is now being extended northward, on the basis of new interpretations of series such as those of Bed VII of the Grotte du Renne at Arcy-sur-Cure (Bon and Bodu 2002; Perpère and Schmider 2002), of Bed K at Le Piage (Bordes 2005), or again at the Grotte Dufour (Bordes and Bon, unpublished). The presence of several such bladelets among the industries of Fontéchevade may indicate, albeit without any certainty, that a Protoaurignacian existed at that site. This would not, however, be exceptional for the region of the Charente; an industry of this type has been identified in Bed 2 of the Grotte Bourgeois-Delaunay in Vouthon (Demars, forthcoming).

Critical analysis of material published in the course of previous studies

Although there is undisputable evidence of Upper Paleolithic materials having come from the cave, the present study of available material does not prove the former existence of clearly individualized beds of this period. This section presents other data that can be brought to bear on this question.

THE DUROUSSEAU-DUGONTIER COLLECTION

Although the excavation that produced the Durousseau-Dugontier collection covered a broad area inside the cave, the collection itself contains only lithics with no stratigraphic attribution; however, Henri-Martin believed that the excavations included Vallade's Beds 1 and 2 (Henri-Martin 1957:204). In the course of the Durousseau-Dugontier excavation, mostly tools were kept. Henri-Martin indicates the presence of only 3 unretouched flakes, 19 unmodified blades or bladelets, 2 burin spalls, and 2 cores. There are 61 tools.

In view of the material from the Durousseau-Dugontier excavations illustrated in Henri-Martin's 1957 publication (Fig. 10.4), it is most probable that these excavations combined all of the Upper Paleolithic material in the cave and perhaps the Mousterian as well. In effect, the collection includes pieces attributable to the Mousterian (Mousterian points), to the Châtelperronian (Châtelperron points), to the Aurignacian (nosed scrapers, busked burins), and to the Gravettian (Gravette points, polyhedral dihedral burins). Given the limited information available, the collection cannot provide precise information about the existence of Upper Paleolithic beds in the site.

VALLADE'S COLLECTION

Vallade's collection was much larger and better documented because Vallade gave his excavation notebook to G. Henri-Martin (Henri-Martin 1953). Based on this notebook, Henri-Martin was able, in her words, to "reconstruct the stratigraphy of the site's Aurignacian beds" (Henri-Martin 1957:22), which included separate beds for the Châtelperronian, Typical Aurignacian (Aurignacian 2 of Abbé Breuil), and a more evolved industry that should probably be assigned to the Upper Perigordian (Henri-Martin 1953, 1957:191).

Figure 10.4
Pieces from Durousseau-Dugontier's excavations. a: Mousterian point; b: Châtelperronian point; c: nosed endscraper; d: busked burin; e: endscraper-dihedral polyhedric burin; f: Gravette point; g: dihedral polyhedric burin (Drawings by J. Bouyssonie in Henri-Martin [1957], reproduced by permission of Elsevier.)

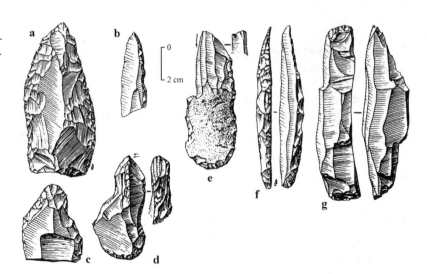

Lugol's series is the largest, and the lithics from that collection inventoried by Henri-Martin numbered 159 for Bed 1, 190 for Bed 2, and 47 for Bed 3. There were also 13 bone artifacts and 1 ornament in Bed 2, as well as 2 bone artifacts in Bed 3. The series stored at the Musée d'Angoulême included 16 pieces from Bed 1, 25 from Bed 2, and 68 pieces with no indication of provenience. Given that only pieces from Lugol's series are illustrated, those are the ones used for the present analysis.

Bed 1: Châtelperronian. Vallade's Bed 1 produced a large proportion of Châtelperron points, with 31 specimens (Fig. 10.5a–d). Endscrapers were essentially represented by endscrapers on flakes and some endscrapers on unretouched blades. There were also some rather untypical burins. Alongside these typically Upper Paleolithic pieces, one finds Mousterian-type tools (Fig. 10.5e,f), which are common in Châtelperronian industries.

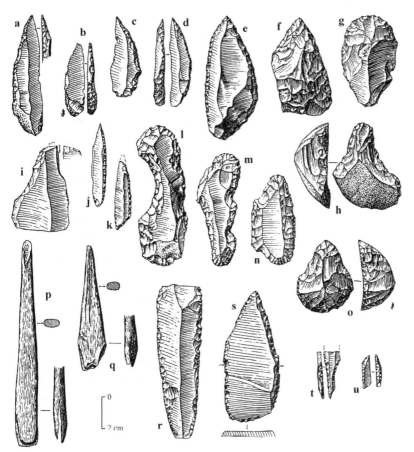

Figure 10.5
Pieces from the Vallades' excavation (a–h, Bed 1; q, Bed 2, r–u, Bed 3). a–d: Châtelperronian points; e: Mousterian point; f: Mousterian sidescraper; g: carinated endscraper; h: nosed endscraper; i: busked burin; j: Gravette point; k: backed bladelet on an oblique truncation; l: strangled blade; m: endscraper on an Aurignacian blade; n: double endscraper on an Aurigancian blade; o: double endscraper (carinated and nosed); p,q: split-based points; r: retouched blade; s: point; t: base of a Font-Robert point (?); u: backed bladelet. (Drawings by J. Bouyssonie in Henri-Martin [1957]. reproduced by permission of Elsevier.)

By contrast, it should be noted that Aurignacian-type endscrap-ers are present in relatively large numbers, with 13 carinated scrap-ers, 5 thick-nosed scrapers, and 10 thick atypical endscrapers. In her description of the Châtelperronian, de Sonneville-Bordes (1972:144) notes that it contains "very rare 'Aurignacian' carinated or nosed scrapers that are also not very typical." However, the pieces illus-trated by Henri-Martin are entirely typical (Fig. 10.5g,h).

As a whole, the industry described is generally characteristic of the Châtelperronian, but the presence of Aurignacian endscrapers implies mixing with the Aurignacian.

Bed 2: Typical Aurignacian. Henri-Martin considered the Aurigna-cian of the Fontéchevade Cave to be a Typical Aurignacian (Breuil's Aurignacian 2) or, in present-day terminology, an Evolved Aurigna-cian. This attribution seems to be based essentially on the presence of busked burins (Fig. 10.5i). However, if one looks at the description of this industry and the illustrated pieces, a different reading is pos-sible. In fact, the presence of backed pieces is completely out of place for an Aurignacian. The different types of backed pieces described (Gravette point [Fig. 10.5j], point with obliquely truncated base [Fig. 10.5 k], and fragments of backed blades) suggest, rather, a Gravettian attribution.

Henri-Martin writes that "the oldest facies of the Aurigna-cian sensu stricto (Breuil's Aurignacian 1), with large strangulated blades predominating, is absent at Fontéchevade" (1957:210). Yet, she reports the presence of two endscrapers on strangulated blades (Fig. 10.5l) and endscrapers on blades whose edges have been totally or partially retouched – and the illustrations indicate that this is often scalar Aurignacian retouch (Fig. 10.5m,n). These pieces are character-istic of Early Aurignacian and are absent in the Evolved Aurignacian.

Likewise, in the bone industry, Henri-Martin notes the presence of five points and point fragments with split bases. She states that "split base bone points, more often sublozenges than triangular in shape, argue for [an Evolved Aurignacian attribution]" (Henri-Martin 1957:211). However, split-base bone points are present only in the Early Aurignacian, never in the Evolved Aurignacian, and in fact, the sections of the pieces illustrated (Fig. 10.5p,q) fall entirely within the variability of Early Aurignacian split-base bone points (Hahn 1988).

The number of endscrapers is very large in this industry (170 specimens in all), but there are only eight burins. Such a relative frequency of these two types is also a marker of the Early Aurignacian (or at least of a very large part of this period).

Finally, the only elements that are truly diagnostic of the Evolved Aurignacian are the carinated busked burins (Fig. 10.5i), but there are only three such specimens. Based on the illustrated pieces, carinated nosed scrapers are present in forms that recall the Evolved Aurignacian (Fig. 10.5o), but this type of scraper is present in all stages of the Aurignacian. Henri-Martin (1957:263) also notes the presence of a fragment of lozenge-shaped point considered characteristic of the Evolved Aurignacian.

Bed 3: Upper Perigordian? In Henri-Martin's study, the attribution of Vallade's third bed was less clear. Nevertheless, she believed it to be well-enough defined to be considered an Upper Perigordian with Font-Robert points. The pieces she describes does support the notion that this is a Gravettian industry, notably because of the presence of armature elements, including backed pieces (Fig. 10.5u), a fragment of Gravette point, or a probable fragment of Font-Robert point (Fig. 10.5t). In addition, the retouch shown on the illustrated blades resembles that of the Gravettian more than that of the Aurignacian (Fig. 10.5r,s) but not conclusively. Henri-Martin (1957:202) notes in the bone industry the presence of a "fragment of point with a transversely striated base" that could correspond to the description of an Isturitz Point, but here again, not conclusively, because the specimens could not be found.

CONCLUSION

The study of the material from Henri-Martin's excavation and those from the 1994–1998 excavations, as well as the analysis of Henri-Martin's publication of the Durousseau-Dugontier and Vallade collections, permits certain conclusions about the presence of Upper Paleolithic materials coming from the cave.

First, it has enabled us to confirm the presence in the site of different industries: Châtelperronian, Aurignacian, and Gravettian. Contrary to what was earlier believed, it appears that several stages of Aurignacian are present: Early Aurignacian (or Aurignacian I),

Evolved Aurignacian (or Aurignacian II), and perhaps even Protoaurignacian. On the other hand, there are doubts about the presence of clearly distinct layers in the upper part of the cave fill.

It is true that the lack of access to Vallade's notes prevents any conclusion to be made regarding the possibility of excavator bias at the time the collection was recovered. In effect, the excavator may have sorted a part of the material a posteriori, as was often the case at this time. It is also impossible to say whether the mixtures are the result of the excavation (failure by the excavators to recognize certain changes in stratigraphy) or of perturbations of the deposits themselves.

The Châtelperronian bed is more uniform and characteristic in terms of the industries it contained, including a large number of Châtelperron points, endscrapers, and burins whose quantities and characteristics correspond to those known from industries of this type. It also contained a relatively small Mousterian component. The only real discordant element is the presence of typical carinated and nosed scrapers, which could only have come from a contamination from the overlying Aurignacian.

The Aurignacian is much less uniform than Henri-Martin's study would lead one to believe. In effect, although this author considered it to be an Evolved Aurignacian, the present study shows that it was probably a mixture of Early and Evolved Aurignacian. It is also probable that a large part of Vallade's collection should be considered an Early Aurignacian. This collection also contains Gravettian-type pieces.

In the Upper Paleolithic material from Henri-Martin's excavation, which she claimed was found only in a single bed in the course of excavation, it is not possible to demonstrate a mixture of the two Aurignacian stages. On the other hand, both Châtelperronian and typically Gravettian pieces are present. Regarding the latter, it is difficult to specify the type of industry found. Henri-Martin (1957:211) spoke of a "a Font-Robert bed of Upper Perigordian," but this attribution is based only on the presence of a Font-Robert point in Vallade's collection. This is a very fragmentary piece, with a tang that, according to the illustration, could equally well be interpreted as a fragment of a Perigordian *pièce à cran*. The only certainty is that Gravettian pieces are present in all the assemblages examined, but it is impossible to identify this Gravettian more precisely.

All of these findings raise the question whether different beds of Upper Paleolithic actually existed in the Cave of Fontéchevade. Given the mixtures observed, it is possible that the material was not recovered from well-defined beds but rather from sediments in secondary position, containing a mixture of the different industries noted previously in this chapter, and indeed, this conclusion is supported by the results of the 1994–1998 excavation. For example, Farrand's geological study (see Chapter 3) shows that the upper levels in the back of the cave (Beds A and B of Henri-Martin's Test Pit 3 (or simply the Test Pit in the 1994–1998 excavations) are made up of sediment flow from the plateau. In fact, it appears that the majority of the sediments making up the fill of the cave had the same origin. Although Upper Paleolithic materials were not found in these particular beds, it is logical to hypothesize that the deposition of the other materials recovered by previous excavators was due to the same process and, consequently, that the archaeological material is in secondary position. This is especially plausible given that the collections studied contain pieces showing alterations caused by transportation. It is also a fact that all of the Upper Paleolithic materials that were recovered during the course of the present excavation were found in sediments that were clearly disturbed, especially in the case of Level X, which is along the sides of the cave walls. Finally, such a mode of deposition would make it possible to explain all the mixtures observed in the Upper Paleolithic industries, as well as the differences in horizontal distributions noted by the different excavators (e.g., an absence of Châtelperronian along the edges of the cave).

11

Description of the Lithic Industries

Harold L. Dibble and Shannon P. McPherron

INTRODUCTION

This chapter presents the basic descriptive data on the lithic assemblages from Fontéchevade. The presentation is organized according to four distinct groups of assemblages, which in fact are not related stratigraphically one to the other. The first group of assemblages is the collection excavated by Henri-Martin, which is now housed at the Musée d'Archéologie Nationale in St. Germain-en-Laye. As described in earlier chapters, this material comes from the front of the cave up to the main profile left by her. Although the material is labeled according to stratigraphic level and was analyzed by us accordingly, no other provenience information is available for the objects.

The other three groups of assemblages are the result of our own excavation. The first, and primary, set comes from the Main Profile, and the levels from this area are numbered (from the top down) with Arabic numbers (with subdivisions indicated by letters; e.g., 1A, 2B, etc.). Some of these sublevels have been combined where appropriate. The second set comes from our excavation in the back of the cave where Henri-Martin had excavated her Test Pit 3 (designated by us as the "Test Pit"). The levels from this area are given letter designations, and all of the subdivisions have been combined here. The third set of assemblages comes from the Witness Section left by Henri-Martin, which is located near the grid east wall of the cave, just outside the dripline. Our original stratigraphy labeled levels from this area as T1, T2, etc., though all of the recovered material has been combined in the following analysis.

The methods we used to describe and analyze the lithic material presented here can be found in Chapter 2.

THE COLLECTION OF HENRI-MARTIN

During the course of our research on Fontéchevade, we analyzed the collection of Henri-Martin in detail, using the same methods applied to the objects coming from our own excavation. Doing so not only

Table 11.1. Inventory, type counts, indices, and measurements of the lithic material from Bed E0 (Henri-Martin collection)

Level E0

#	Type	N	Dimensional data	N	Mean	S.D.
10	Convex single scraper	1	Complete flakes			
11	Concave single scraper	1	Length	69	54.0	16.7
42	Notch	4	Width	69	37.3	11.4
43	Denticulate	2	Thickness	69	12.3	5.1
48	Abrupt/alternating retouch	11	Weight	69	39.5	43.4
64	Truncated-faceted piece	2	Scrapers			
			Length	2	68.1	2.0
			Width	2	49.8	4.5
Real count		19	Thickness	2	16.8	4.6
Essential count		8	Weight	2	74.5	19.1
Complete and proximal flakes		89	Notches and denticulates			
Flake fragments and shatter		3	Length	6	58.8	10.6
Cores and core fragments		15	Width	6	38.3	13.2
Quartz cobbles		13	Thickness	6	18.2	17.1
Unworked		395	Weight	6	71.0	89.7
			Cores			
			Length	15	63.5	15.8
Typological indices			Width	15	52.6	11.5
			Thickness	15	28.6	9.8
Real count		Essential count	Weight	15	130.9	96.1

Real count		Essential count	
Ilty	0.0		
IR	10.5	IR	25.0
IAU	0.0	IAU	0.0
I	0.0		
II	10.5	II	25.0
III	0.0	III	0.0
IV	10.5	IV	25.0

Cortex (complete flakes and tools combined)

0%	17	Primary	46.4%
1–10%	15	Secondary	39.1%
10–40%	11	Tertiary	14.5%
40–60%	13		
60–90%	3		
90–99%	5		
100%	5		

Technological indices

IL	1.04
Ilam	3.16
IF	16.44
ÍFs	10.96

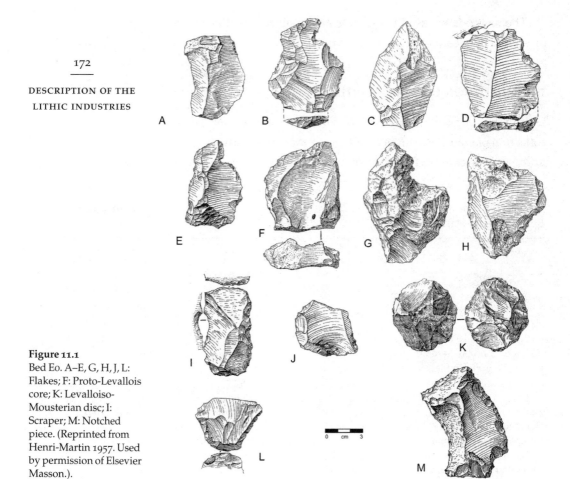

Figure 11.1
Bed E0. A–E, G, H, J, L:
Flakes; F: Proto-Levallois
core; K: Levalloiso-
Mousterian disc; I:
Scraper; M: Notched
piece. (Reprinted from
Henri-Martin 1957. Used
by permission of Elsevier
Masson.).

enabled us to make direct comparisons between the two collections (see the end of this chapter) but it also brings the level of description of the earlier collection up to more modern standards. All of the illustrations of her material that are presented in this chapter are reprinted from her monograph (Henri-Martin 1957), along with the descriptions that she employed there.

Bed E0

The assemblage from Bed E0 consists of 126 artifacts, a few quartz cobbles, and almost 400 unworked objects, primarily thermal-fractured flint (see Table 11.1 and Figs. 11.1 and 11.2). The technology

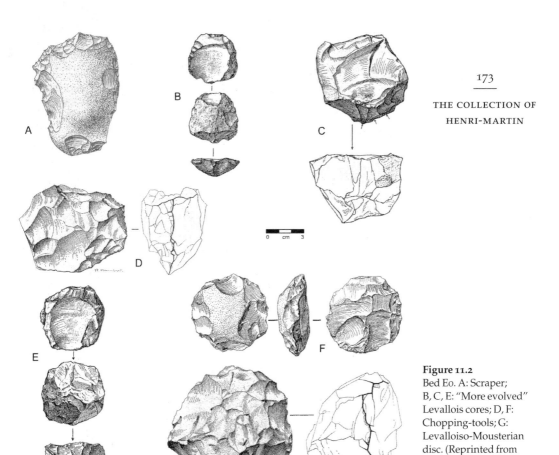

Figure 11.2
Bed Eo. A: Scraper;
B, C, E: "More evolved"
Levallois cores; D, F:
Chopping-tools; G:
Levalloiso-Mousterian
disc. (Reprinted from
Henri-Martin 1957. Used
by permission of Elsevier
Masson.)

is nondescript, with only one Levallois product. Most of the striking platforms are plain, with only eight faceted platforms and four dihedral ones. The cores are also quite simple, with only one or, at most, two removals. The low number of cores and the few removals exhibited on each are not totally in line with the blank-to-core ratio (about 6.5 blanks per core) nor with the fact that more than half of the flakes are either partially or completely non-cortical.

There are relatively few retouched tools – a couple of scrapers, some notches and denticulates, and two truncated-faceted pieces. Most of the pieces show a significant degree of damage on the edges.

Bed E1

Bed E1 contained even less material than the overlying E0, with about half the existing collection composed of pieces that are unworked (see Table 11.2 and Fig. 11.3). Again, nothing really stands out in this industry as far as being diagnostic of a particular technology, and there are too few retouched pieces to make any significant comments.

Table 11.2. Inventory, type counts, indices, and measurements of the lithic material from Bed E1 (Henri-Martin collection)

Level E1

#	Type	N		Dimensional data	N	Mean	S.D.
1	Typical Levallois flake	3		Complete flakes			
2	Atypical Levallois flake	1		Length	34	54.3	17.2
10	Convex single scraper	1		Width	34	33.0	10.8
38	Naturally backed knife	2		Thickness	34	11.1	6.0
43	Denticulate	1		Weight	34	30.6	34.4
48	Abrupt/alternating retouch	7		Scrapers			
				Length	1	54.9	–
				Width	1	30.0	–
Real count		15		Thickness	1	14.6	–
Essential count		2		Weight	1	26.0	–
Complete and proximal flakes		45		Notches and denticulates			
Flake fragments and shatter		2		Length	1	58.3	–
Cores and core fragments		1		Width	1	39.5	–
Quartz cobbles		2		Thickness	1	18.8	–
Unworked		44		Weight	1	47.0	–
				Cores			
				Length	1	48.7	–
				Width	1	48.7	–
Typological indices				Thickness	1	31.6	–
				Weight	1	62 0	–

Typological indices

Real count		Essential count	
ILty	26.67		
IR	6.67	IR	50.00
IAU	0.00	IAU	0.00
I	26.67		
II	6.67	II	50.00
III	0.00	III	0.00
IV	6 67	IV	50.00

Cortex (complete flakes and tools combined)

0%	19	Primary	73.5%
1–10%	6	Secondary	23.5%
10–40%	6	Tertiary	2.9%
40–60%	1		
60–90%	1		
90–99%	1		
100%	0		

Technological indices

IL	10.00
ILam	10.42
IF	27.91
IFs	16.28

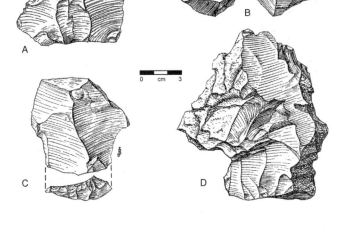

Figure 11.3
Bed E1. A, C: Flakes; B, D:
"Massive endscrapers"
or choppers. (Reprinted
from Henri-Martin 1957.
Used by permission of
Elsevier Masson.)

The overwhelming proportion of blanks are non-cortical, and only one core is represented in the entire assemblage.

Bed E1′

This bed, one of the largest from Henri-Martin's excavation, is very rich in unretouched flakes, but again shows a general lack of retouched tools (see Table 11.3 and Figs. 11.4 and 11.5). Although there are a number of Levallois flakes, the overall Levallois Index is still low, whereas the Faceting Index is moderate. There are a few chopping-tools, in addition to a small number of scrapers, notches, and denticulates and two truncated-faceted pieces. Cores, however, are well represented, though usually very simple in terms of their preparation. We determined that more than half of the assemblage was unworked.

Table 11.3. Inventory, type counts, indices, and measurements of the lithic material from Bed E1′ (Henri-Martin collection)

Level E1′

#	Type	N
1	Typical Levallois flake	10
2	Atypical Levallois flake	4
5	Pseudo-Levallois point	2
9	Straight single scraper	1
10	Convex single scraper	3
11	Concave single scraper	2
23	Convex transverse scraper	1
26	Abrupt scraper	2
29	Alternate scraper	1
30	Typical endscraper	1
31	Atypical endscraper	1
33	Atypical burin	1
38	Naturally backed knife	10
42	Notch	3
43	Denticulate	6
48	Abrupt/alternating retouch	77
58	Tanged tool	1
61	Chopping-tool	5
64	Truncated-faceted piece	2

Dimensional data	N	Mean	S.D.
Complete flakes			
Length	500	51.9	14.0
Width	500	35.6	10.6
Thickness	500	11.8	5.4
Weight	497	33.5	32.0
Scrapers			
Length	10	52.3	11.6
Width	10	38.7	8.4
Thickness	10	14.2	2.8
Weight	10	35.5	12.8
Notches and denticulates			
Length	9	47.5	4.0
Width	9	33.7	9.6
Thickness	9	12.5	2.8
Weight	9	23.8	9.9
Cores			
Length	61	66.7	19.1
Width	61	52.5	14.8
Thickness	61	31.9	12.8
Weight	61	147.3	145.8

Real count	131
Essential count	28
Complete and proximal flakes	696
Flake fragments and shatter	13
Cores and core fragments	61
Quartz cobbles	26
Unworked	1082

Cortex

0%	138	Primary	50.6%
1–10%	105	Secondary	44.6%
10–40%	120	Tertiary	4.8%
40–60%	48		
60–90%	46		
90–99%	16		
100%	7		

Typological indices

Real count		Essential count	
ILty	10.69		
IR	7.63	IR	35.71
IAU	0.00	IAU	0.00
I	10.69		
II	9.16	II	42.86
III	2.29	III	10.71
IV	4.58	IV	21.43

Technological indices

IL	1.95
Ilam	2.49
IF	20.32
ÍFs	10.08

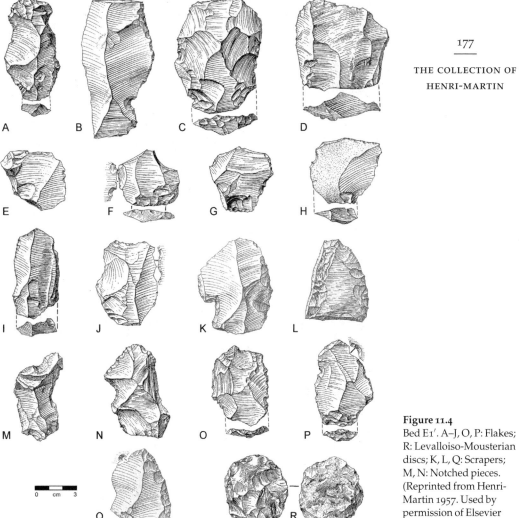

Figure 11.4
Bed E1′. A–J, O, P: Flakes;
R: Levalloiso-Mousterian
discs; K, L, Q: Scrapers;
M, N: Notched pieces.
(Reprinted from Henri-
Martin 1957. Used by
permission of Elsevier
Masson.)

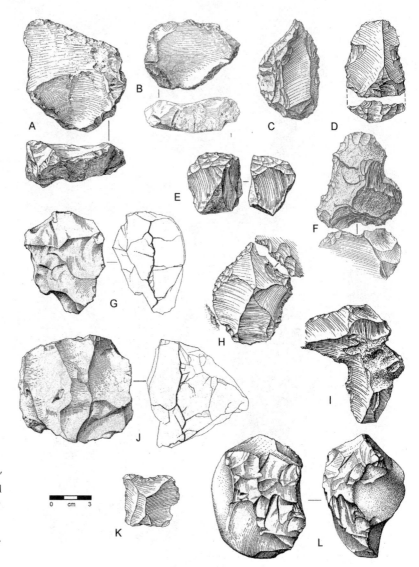

Figure 11.5
Bed E1′. A, B: "Proto-Levallois" cores; C: Scraper; D, H, K: Flakes; E: "Massive endscrapers" or choppers; F, I: Notched pieces; G, J, L: Chopping-tools. (Reprinted from Henri-Martin 1957. Used by permission of Elsevier Masson.)

Bed E1″

The largest of the Henri-Martin collections, Bed E1″ has a much wider range of types represented, including a fair number of scrapers, some Upper Paleolithic types (burins, backed knives), and choppers and chopping-tools (see Table 11.4 and Figs. 11.6 and 11.7). Cores are numerous as well, and the observation of cortex suggests that most of the stages of reduction are represented. However, much of the material exhibits edge damage (including those pieces classified as type 48), and there are many unworked pieces as well.

Table 11.4. Inventory, type counts, indices, and measurements of the lithic material from Bed E1″ (Henri-Martin collection)

Level E1″

#	Type	N
1	Typical Levallois flake	8
2	Atypical Levallois flake	3
5	Pseudo-Levallois point	6
9	Straight single scraper	6
10	Convex single scraper	3
11	Concave single scraper	1
13	Double straight-convex scraper	1
19	Convex convergent scraper	1
21	Dejete scraper	1
24	Concave transvers scraper	1
25	Scraper on interior	1
32	Typical burin	1
33	Atypical burin	1
38	Naturally backed knife	7
39	Raclette	1
40	Truncation	1
42	Notch	13
43	Denticulate	4
45	Retouch on interior	2
48	Abrupt/alternating retouch	98
54	End-notched flake	1
56	Rabot	1
59	Chopper	2
61	Chopping-tool	10
64	Truncated-faceted piece	1

Real count	174
Essential count	50
Complete and proximal flakes	712
Flake fragments and shatter	30
Cores and core fragments	82
Quartz cobbles	14
Unworked	1661

Typological indices

Real count		Essential count	
ILty	6.32		
IR	8.62	IR	30.00
IAU	0.00	IAU	0.00
I	6.32		
II	12.07	II	42.00
III	1.72	III	6.00
IV	2.30	IV	8.00

Dimensional data	N	Mean	S.D.
Complete flakes			
Length	511	49.5	13.4
Width	510	34.1	10.3
Thickness	509	11.3	4.8
Weight	509	29.8	28.3
Scrapers			
Length	15	51.4	10.6
Width	15	34.8	7.5
Thickness	15	11.2	3.4
Weight	15	28.6	16.8
Notches and denticulates			
Length	18	57.5	21.7
Width	18	38.9	16.7
Thickness	18	21.3	15.6
Weight	18	80.7	112.9
Cores			
Length	81	70.1	18.6
Width	82	52.5	13.8
Thickness	82	31.4	12.4
Weight	81	146.8	126.6

Cortex

0%	163	Primary	50.6%
1–10%	93	Secondary	43.9%
10–40%	127	Tertiary	5.5%
40–60%	48		
60–90%	47		
90–99%	14		
100%	14		

Technological indices

IL	1.55
Ilam	0.83
IF	14.50
ÍFs	5.19

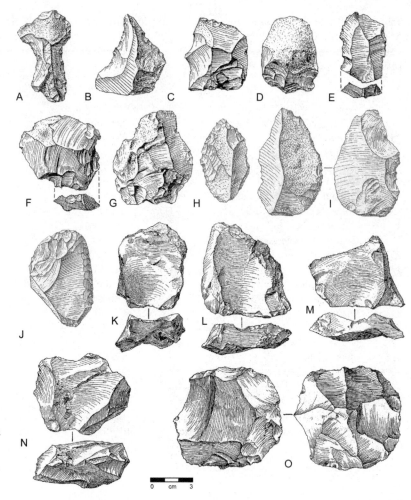

Figure 11.6.
Bed E1″. A, B: Notched
pieces; C–G: Flakes;
H–J: Scrapers; K–N:
"Proto-Levallois" cores;
O: Levalloiso-Mousterian
discs. (Reprinted from
Henri-Martin 1957. Used
by permission of Elsevier
Masson.)

Figure 11.7
Bed E1″. A: "Proto-
Levallois" core; B, C:
Levalloiso-Mousterian
discs. (Reprinted from
Henri-Martin 1957. Used
by permission of Elsevier
Masson.)

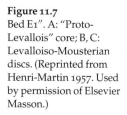

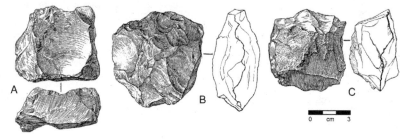

Bed E2

Bed E2 is not a very rich layer, with only about 100 total artifacts and more than four times that number of unworked pieces (see Table 11.5 and Fig. 11.8). There are no Levallois products in this bed, although the Faceting Index is relatively high. Two scrapers and a few notches are the only retouched pieces.

Table 11.5. Inventory, type counts, indices, and measurements of the lithic material from Bed E2 (Henri-Martin collection)

Level E2

#	Type	N	Dimensional data	N	Mean	S.D.
10	Convex single scraper	1	Complete flakes			
23	Convex transverse scraper	1	Length	63	52.1	20.2
38	Naturally backed knife	3	Width	63	38.4	13.4
42	Notch	3	Thickness	63	12.6	6.0
48	Abrupt/alternating retouch	1	Weight	62	43.0	49.4
			Scrapers			
			Length	2	47.3	3.0
Real count		9	Width	2	47.9	8.4
Essential count		5	Thickness	2	22.8	6.9
Complete and proximal flakes		76	Weight	2	78.0	48.1
Flake fragments and shatter		2	Notches and denticulates			
Cores and core fragments		17	Length	3	67.0	11.0
Quartz cobbles		4	Width	3	40.4	7.6
Unworked		421	Thickness	3	15.5	5.9
			Weight	3	52.3	33.7
			Cores			
Typological indices			Length	17	75.2	24.3
			Width	17	55.4	16.4
Real count		Essential count	Thickness	17	35.3	9.9
			Weight	17	201.1	186.6

Real count		Essential count	
ILty	0.00		
IR	22.22	IR	40.00
IAU	0.00	IAU	0.00
I	0.00		
II	22.22	II	40.00
III	0.00	III	0.00
IV	0.00	IV	0.00

Cortex

	N		%
0%	14	Primary	36.9%
1–10%	10	Secondary	52.3%
10–40%	16	Tertiary	10.8%
40–60%	9		
60–90%	9		
90–99%	3		
100%	4		

Technological indices

IL	0.00
Ilam	0.00
IF	29.58
ÍFs	11.27

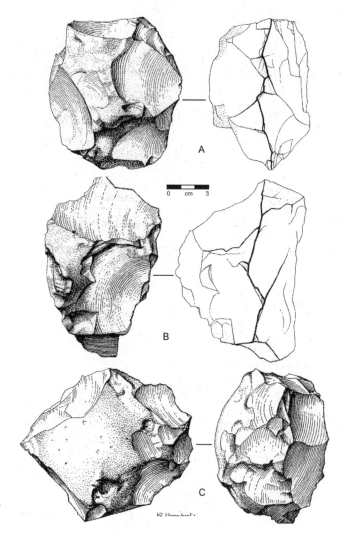

Figure 11.8
Bed E2. A–C: Chopping-
tools. (Reprinted from
Henri-Martin 1957. Used
by permission of Elsevier
Masson.)

Bed E2′

Bed E2′ is about twice as rich as E2, though the number of retouched
pieces is even lower (see Table 11.6 and Fig. 11.9). Although Henri-
Martin reported a considerable number of both cores and core
tools from this level, our own analysis suggests that most of these
were actually unworked. There are no Levallois products from this
bed.

Table 11.6. Inventory, type counts, indices, and measurements of the lithic material from Bed E2' (Henri-Martin collection)

Level E2'

#	Type	N
38	Naturally backed knife	6
42	Notch	1
43	Denticulate	2
48	Abrupt/alternating retouch	7

Real count	16
Essential count	3
Complete and proximal flakes	181
Flake fragments and shatter	5
Cores and core fragments	11
Quartz cobbles	13
Unworked	640

Typological indices

Real count		Essential count	
ILty	0.00		
IR	0.00	IR	0.00
IAU	0.00	IAU	0.00
I	0.00		
II	0.00	II	0.00
III	0.00	III	0.00
IV	12.50	IV	66.67

Technological indices

IL	0.00
Ilam	0.00
IF	13.91
ÍFs	4.64

Dimensional data	N	Mean	S.D.
Complete flakes			
Length	127	49.0	16.1
Width	127	33.6	12.0
Thickness	127	11.2	5.2
Weight	126	28.8	27.7
Scrapers			
Length	0	–	–
Width	0	–	–
Thickness	0	–	–
Weight	0	–	–
Notches and denticulates			
Length	3	64.1	9.8
Width	3	60.3	7.4
Thickness	3	25.2	13.0
Weight	3	107.0	47.7
Cores			
Length	11	71.3	30.1
Width	11	45.0	20.3
Thickness	11	29.9	14.9
Weight	11	163.5	230.4

Cortex

0%	40	Primary	43.1%
1–10%	13	Secondary	53.7%
10–40%	37	Tertiary	3.3%
40–60%	18		
60–90%	11		
90–99%	4		
100%	0		

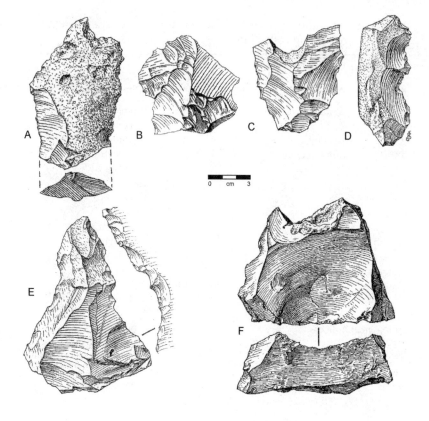

Figure 11.9
Bed E2′. A–C: Flakes;
D, E: Notched pieces; F:
"Proto-Levallois" core.
(Reprinted from Henri-
Martin 1957. Used by
permission of Elsevier
Masson.)

Bed E2″

Bed E2″ is a relatively rich bed, in spite of the fact that there are
more than 800 unworked pieces in the collection (see Table 11.7 and
Fig. 11.10). We only considered one piece to be a chopping-tool (vs.
the 112 reported by Henri-Martin), and various notched types round
out the list of retouched pieces. There are two atypical Levallois
flakes, although the overall Levallois Index is still low.

Figure 11.10
Bed E2″. A–D: Flakes.
(Reprinted from Henri-
Martin 1957. Used by
permission of Elsevier
Masson.)

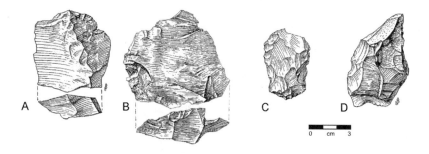

Table 11.7. Inventory, type counts, indices, and measurements of the lithic material from Bed E2″ (Henri-Martin collection)

Level E2″

#	Type	N
2	Atypical Levallois flake	2
5	Pseudo-Levallois point	3
38	Naturally backed knife	10
42	Notch	7
43	Denticulate	3
48	Abrupt/alternating retouch	13
54	End-notched flake	2
61	Chopping-tool	1

Real count	41
Essential count	13
Complete and proximal flakes	429
Flake fragments and shatter	22
Cores and core fragments	36
Quartz cobbles	9
Unworked	845

Typological indices

Real count		Essential count	
ILty	4.88		
IR	0.00	IR	0.00
IAU	0.00	IAU	0.00
I	4.88		
II	7.32	II	23.08
III	0.00	III	0.00
IV	7.32	IV	23.08

Technological indices

IL	0.43
Ilam	1.61
IF	12.81
ÍFs	4.02

Dimensional data	N	Mean	S.D.
Complete flakes			
Length	334	50.8	15.9
Width	332	35.7	11.5
Thickness	334	12.3	5.5
Weight	332	34.9	36.1
Scrapers			
Length	0	–	–
Width	0	–	–
Thickness	0	–	–
Weight	0	–	–
Notches and denticulates			
Length	12	52.3	13.8
Width	12	36.3	11.2
Thickness	12	13.0	6.7
Weight	12	36.2	31.5
Cores			
Length	36	76.9	22.2
Width	35	52.0	15.6
Thickness	36	37.2	14.8
Weight	36	203.1	188.2

Cortex

0%	74	Primary	43.0%
1–10%	71	Secondary	47.5%
10–40%	91	Tertiary	9.5%
40–60%	39		
60–90%	30		
90–99%	22		
100%	10		

Summary of the Henri-Martin collection

In general, our own analysis of Henri-Martin's collection is not entirely inconsistent with that reported by her. Generally, we found low numbers of retouched pieces, very few Levallois products, and moderate degrees of platform preparation.

However, in two primary areas there were major inconsistencies between what we recorded and what was reported by Henri-Martin. First, we identified a higher proportion of pieces in her collection as unworked. In fact, of the 7835 pieces that we examined from her collection, more than 5000, or about 65 percent, showed no signs of intentional knapping – virtually all of these were spalls of thermally fractured flint that outcrops from the cave walls. These spalls were also common in our own excavation, and they presented some difficulty in deciding whether they were natural or artifactual.

Second, her counts of retouched artifacts – scrapers and notches/denticulates – are higher than what we found in the collection. Probably this reflects our more conservative tendency to view much of the material as edge damaged rather than as deliberate retouch. We are probably not alone in this interpretation – Bordes himself (1953; Bordes and Bourgon 1951:17) also thought that the "retouched" pieces characterized in the Tayacian were most probably the result of damage. Interestingly, in the collection housed at the Musée d'Archéologie Nationale, one box of objects had the label "Podoliths, according to F. Bordes."

Regardless of the discrepancy between our analysis and that of Henri-Martin, it is clear that our view of her collection is strikingly similar to our view of our own collection. This comparison is presented later in this chapter, after the description of the material resulting from the 1994–1998 excavation.

THE 1994–1998 COLLECTION

The following is a description of the lithic material recovered during the course of the new excavations at Fontéchevade organized by level and area excavated (Main Profile, Test Pit, and Witness Section).

Level 1A

Level 1A is the uppermost level recognized in the Main Profile, just beneath the surface. As such, it should be viewed with some caution as some of the material could be derived.

Table 11.8. Inventory, type counts, indices, and measurements of the lithic material from Level 1A (current collection)

Level 1A

#	Type	N
2	Atypical Levallois flake	1
10	Convex single scraper	1
19	Convex convergent scraper	1
26	Abrupt scraper	1
29	Alternate scraper	1
37	Atypical backed knife	1
42	Notch	6
43	Denticulate	1
45	Retouch on interior	1
48	Abrupt/alternating retouch	54
61	Chopping-tool	1

Real count	69
Essential count	13
Complete and proximal flakes	135
Flake fragments and shatter	20
Cores and core fragments	5
Quartz cobbles	71
Number of buckets excavated	109
Artifacts per bucket	1.59
Wet-screen data	
N samples	80
N artifacts	196
Total weight	225
Mean weight	1.1

Typological indices

Real count		Essential count	
ILty	1.45		
IR	5.80	IR	30.77
IAU	0.01	IAU	0.08
I	1.45		
II	5.80	II	30.77
III	1.45	III	7.69
IV	1.45	IV	7.69

Technological indices

IL	0.55
Ilam	4.14
IF	12.00
ÍFs	4.00

Dimensional data	N	Mean	S.D.
Complete flakes			
Length	87	39.2	13.0
Width	87	26.7	9.8
Thickness	86	8.9	4.2
Weight	86	17.9	19.4
Scrapers			
Length	4	45.9	7.4
Width	4	30.5	4.2
Thickness	4	15.2	13.1
Weight	4	35.0	35.9
Notches and denticulates			
Length	7	50.3	12.3
Width	7	31.1	5.8
Thickness	7	16.1	5.6
Weight	7	35.1	17.8
Cores			
Length	5	62.2	12.4
Width	5	43.1	9.1
Thickness	5	26.7	7.8
Weight	5	74.8	15.6
Quartz Cobbles			
Length	51	73.4	24.4
Weight	51	260.0	305.5

Cortex

0%	20	Primary	40.2%
1–10%	15	Secondary	49.4%
10–40%	19	Tertiary	10.3%
40–60%	10		
60–90%	14		
90–99%	3		
100%	6		

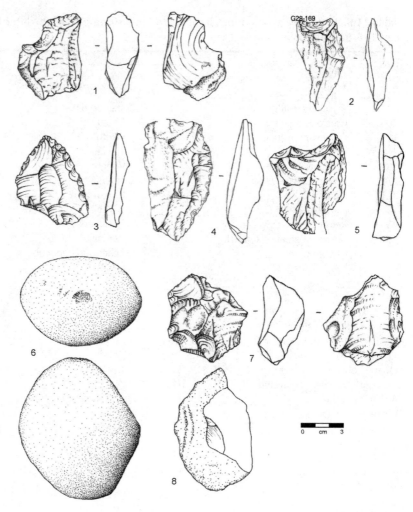

Figure 11.11
Lithic artifacts from Level
1A. 1, 5, 7, 8: Notches; 2:
Unworked local chert; 3:
Convergent scraper on
non-local flint; 4: Flake; 6:
Hammerstone.

The artifactual material from this level is not particularly rich, and there are very few retouched pieces relative to the number of unretouched or edge-damaged flakes (see Table 11.8 and Fig. 11.11). The one atypical Levallois flake is the only piece that can be attributed to that technology, and there are a fair number (N = 34) of angular flakes in the assemblage.

Level 1B

The assemblage from Level 1B is very small, with only a little more than a dozen pieces represented, but the level itself is very thin (see Table 11.9).

Table 11.9. Inventory, type counts, indices, and measurements of the lithic material from Level 1B (current collection)

Level 1B

#	Type	N	Dimensional data	N	Mean	S.D.
43	Denticulate	1	Complete flakes			
			Length	8	31.8	13.7
			Width	8	23.5	11.6
Real count		1	Thickness	8	5.6	3.0
Essential count		1	Weight	8	8.8	12.6
Complete and proximal flakes		14	Scrapers			
Flake fragments and shatter		2	Length	0	–	–
Cores and core fragments		0	Width	0	–	–
Quartz cobbles		0	Thickness	0	–	–
Number of buckets excavated		29	Weight	0	–	–
Artifacts per bucket		0.59	Notches and denticulates			
Wet-screen data			Length	1	33.6	–
N samples		19	Width	1	16.7	–
N artifacts		44	Thickness	1	6.9	–
Total Weight		27	Weight	1	5.0	–
Mean Weight		0.6	Cores			
			Length	0	–	–
			Width	0	–	–

Typological indices

| Thickness | 0 | – | – |

Real count		**Essential count**		Weight	0	–	–
				Quartz cobbles			
ILty	0.00			Length	4	84.1	12.3
IR	0.00	IR	0.00	Weight	4	278.0	42.1
IAU	0.00	IAU	0.00				
I	0.00						
II	0.00	II	0.00	**Cortex**			
III	0.00	III	0.00				
IV	100.00	IV	100.00	0%	0	Primary	0.0%
				1–10%	0	Secondary	37.5%
				10–40%	1	Tertiary	62.5%
				40–60%	0		

Technological indices

		60–90%	2
IL	0.00	90–99%	3
Ilam	11.11	100%	2
IF	7.69		
ÍFs	7.69		

Level 2A

Level 2A yielded only four scrapers and the same number of notches/denticulates, though it also included six choppers or cores (Table 11.10 and Figs. 11.12–11.15). There is no Levallois present in the assemblage, and there are only six flakes with faceted platforms.

Figure 11.12
Lithic artifacts from Level 2A. 1: Interior scraper on non-local flint; 2: Notch; 3, 5, 6: Cores; 4: Flake.

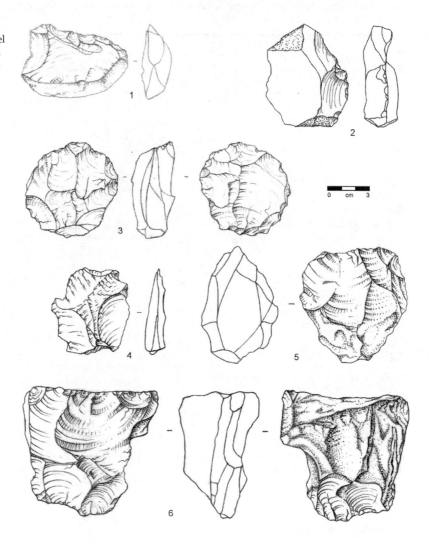

Table 11.10. Inventory, type counts, indices, and measurements of the lithic material from Level 2A (current collection)

Level 2A

#	Type	N
5	Pseudo-Levallois point	2
9	Straight single scraper	1
10	Convex single scraper	1
25	Scraper on interior	2
38	Naturally backed knife	5
42	Notch	3
43	Denticulate	1
48	Abrupt/alternating retouch	52
59	Chopper	6
62	Divers	4

Real count	77
Essential count	18
Complete and proximal flakes	116
Flake fragments and shatter	10
Cores and core fragments	15
Quartz cobbles	228
Number of buckets excavated	189
Artifacts per bucket	0.84
Wet-screen data	
N samples	121
N artifacts	193
Total weight	223
Mean weight	1.2

Typological indices

Real count		Essential count	
ILty	0.00		
IR	5.19	IR	22.22
IAU	0.00	IAU	0.00
I	0.00		
II	7.79	II	33.33
III	0.00	III	0.00
IV	1.30	IV	5.56

Technological indices

IL	0.00
Ilam	1.42
IF	10.62
ÍFs	5.31

Dimensional data	N	Mean	S.D.
Complete flakes			
Length	70	38.0	12.2
Width	67	26.1	9.4
Thickness	70	9.0	4.6
Weight	69	15.2	17.0
Scrapers			
Length	3	32.4	5.7
Width	3	24.5	7.2
Thickness	3	9.2	3.2
Weight	3	13.0	12.3
Notches and denticulates			
Length	4	50.7	9.7
Width	4	42.0	14.9
Thickness	4	13.7	2.2
Weight	4	41.8	27.3
Cores			
Length	15	59.5	16.7
Width	15	46.1	12.6
Thickness	15	27.1	11.9
Weight	15	118.6	129.9
Quartz cobbles			
Length	174	83.2	23.5
Weight	174	385.7	335.4

Cortex

0%	18	Primary	47.1%
1–10%	15	Secondary	40.0%
10–40%	15	Tertiary	12.9%
40–60%	4		
60–90%	9		
90–99%	3		
100%	6		

DESCRIPTION OF THE
LITHIC INDUSTRIES

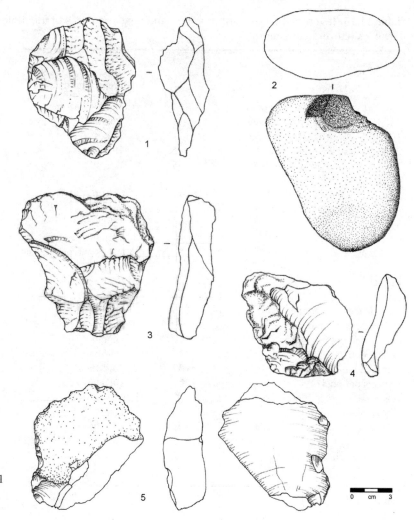

Figure 11.13
Lithic artifacts from Level
2A. 1: Core; 2: Quartz
cobble; 3–5: Flakes.

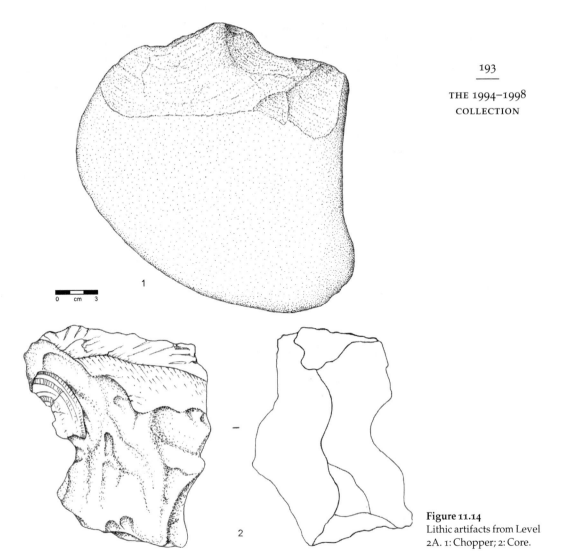

0 cm 3

1

2

Figure 11.14
Lithic artifacts from Level
2A. 1: Chopper; 2: Core.

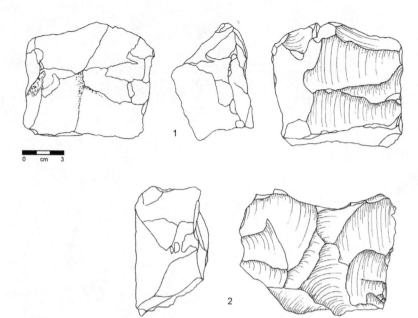

Figure 11.15
Lithic artifacts from Level
2A. 1, 2: Cores.

Levels 2B–2D

Because all of these levels are lacking in archaeological material, they are combined in this presentation. Nonetheless, only one retouched piece, a notch, and no cores or core fragments are found in these levels (see Table 11.11 and Fig. 11.16).

Figure 11.16
Notch on local flint from
Level 2D.

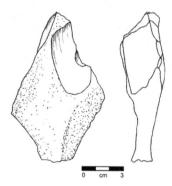

Table 11.11. Combined inventory, type counts, indices, and measurements of the lithic material from Levels 2B–2D (current collection)

Levels 2B–2D

#	Type	N	Dimensional data	N	Mean	S.D.
5	Pseudo-Levallois point	2	Complete flakes			
			Length	5	54.7	20.5
			Width	5	36.5	13.7
Real count		0	Thickness	5	13.6	8.4
Essential count		0	Weight	5	42.6	33.2
Complete and proximal flakes		7	Scrapers			
Flake fragments and shatter		0	Length	0	–	–
Cores and core fragments		0	Width	0	–	–
Quartz cobbles		17	Thickness	0	–	–
Number of buckets excavated		27	Weight	0	–	–
Artifacts per bucket		0.26	Notches and denticulates			
Wet-screen data			Length	1	65.5	–
N samples		13	Width	1	37.9	–
N artifacts		30	Thickness	1	13.4	–
Total weight		26	Weight	1	36.0	–
Mean weight		0.9	Cores			
			Length	0	–	–
			Width	0	–	–
Technological indices			Thickness	0	–	–
			Weight	0	–	–
IL		0.00	Quartz cobbles			
Ilam		0.00	Length	14	92.2	19.5
IF		12.50	Weight	14	499.6	255.5
ÍFs		0.00				

Cortex

0%	0	Primary	0.4
1–10%	2	Secondary	0.2
10–40%	1	Tertiary	0.4
40–60%	0		
60–90%	0		
90–99%	1		
100%	1		

Level 3A

Level 3A has four Levallois elements (all of which are unretouched), only a few scrapers and notches/denticulates, and four choppers or chopping-tools (see Table 11.12 and Figs. 11.17–11.19). It does have, however, a large number of quartz cobbles, virtually none of which show any sign of having been used as hammerstones. Only about 2 percent (N = 12) of the flakes exhibit faceted platforms.

Table 11.12. Inventory, type counts, indices, and measurements of the lithic material from Level 3A (current collection)

Level 3A

#	Type	N
1	Typical Levallois flake	3
2	Atypical Levallois flake	1
8	Limace	1
10	Convex single scraper	4
38	Naturally backed knife	6
42	Notch	3
43	Denticulate	1
48	Abrupt/alternating retouch	23
54	End-notched flake	1
59	Chopper	3
61	Chopping-tool	1
62	Divers	3

Real count	50
Essential count	17
Complete and proximal flakes	80
Flake fragments and shatter	10
Cores and core fragments	11
Quartz cobbles	170
Number of buckets excavated	233
Artifacts per bucket	0.51
Wet-screen data	
N samples	159
N artifacts	128
Total weight	137
Mean weight	1.1

Typological indices

Real count		Essential count	
ILty	8.00		
IR	8.00	IR	23.53
IAU	0.00	IAU	0.00
I	8.00		
II	10.00	II	29.41
III	0.00	III	0.00
IV	2.00	IV	5.88

Dimensional data	N	Mean	S.D.
Complete flakes			
Length	53	46.8	19.4
Width	53	28.9	9.2
Thickness	53	9.2	5.6
Weight	53	26.1	35.5
Scrapers			
Length	4	64.0	21.9
Width	4	45.6	24.2
Thickness	4	18.4	14.1
Weight	4	80.8	77.7
Notches and denticulates			
Length	4	46.5	14.7
Width	4	28.1	8.6
Thickness	4	15.2	4.5
Weight	4	36.8	25.6
Cores			
Length	11	66.4	20.3
Width	11	52.0	13.9
Thickness	11	25.7	12.7
Weight	11	135.8	125.9
Quartz cobbles			
Length	127	72.6	26.0
Weight	127	275.9	319.2

Cortex

0%	13	Primary	35.8%
1–10%	6	Secondary	41.5%
10–40%	9	Tertiary	22.6%
40–60%	8		
60–90%	5		
90–99%	6		
100%	6		

Technological indices

IL	2.94
ILam	5.83
IF	21.52
ÍFs	16.46

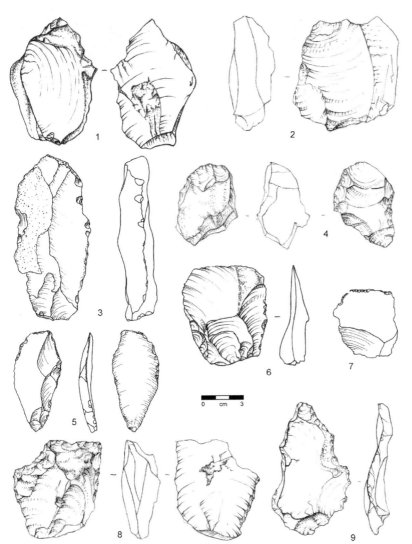

Figure 11.17
Lithic artifacts from Level
3A. 1, 3, 5–7, 9: Flakes
(5–7 on non-local flint); 2,
4: Single-surface cores; 8:
Notched piece.

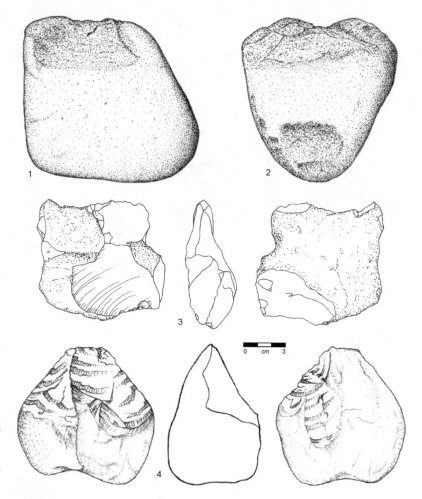

Figure 11.18
Lithic artifacts from Level
3A. 1–4: "Tested" cores.
All on quartz cobbles
except 3, which is on local
chert.

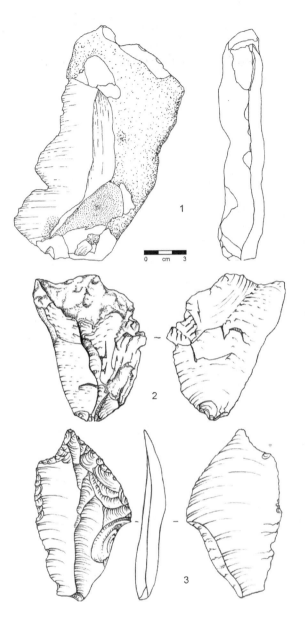

Figure 11.19
Lithic artifacts from
Level 3A. 1: Unworked
local chert; 2: Flake; 3:
Multiply retouched flake
on non-local flint.

Level 3B

Level 3B is another very small assemblage, with only one retouched piece (see Table 11.13 and Fig. 11.20).

Table 11.13. Inventory, type counts, indices, and measurements of the lithic material from Level 3B (current collection)

Level 3B

#	Type	N
9	Straight single scraper	1
38	Naturally backed knife	1
48	Abrupt/alternating retouch	7

Real count	9
Essential count	1
Complete and proximal flakes	13
Flake fragments and shatter	0
Cores and core fragments	2
Quartz cobbles	30
Number of buckets excavated	46
Artifacts per bucket	0.35
Wet-screen data	
N samples	23
N artifacts	11
Total weight	13
Mean weight	1.2

Typological indices

Real count		Essential count	
ILty	0.00		
IR	11.11	IR	100.00
IAU	0.00	IAU	0.00
I	0.00		
II	11.11	II	100.00
III	0.00	III	0.00
IV	0.00	IV	0.00

Technological indices

IL	0.00
Ilam	6.67
IF	0.00
ÍFs	0.00

Dimensional data	N	Mean	S.D.
Complete flakes			
Length	10	47.5	15.9
Width	10	28.1	9.6
Thickness	10	12.6	7.7
Weight	10	26.8	23.5
Scrapers			
Length	1	77.8	0.0
Width	1	51.3	0.0
Thickness	1	16.2	0.0
Weight	1	81.0	0.0
Notches and denticulates			
Length	0	–	–
Width	0	–	–
Thickness	0	–	–
Weight	0	–	–
Cores			
Length	0	–	–
Width	0	–	–
Thickness	0	–	–
Weight	0	–	–
Quartz cobbles			
Length	27	56.5	16.5
Weight	27	108.1	89.0

Cortex

0%	1	Primary	10.0%
1–10%	0	Secondary	60.0%
10–40%	3	Tertiary	30.0%
40–60%	1		
60–90%	2		
90–99%	2		
100%	1		

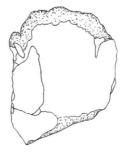

Figure 11.20
Single surface core from
Level 3B.

Levels 3C and 3D

Levels 3C and 3D, combined because of the extreme rarity of the objects found there, yielded seven scrapers and three notches/denticulates in total (see Table 11.14 and Figs. 11.21 and 11.22). There

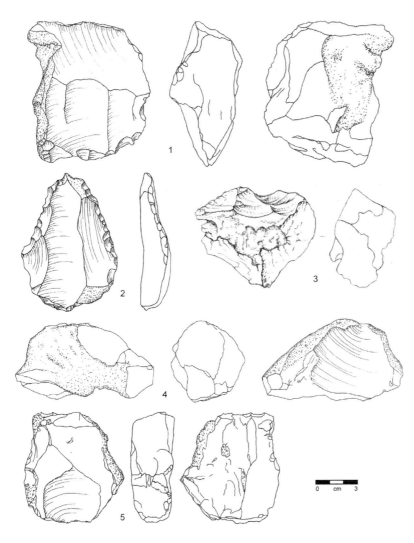

Figure 11.21
Lithic artifacts from
Levels 3C and 3D. 1, 3,
5: Cores; 2: Denticulate
and scraper on Levallois
flake (local chert); 4:
Unworked piece of local
chert.

Table 11.14. Combined inventory, type counts, indices, and measurements of the lithic material from Levels 3C–3D (current collection)

Levels 3C–3D

#	Type	N
9	Straight single scraper	2
10	Convex single scraper	1
25	Scraper on interior	2
26	Abrupt scraper	2
38	Naturally backed knife	4
42	Notch	1
43	Denticulate	2
48	Abrupt/alternating retouch	50
61	Chopping-tool	1
62	Divers	1

Real count	66
Essential count	12
Complete and proximal flakes	57
Flake fragments and shatter	11
Cores and core fragments	6
Quartz cobbles	156
Number of buckets excavated	142
Artifacts per bucket	0.61
Wet-screen data	
N samples	86
N artifacts	45
Total weight	70
Mean weight	1.6

Typological indices

Real count		Essential count	
ILty	0.00		
IR	10.61	IR	58.33
IAU	0.00	IAU	0.00
I	0.00		
II	10.61	II	58.33
III	0.00	III	0.00
IV	3.03	IV	16.67

Technological indices

IL	1.05
Ilam	1.18
IF	14.52
ÍFs	11.29

Dimensional data	N	Mean	S.D.
Complete flakes			
Length	32	46.0	21.4
Width	32	28.1	11.5
Thickness	32	11.2	5.4
Weight	32	31.0	48.9
Scrapers			
Length	5	40.0	14.3
Width	5	28.0	9.5
Thickness	5	12.2	2.0
Weight	5	20.0	12.8
Notches and denticulates			
Length	3	47.2	16.7
Width	3	29.0	14.7
Thickness	3	7.7	2.9
Weight	3	22.0	22.7
Cores			
Length	6	64.6	11.5
Width	6	46.5	6.0
Thickness	6	26.2	4.1
Weight	6	105.2	28.3
Quartz cobbles			
Length	126	54.2	17.8
Weight	126	101.8	140.1

Cortex

0%	7	Primary	33.3%
1–10%	5	Secondary	41.7%
10–40%	8	Tertiary	25.0%
40–60%	4		
60–90%	3		
90–99%	2		
100%	7		

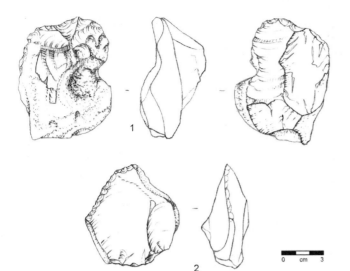

Figure 11.22
Lithic artifacts from
Levels 3C and 3D. 1:
Flake; 2: Single scraper on
local chert.

are no Levallois products. However, the number of quartz cobbles is
very large, almost double the number of other lithics combined.

Level 4

Level 4 has one scraper and four notches/denticulates, with the
rest of the Bordian "real count" being edge-damaged pieces (see Table 11.15 and Fig. 11.23).

Figure 11.23
Convergent scraper on
local chert from Level 4.

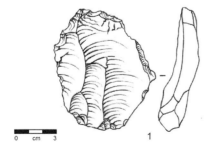

Table 11.15. Inventory, type counts, indices, and measurements of the lithic material from Level 4 (current collection)

Level 4

#	Type	N
19	Convex convergent scraper	1
42	Notch	2
43	Denticulate	1
48	Abrupt/alternating retouch	14
54	End-notched flake	1

Real count	19
Essential count	5
Complete and proximal flakes	19
Flake fragments and shatter	4
Cores and core fragments	2
Quartz cobbles	7
Number of buckets excavated	22
Artifacts per bucket	1.36
Wet-screen data	
N samples	11
N artifacts	9
Total Weight	18
Mean Weight	2.0

Typological indices

Real count		Essential count	
ILty	0.00		
IR	5.26	IR	20.00
IAU	0.00	IAU	0.00
I	0.00		
II	5.26	II	20.00
III	0.00	III	0.00
IV	5.26	IV	20.00

Technological indices

IL	0.00
Ilam	0.00
IF	8.70
ÍFs	8.70

Dimensional data	N	Mean	S.D.
Complete flakes			
Length	12	35.7	12.4
Width	12	26.2	8.3
Thickness	12	8.2	2.8
Weight	12	13.9	15.2
Scrapers			
Length	1	53.2	0.0
Width	1	41.1	0.0
Thickness	1	8.6	0.0
Weight	1	31.0	0.0
Notches and denticulates			
Length	4	37.6	13.1
Width	4	26.6	2.3
Thickness	4	8.9	3.4
Weight	4	16.0	14.1
Cores			
Length	2	82.3	31.6
Width	2	62.0	32.9
Thickness	2	37.8	19.2
Weight	2	325.5	357.1
Quartz cobbles			
Length	5	54.0	11.7
Weight	5	77.4	50.0

Cortex

0%	6	Primary	47.1%
1–10%	2	Secondary	23.5%
10–40%	3	Tertiary	29.4%
40–60%	0		
60–90%	1		
90–99%	3		
100%	2		

Level 5

Level 5 is the largest of the excavated assemblages, with a total of 36 retouched tools, including 2 truncated-faceted pieces (see Table 11.16 and Figs. 11.24–28). Edge-damaged pieces are very well represented, however, and there are a relatively high number of cores. Quartz cobbles again dominate the assemblage.

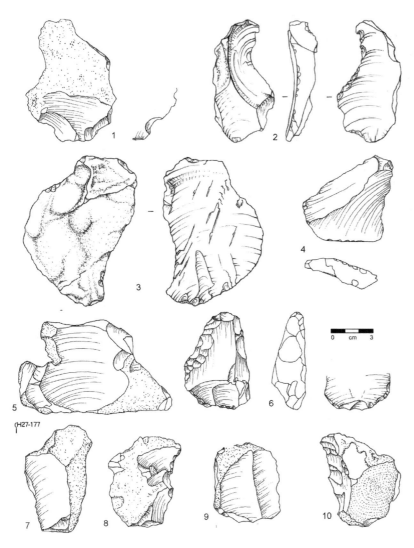

Figure 11.24
Lithic artifacts from Level 5. 1, 10: Notches; 2–4, 9: Flakes; 5: Core; 6: Convergent scraper on non-local flint; 7: Unworked local chert; 8: Denticulate.

Table 11.16. Inventory, type counts, indices, and measurements of the lithic material from Level 5 (current collection)

Level 5

#	Type	N
9	Straight single scraper	1
11	Concave single scraper	1
19	Convex convergent scraper	1
20	Concave convergent scraper	1
26	Abrupt scraper	3
27	Scraper with thinned back	1
29	Alternate scraper	1
32	Typical burin	1
38	Naturally backed knife	2
42	Notch	12
43	Denticulate	10
48	Abrupt/alternating retouch	113
54	End-notched flake	1
61	Chopping-tool	1
62	Divers	2
64	Truncated-faceted piece	2

Real count	151
Essential count	36
Complete and proximal flakes	165
Flake fragments and shatter	23
Cores and core fragments	20
Quartz cobbles	58
Number of buckets excavated	215
Artifacts per bucket	1.13
Wet-screen data	
N samples	154
N artifacts	182
Total weight	229
Mean weight	1.3

Typological indices

Real count		Essential count	
Ilty	0.00		
IR	5.96	IR	25.00
IAU	0.00	IAU	0.00
I	0.00		
II	5.96	II	25.00
III	0.66	III	2.78
IV	6.62	IV	27.78

Dimensional data	N	Mean	S.D.
Complete flakes			
Length	106	42.1	15.7
Width	106	28.4	10.7
Thickness	106	11.0	5.4
Weight	106	24.9	31.3
Scrapers			
Length	8	55.2	12.4
Width	8	37.8	11.5
Thickness	8	13.6	3.4
Weight	8	39.6	23.1
Notches and denticulates			
Length	23	45.3	13.9
Width	21	32.6	8.7
Thickness	23	12.9	6.7
Weight	23	25.9	19.9
Cores			
Length	20	70.3	22.9
Width	20	51.7	14.8
Thickness	20	29.7	12.2
Weight	20	173.3	175.1
Quartz cobbles			
Length	45	52.6	23.0
Weight	45	115.2	185.0

Cortex

0%	23	Primary	30.8%
1–10%	13	Secondary	43.6%
10–40%	23	Tertiary	25.6%
40–60%	9		
60–90%	19		
90–99%	16		
100%	14		

Technological indices

IL	0.40
Ilam	2.13
IF	13.86
ÍFs	8.43

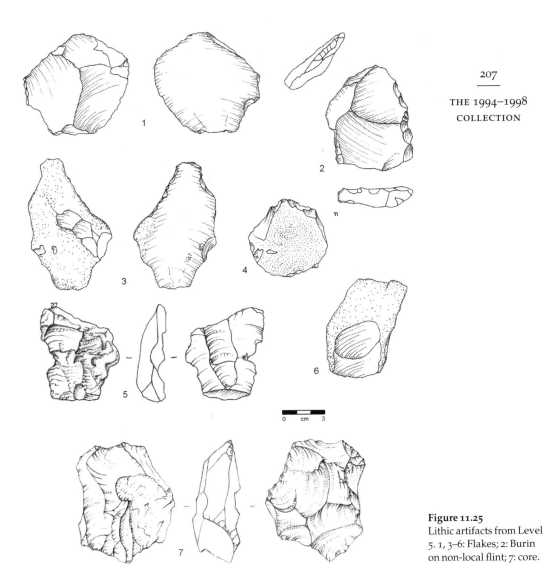

Figure 11.25
Lithic artifacts from Level
5. 1, 3–6: Flakes; 2: Burin
on non-local flint; 7: core.

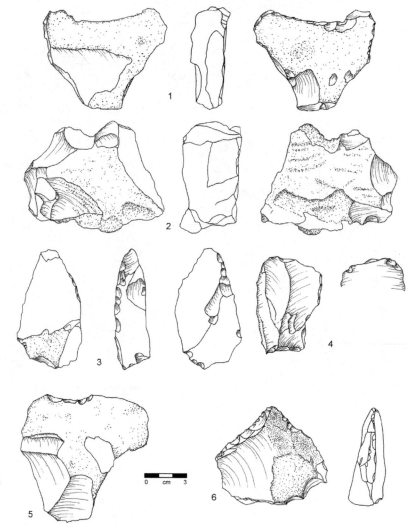

Figure 11.26
Lithic artifacts from Level
5. 1, 4, 6: Flakes; 2: Core;
3: Alternate scraper; 5:
End-notched piece.

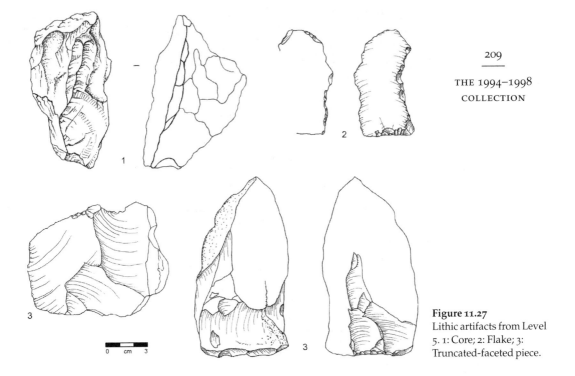

Figure 11.27
Lithic artifacts from Level
5. 1: Core; 2: Flake; 3:
Truncated-faceted piece.

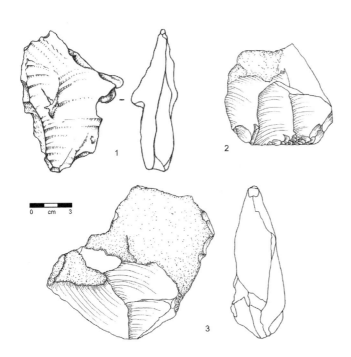

Figure 11.28
Lithic artifacts from Level
5. 1, 3: Flakes; 2: Core.

Level 6

Level 6 is another very small level, with only one scraper represented (see Table 11.17).

Table 11.17. Inventory, type counts, indices, and measurements of the lithic material from Level 6 (current collection)

Level 6

#	Type	N
10	Convex single scraper	1
48	Abrupt/alternating retouch	3
62	Divers	1

Real count	5
Essential count	2
Complete and proximal flakes	7
Flake fragments and shatter	1
Cores and core fragments	1
Quartz cobbles	15
Number of buckets excavated	67
Artifacts per bucket	0.16
Wet-screen data	
N samples	30
N artifacts	13
Total weight	14
Mean weight	1.1

Typological indices

Real count		Essential count	
ILty	0.00		
IR	20.00	IR	50.00
IAU	0.00	IAU	0.00
I	0.00		
II	20.00	II	50.00
III	0.00	III	0.00
IV	0.00	IV	0.00

Technological indices

IL	10.00
Ilam	0.00
IF	0.00
ÍFs	0.00

Dimensional data	N	Mean	S.D.
Complete flakes			
Length	2	41.7	12.6
Width	2	22.4	8.7
Thickness	2	7.7	3.8
Weight	2	11.5	12.0
Scrapers			
Length	1	84.8	–
Width	1	40.8	–
Thickness	1	9.7	–
Weight	1	49.0	–
Notches and denticulates			
Length	0	–	–
Width	0	–	–
Thickness	0	–	–
Weight	0	–	–
Cores			
Length	0	–	–
Width	0	–	–
Thickness	0	–	–
Weight	0	–	–
Quartz cobbles			
Length	13	53.3	25.3
Weight	13	126.6	216.7

Cortex			
0%	2	Primary	100.0%
1–10%	1	Secondary	0.0%
10–40%	0	Tertiary	0.0%
40–60%	0		
60–90%	0		
90–99%	0		
100%	0		

Level 7

Level 7 is very small level, with only a few flakes and no retouched
tools (see Table 11.18).

Table 11.18. Inventory, type counts, indices, and measurements of the lithic material from Level 7 (current collection)

Level 7

#	Type	N	Dimensional data	N	Mean	S.D.
38	Naturally backed knife	1	Complete flakes			
48	Abrupt/alternating retouch	1	Length	5	30.3	10.0
			Width	5	18.5	5.1
			Thickness	5	6.2	3.1
Real count		2	Weight	5	4.8	3.4
Essential count		0	Scrapers			
Complete and proximal flakes		8	Length	0	–	–
Flake fragments and shatter		0	Width	0	–	–
Cores and core fragments		0	Thickness	0	–	–
Quartz cobbles		7	Weight	0	–	–
Number of buckets excavated		196	Notches and denticulates			
Artifacts per bucket		0.04	Length	0	–	–
Wet-screen data			Width	0	–	–
N samples		18	Thickness	0	–	–
N artifacts		8	Weight	0	–	–
Total weight		9	Cores			
Mean weight		1.1	Length	0	–	–
			Width	0	–	–
			Thickness	0	–	–

Typological indices

Real count		Essential count	
ILty	0.00		
IR	0.00	IR	–
IAU	0.00	IAU	–
I	0.00		
II	0.00	II	–
III	0.00	III	–
IV	0.00	IV	–

Dimensional data	N	Mean	S.D.
Weight	0	–	–
Quartz cobbles			
Length	7	56.5	23.0
Weight	7	115.7	96.6

Cortex

0%	1	Primary	40.0%
1–10%	1	Secondary	20.0%
10–40%	1	Tertiary	40.0%
40–60%	0		
60–90%	0		
90–99%	1		
100%	1		

Technological indices

IL	0.00
Ilam	0.00
IF	0.00
ÍFs	0.00

Level X

Level X contains a fair amount of material including one Levallois flake and some retouched tools (see Table 11.19 and Fig. 11.29).

Table 11.19. Inventory, type counts, indices, and measurements of the lithic material from Level X (current collection)

Level X

#	Type	N
1	Typical Levallois flake	1
5	Pseudo-Levallois point	1
9	Straight single scraper	1
34	Typical percoir	1
42	Notch	2
43	Denticulate	2
48	Abrupt/alternating retouch	26
54	End-notched flake	1
61	Chopping-tool	1
64	Truncated-faceted piece	1

Real count	36
Essential count	8
Complete and proximal flakes	72
Flake fragments and shatter	9
Cores and core fragments	2
Quartz cobbles	77
Number of buckets excavated	282
Artifacts per bucket	0.32
Wet-screen data	
N samples	125
N artifacts	106
Total weight	139
Mean weight	1.3

Typological indices

Real count		Essential count	
ILty	2.78		
IR	2.78	IR	12.50
IAU	0.00	IAU	0.00
I	2.78		
II	5.56	II	25.00
III	2.78	III	12.50
IV	5.56	IV	25.00

Technological indices

IL	1.11
Ilam	11.11
IF	14.29
ÍFs	10.39

Dimensional data	N	Mean	S.D.
Complete flakes			
Length	42	38.9	14.5
Width	42	25.6	8.9
Thickness	42	7.9	4.7
Weight	41	18.4	25.3
Scrapers			
Length	1	55.6	0.0
Width	1	34.9	0.0
Thickness	1	9.4	0.0
Weight	1	25.0	0.0
Notches and denticulates			
Length	5	43.0	12.0
Width	5	33.1	8.4
Thickness	5	10.0	1.7
Weight	5	22.2	15.2
Cores			
Length	2	65.2	3.8
Width	2	57.3	3.5
Thickness	2	36.5	1.8
Weight	2	126.5	4.9
Quartz cobbles			
Length	62	76.6	24.4
Weight	62	301.3	258.9

Cortex

0%	13	Primary	42.2%
1–10%	6	Secondary	37.8%
10–40%	7	Tertiary	20.0%
40–60%	3		
60–90%	7		
90–99%	2		
100%	7		

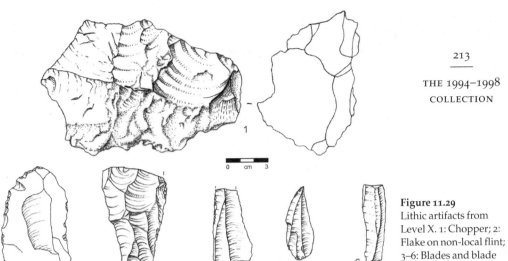

Figure 11.29
Lithic artifacts from
Level X. 1: Chopper; 2:
Flake on non-local flint;
3–6: Blades and blade
fragments, all on non-
local flint.

However, flakes with abrupt and/or alternating retouch predominate in the real counts. Two cores and a number of quartz cobbles also come from this level.

Levels A–D (Test Pit)

Work in the back of the cave in the area referred to as the Test Pit (originally dug by Henri-Martin) concentrated only on the cleaning of the walls to better expose the stratigraphy in that part of the cave. As such, the amount of sediment removed, and consequently the amount of lithic material recovered from this area, was relatively low. In spite of the difficulty in correlating the stratigraphic sequence from this area with that apparent in the Main Profile, the lithic assemblages from the back of the cave very much resemble what was found in the Main Profile. Thus, although there are a few scrapers and some possible deliberate notches/denticulates, the primary "type" represented are the ones that clearly reflect edge damage (see Tables 11.20–11.23 and Fig. 11.30). Quartz cobbles continue to be present in high numbers as well.

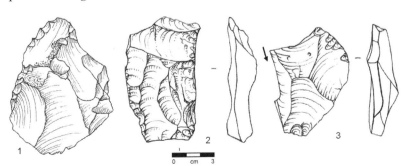

Figure 11.30
Lithic artifacts from
Levels A, B. 1: Single
scraper on non-local flint
(Level A); 2: Notch; 3:
Burin on non-local flint
(2 and 3 from Level B).

Table 11.20. Inventory, type counts, indices, and measurements of the lithic material from Test Pit Level A (current collection)

Level A

#	Type	N		Dimensional data	N	Mean	S.D.
1	Typical Levallois flake	1		Complete flakes			
12	Double straight scraper	1		Length	9	39.9	16.9
29	Alternate scraper	1		Width	9	27.7	12.8
32	Typical burin	1		Thickness	9	7.3	4.9
42	Notch	1		Weight	9	16.1	24.7
43	Denticulate	1		Scrapers			
48	Abrupt/alternating retouch	2		Length	2	54.2	1.5
62	Divers	1		Width	2	30.1	4.3
				Thickness	2	8.3	1.6
				Weight	2	24.5	17.7
Real count		9		Notches and denticulates			
Essential count		6		Length	2	43.9	15.0
Complete and proximal flakes		19		Width	2	45.6	13.6
Flake fragments and shatter		5		Thickness	2	11.8	3.0
Cores and core fragments		2		Weight	2	28.5	19.1
Quartz cobbles		22		Cores			
Number of buckets excavated		84		Length	2	58.0	11.8
Artifacts per bucket		0.38		Width	2	31.7	0.3
Wet-screen data				Thickness	2	19.1	10.4
N samples		26		Weight	2	44.5	27.6
N artifacts		8		Quartz cobbles			
Total weight		7		Length	14	83.0	24.7
Mean weight		0.9		Weight	14	448.9	455.4

Typological indices

Real count		Essential count			Cortex			
ILty	11.11				0%	5	Primary	60.0%
IR	22.22	IR	33.33		1–10%	1	Secondary	40.0%
IAU	0.00	IAU	0.00		10–40%	3	Tertiary	0.0%
I	11.11				40–60%	0		
II	22.22	II	33.33		60–90%	1		
III	11.11	III	16.67		90–99%	0		
IV	11.11	IV	16.67		100%	0		

Technological indices

IL	3.70
Ilam	19.23
IF	6.67
ÍFs	0.00

Table 11.21. Inventory, type counts, indices, and measurements of the lithic material from Test Pit Level B (current collection)

Level B

#	Type	N
9	Straight single scraper	2
10	Convex single scraper	1
11	Concave single scraper	0
26	Abrupt scraper	1
38	Naturally backed knife	2
42	Notch	1
48	Abrupt/alternating retouch	26
59	Chopper	1

	N
Real count	34
Essential count	6
Complete and proximal flakes	53
Flake fragments and shatter	12
Cores and core fragments	3
Quartz cobbles	151
Number of buckets excavated	397
Artifacts per bucket	0.19
Wet-screen data	
N samples	88
N artifacts	63
Total weight	86
Mean weight	1.4

Dimensional data	N	Mean	S.D.
Complete flakes			
Length	39	38.7	15.5
Width	39	27.9	12.8
Thickness	39	7.8	4.8
Weight	39	17.6	27.1
Scrapers			
Length	4	46.1	19.0
Width	4	34.1	8.7
Thickness	4	7.1	2.0
Weight	4	19.8	19.5
Notches and denticulates			
Length	1	57.9	–
Width	1	34.7	–
Thickness	1	11.2	–
Weight	1	36.0	–
Cores			
Length	3	47.8	4.6
Width	3	34.5	2.7
Thickness	3	28.8	8.0
Weight	3	53.0	20.0
Quartz cobbles			
Length	125	52.9	19.3
Weight	125	96.7	157.0

Typological indices

Real count		Essential count	
ILty	0.00		
IR	11.76	IR	66.67
IAU	0.00	IAU	0.00
I	0.00		
II	11.76	II	66.67
III	0.00	III	0.00
IV	0.00	IV	0.00

Technological indices

IL	0.00
Ilam	11.49
IF	13.79
ÍFs	5.17

Cortex

0%	13	Primary	55.0%
1–10%	9	Secondary	27.5%
10–40%	7	Tertiary	17.5%
40–60%	3		
60–90%	1		
90–99%	3		
100%	4		

Table 11.22. Inventory, type counts, indices, and measurements of the lithic material from Test Pit Level C (current collection)

Level C

#	Type	N
1	Typical Levallois flake	1
38	Naturally backed knife	2
42	Notch	1
48	Abrupt/alternating retouch	4
61	Chopping-tool	1

Real count	9
Essential count	2
Complete and proximal flakes	15
Flake fragments and shatter	2
Cores and core fragments	0
Quartz cobbles	133
Number of buckets excavated	164
Artifacts per bucket	0.12
Wet-screen data	
N samples	44
N artifacts	32
Total weight	42
Mean weight	1.3

Typological indices

Real count		Essential count	
ILty	11.11		
IR	0.00	IR	0.00
IAU	0.00	IAU	0.00
I	11.11		
II	0.00	II	0.00
III	0.00	III	0.00
IV	0.00	IV	0.00

Technological indices

IL	3.85
Ilam	0.00
IF	16.67
ÍFs	8.33

Dimensional data	N	Mean	S.D.
Complete flakes			
Length	8	37.3	8.1
Width	8	29.4	5.8
Thickness	8	9.3	4.0
Weight	8	13.6	9.1
Scrapers			
Length	0	–	–
Width	0	–	–
Thickness	0	–	–
Weight	0	–	–
Notches and denticulates			
Length	1	60.5	–
Width	1	35.3	–
Thickness	1	13.0	–
Weight	1	51.0	–
Cores			
Length	0	–	–
Width	0	–	–
Thickness	0	–	–
Weight	0	–	–
Quartz cobbles			
Length	106	60.7	20.4
Weight	107	136.2	144.7

Cortex

0%	0	Primary	28.6%
1–10%	2	Secondary	42.9%
10–40%	2	Tertiary	28.6%
40–60%	1		
60–90%	0		
90–99%	0		
100%	2		

Table 11.23. Inventory, type counts, indices, and measurements of the lithic material from Test Pit Level D (current collection)

Level D

#	Type	N
42	Notch	1
44	Bec burinante alterne	1
48	Abrupt/alternating retouch	3

	N
Real count	5
Essential count	2
Complete and proximal flakes	7
Flake fragments and shatter	0
Cores and core fragments	0
Quartz cobbles	153
Number of buckets excavated	25
Artifacts per bucket	0.36
Wet-screen data	
N samples	5
N artifacts	2
Total weight	8
Mean weight	4.0

Typological indices

Real count		Essential count	
ILty	0.00		
IR	0.00	IR	0.00
IAU	0.00	IAU	0.00
I	0.00		
II	0.00	II	0.00
III	0.00	III	0.00
IV	0.00	IV	0.00

Technological indices

IL	0.00
Ilam	11.11
IF	0.00
Level D	

Dimensional data	N	Mean	S.D.
Complete flakes			
Length	3	58.2	17.8
Width	3	28.1	18.3
Thickness	3	9.4	3.9
Weight	3	27.0	24.9
Scrapers			
Length	0	–	–
Width	0	–	–
Thickness	0	–	–
Weight	0	–	–
Notches and denticulates			
Length	1	47.5	–
Width	1	45.7	–
Thickness	1	13.3	–
Weight	1	36.0	–
Cores			
Length	0	–	–
Width	0	–	–
Thickness	0	–	–
Weight	0	–	–
Quartz cobbles			
Length	111	64.4	24.8
Weight	111	136.8	149.0

Cortex

0%	0	Primary	0.0%
1–10%	0	Secondary	100.0%
10–40%	1	Tertiary	0.0%
40–60%	2		
60–90%	1		
90–99%	0		
100%	0		

Witness Section

As noted earlier in this report, Henri-Martin had left a portion of deposits just outside of the cave's dripline unexcavated, which were intended to serve as a Témoin or Witness Section that could be used at some time in the future to verify her own findings. Our own plan was to concentrate instead on the area within the cave that represented her stopping point at the Main Profile. However, we decided to take

Table 11.24. Combined inventory, type counts, indices, and measurements of the lithic material from Witness Section (current collection)

Witness bed

#	Type	N	Dimensional data	N	Mean	S.D.
62	Divers	2	Complete flakes			
			Length	6	29.1	6.9
			Width	6	21.2	7.4
Real count		2	Thickness	6	6.8	3.3
Essential count		2	Weight	6	6.3	7.0
Complete and proximal flakes		6	Scrapers			
Flake fragments and shatter		2	Length	0	–	–
Cores and core fragments		0	Width	0	–	–
Quartz cobbles		11	Thickness	0	–	–
Number of buckets excavated		216	Weight	0	–	–
Artifacts per bucket		0.05	Notches and denticulates			
Wet-screen data			Length	0	–	–
N samples		28	Width	0	–	–
N artifacts		13	Thickness	0	–	–
Total weight		20	Weight	0	–	–
Mean weight		1.5	Cores			
			Length	0	–	–
			Width	0	–	–

Typological indices

Real count				Thickness	0	–	–
		Essential count		Weight	0	–	–
				Quartz cobbles			
ILty	0.00			Length	9	67.8	21.1
IR	0.00	IR	0.00	Weight	9	202.8	156.6
IAU	0.00	IAU	0.00				
I	0.00						
II	0.00	II	0.00				
III	0.00	III	0.00	**Cortex**			
IV	0.00	IV	0.00				

Cortex			
0%	3	Primary	50.0%
1–10%	1	Secondary	12.5%
10–40%	0	Tertiary	37.5%
40–60%	1		
60–90%	0		
90–99%	3		
100%	0		

Technological indices

IL	0.00
Ilam	12.50
IF	0.00
ÍFs	0.00

a small sample of material from the Witness Section just to ensure that the material there was not qualitatively different from the other excavated areas. Although the area of the Witness Section did exhibit a much greater degree of faunal preservation, the characteristics of the lithic material from there are essentially the same as that from other parts of the site, though admittedly the amount of material recovered was very small (see Table 11.24).

Summary of the 1994–1998 Collection

In the area of the Main Profile in Levels 1A through 5, our excavations removed a total of 1012 7-liter buckets of sediment, which corresponds roughly to just more than 5 m³ of compacted sediment. Even though these were the richest levels from that area, yielding a total of 850 lithic artifacts, the density of artifactual material was extremely low – only 0.84 artifacts per bucket or about 170 artifacts per cubic meter. This figure refers to the numbered objects, which were all pieces larger than 2.5 cm in maximum dimension. Additional lithic material smaller than this cutoff was recovered through wet-screening of the buckets, but even the representation of small flakes and other lithic debris was extremely poor – of a total of 666 screened buckets of sediments, only 838 artifacts were found, with an average weight of 1.15 g each, representing slightly more than one per bucket or just more than 100 small artifacts per cubic meter. Compared to what was recently recovered from similar excavations at Pech de l'Azé IV – more than 2100 lithic artifacts larger than 2.5 cm and more than 17,500 small artifacts per cubic meter – the paucity of material at Fontéchevade is clear.

In terms of the overall composition of the assemblages, there are relatively few retouched tools (about 10 percent of the total), and of these, denticulates and notches outnumber scrapers. There are also some choppers and chopping-tools, though whether these represent actual tools or cores is difficult to determine. Levallois products are essentially absent. The most common Bordian type, however, is the combined abrupt and alternating retouch on thin or thick flakes (type 48 in our terminology), which are essentially edge-damaged pieces. Altogether, more than 65 percent of the pieces exhibit clear damage, whether or not they were assigned a type number of 48.

Approximately 23 percent of the lithic assemblage, not including pieces made on quartz, are on other exotic materials. Most often, these materials are other flint types, though some chalcedony and jasper occur in the assemblage. Of the flakes, nearly 24 percent are on exotic materials, versus almost 36 percent of the tools and slightly more than 5 percent of the cores. Although this difference is statistically significant (chi-square = 23.01, $df = 2$), the overall small number of tools somewhat lessens the behavioral significance of this difference.

Finally, it should be noted that our excavation also recorded a large number of unworked objects. To some extent this was deliberate – we wanted to gather orientation and other data on unworked pieces as well as artifacts to compare the orientations of each class (see Chapter 12). It also reflects the difficulty that excavators had in determining natural versus artifactual material, and so early on in the excavation, the decision was made to provenience all objects of which the excavators were unsure, thus allowing the more experienced analysts an opportunity to study them more carefully after they were washed. Counts of unworked objects were not given in the above tables, however, because recovery of these objects was not systematic and most easily recognized non-artifactual pieces of chert were simply discarded at the time of excavation.

COMPARISONS BETWEEN THE TWO COLLECTIONS

Given that Henri-Martin excavated primarily in the front of the cave and that our own excavations were focused primarily within it, the obvious question is whether the two collections are truly comparable. It would not be difficult to imagine, for example, that different kinds of activities or, indeed, different occupations are represented in the two areas. Our own excavations were too limited to adequately explore the possibility of spatial variation, and because horizontal provenience is not available for Henri-Martin's collection, this question cannot be addressed within her excavation either. Another possibility is that a certain degree of excavator bias was operating that could have some effect on the composition of Henri-Martin's collection as it is presently known (Dibble 1995; Dibble et al. 2006).

Our goal here, however, is not to combine the two collections but rather to determine the degree to which our overall interpretations of the site, especially in terms of formation processes, can be applied to the part excavated by Henri-Martin. As we see in Chapter 12, it appears on the basis of our excavation that the archaeological material is largely derived from the overlying plateau, having entered the cave through one or more chimneys at its rear. Whether these

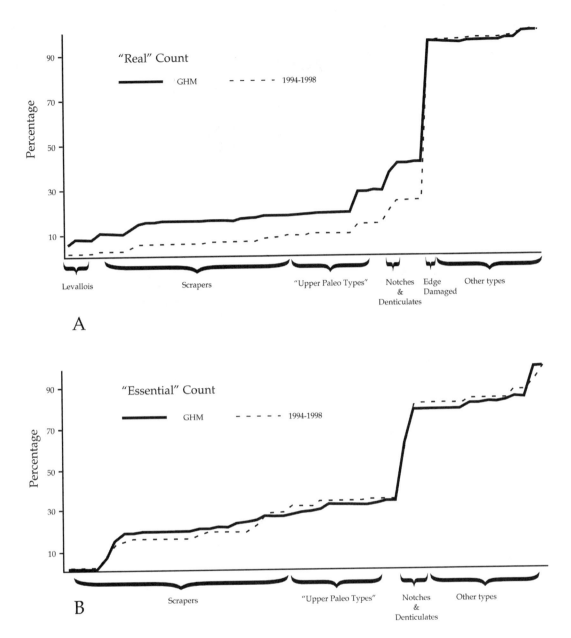

A

B

interpretations can be extended to the area excavated by Henri-Martin depends in large part on whether the nature of the collections is essentially the same or not.

As shown earlier, the typology of the Tayacian of Fontéchevade is largely based on an absence of scrapers and a relative abundance of notches and denticulates. However, in the total, or "real" type list (see Debénath and Dibble 1994), the type most heavily represented is the abrupt and alternating retouch (type 48), which is essentially edge damage. In looking at the real count (see Fig. 11.31), it is clear

Figure 11.31
Typological cumulative graphs of the lithic material from both the current (1994–1998) excavations and those of Henri-Martin. A: Total real counts; B: Essential counts, composed primarily of retouched pieces.

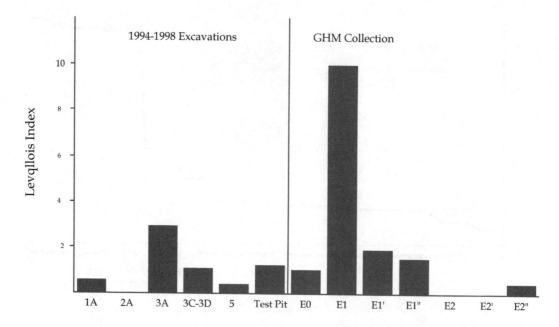

Figure 11.32
Bar graph comparing
the Levallois Index of
both current (1994–1998)
excavations and those of
Henri-Martin.

that both collections share this feature, differing only in terms of a slightly higher Levallois count in Level E1 (see Fig. 11.32) in the Henri-Martin collection. However, if we take out the unretouched component by comparing them on the basis of the "essential" count, the two collections appear to be virtually identical.

The other distinctive characteristic of the Tayacian is its slightly elevated Faceting Index, and again the two collections are virtually identical in terms of overall kinds of platform preparation (Fig. 11.33). In both cases, plain platforms dominate, with roughly equal representation of both faceted and dihedral platforms.

In terms of flake exterior scar morphology, both collections are essentially similar in exhibiting mostly unidirectional preparation,

Figure 11.33
Comparison of platform
surface preparation of
both current (1994–1998)
excavations and those
of Henri-Martin (Chi-
square = 5.71, $df = 2$, $P >$
.05).

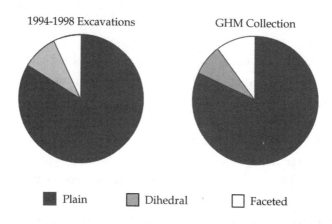

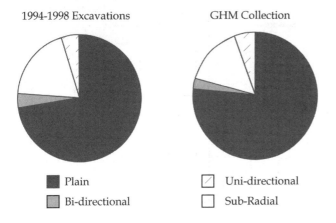

1994-1998 Excavations GHM Collection

■ Plain ⬚ (hatched) Uni-directional

▨ Bi-directional ☐ Sub-Radial

Figure 11.34
Comparison of scar morphology of both current (1994–1998) excavations and those of Henri-Martin (Chi-square = 1.29, $df = 3$, $P > .05$)

with some subradial and some radial (Fig. 11.34). Blank-to-core ratios are not significantly different in the two collections taken as a whole, although cortical flakes are slightly more represented in our collection than in Henri-Martin's.

Differences are apparent between the two collections in flake dimensions. Our excavation yielded significantly smaller flakes on average than those present in the Henri-Martin collection, and, as just mentioned, our collection is more cortical (see Figs. 11.35–11.41). These findings suggest that both smaller flakes and more cortical ones were systematically discarded by Henri-Martin. However, dimension ratios (length to width, width to thickness) are not significantly different in the two collections.

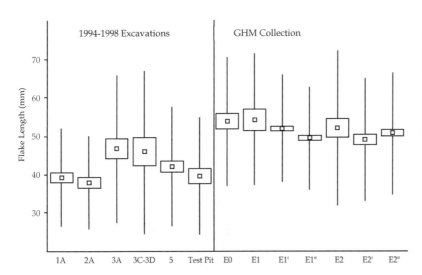

Figure 11.35
Box-whisker comparisons of flake length (complete flakes only) of both current (1994–1998) excavations and those of Henri-Martin ($t = -11.361$, $df = 2043$, $P < .0001$).

Figure 11.36
Box-whisker comparisons of flake width (complete flakes only) of both current (1994–1998) excavations and those of Henri-Martin ($t = -12.386$, $df = 2037$, $P < .0001$).

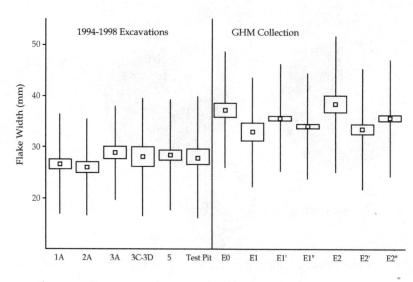

Figure 11.37
Box-whisker comparisons of flake thickness (complete flakes only) of both current (1994–1998) excavations and those of Henri-Martin ($t = -7.5656$, $df = 2040$, $P < .0001$).

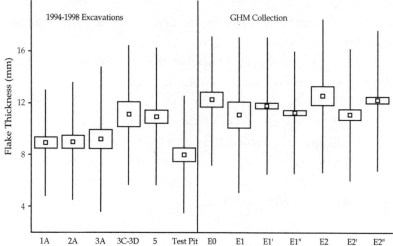

Figure 11.38
Box-whisker comparisons of flake weight (complete flakes only) of both current (1994–1998) excavations and those of Henri-Martin ($t = -6.43$, $df = 2032$, $P < .0001$).

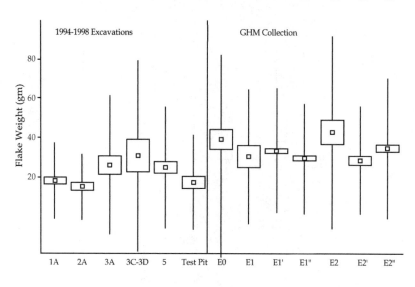

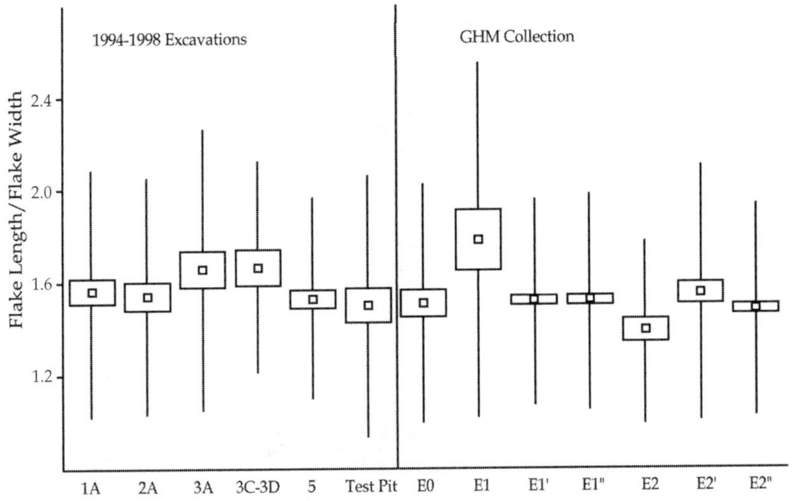

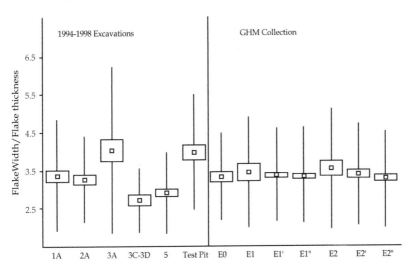

Figure 11.39
Box-whisker comparisons of the ratio of flake length to flake width (complete flakes only) of both current (1994–1998) excavations and those of Henri-Martin ($t = 1.7683$, $df = 2037$, $P = 0.077$).

Figure 11.40
Box-whisker comparisons of the ratio of flake width to flake thickness (complete flakes only) of both current (1994–1998) excavations and those of Henri-Martin ($t = 0.0453$, $df = 2035$, $P = 0.964$).

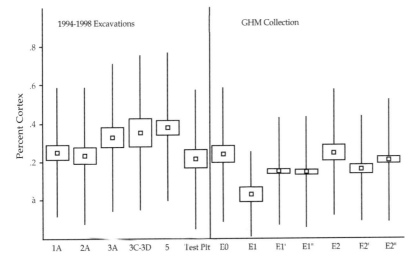

Figure 11.41
Box-whisker comparisons of the percentage of cortex (complete flakes only) of both current (1994–1998) excavations and those of Henri-Martin ($t = 7.2268$, $df = 1934$, $P < 0.0001$).

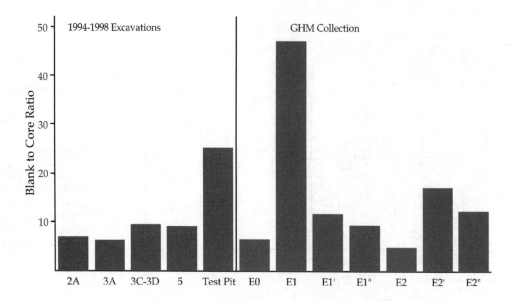

Figure 11.42
Box-whisker compar-
isons of the ratio of
blanks (complete or
proximal flakes or tools)
to cores of both current
(1994–1998) excava-
tions and those of Henri-
Martin.

What these analyses show is that in most respects the collections
from our own excavation and those from Henri-Martin are virtually
identical, with only a small degree of bias in the latter related to size.
Given the time when she was excavating, this is not a surprising
difference. Therefore, it is clear that the overall nature of the industries is the same, which means that interpretations drawn from our
collection can be extended to hers.

At this point, it is not necessary to present more detailed descriptions of either collection, since as is shown in Chapter 12, there is
little doubt that this is not a homogeneous assemblage.

PART III

ANALYSIS AND CONCLUSIONS

Philip G. Chase

André Debénath

Harold L. Dibble

Shannon P. McPherron

12

Processes of Site Formation and Their Implications

When Henri-Martin interpreted the data from her excavations at Fontéchevade, she did not have the benefit of the huge body of research into site-formation processes and lithic and faunal taphonomy that has developed since that time. The findings of this research, as well as the methods that were developed to investigate them, were fundamental to our interpretation of the site and of material from both her excavations and ours. This chapter describes our analysis of site-formation processes at Fontéchevade and lays out the implications of this analysis for the overall understanding of the hominin occupation of the site and of the nature of the Tayacian industry.

ORIGINS OF THE SEDIMENTS, LITHICS, AND FAUNAL REMAINS

Origin of the sediments

The sediments from which the artifacts and fauna were recovered seem to come from two sources. The first was the dolomite bedrock and enclosed chert nodules, from which blocks were removed, probably by solution processes. The dolomite was subsequently largely dissolved from the sediments. The second source was the sediments that overlay the cave and that entered through various chimneys.

Several lines of evidence support this conclusion. Chapter 3 summarizes the sedimentary evidence. The silty loam and quartz cobbles, pebbles, and granules that compose the bulk of the sediment cannot have been derived from the bedrock (arguments against the quartz cobbles having served as hammerstones are presented later in this chapter), and there is no evidence of either aeolian or fluviatile deposition, apart from the karstic clays of Level 8 that predate the hominin occupation of the site. In fact, two active chimneys are observable in the cave today. One is located at the end of the excavated portion of the side passage that Henri-Martin called the "Diverticule." The second is located at the back of the cave near the Test Pit, where the top of the sediments climbs toward the roof of the cave. Fine sediments are still entering the cave through both chimneys (see Fig. 12.1). That the back chimney is connected to the surface is confirmed by the presence of roots protruding from the sediments. Furthermore, the electrical resistivity survey reported in Chapter 5 discovered areas of low resistivity, which indicate deep sediments overlying the bedrock; these too are possible chimneys. One of these is located above the active chimney at the back of the cave and corresponds to a shallow depression on the surface.

Origin of the faunal remains

Faunal remains from the Test Pit near the back of the cave consisted of poorly fossilized bones with either fresh surfaces or surfaces severely corroded by chemical action. However, they also included several highly fossilized and highly abraded bones (see Chapter 8). These findings are entirely consistent with a redeposition through chimneys or other openings from surface deposits. As seen in the following section, analysis of the lithics from both the Henri-Martin collection and the 1994–1998 excavations indicated that they were derived from elsewhere, most likely from the overlying plateau.

The analysis of the faunal remains from the excavations (Chapter 8) showed that humans were responsible for only a small portion of the material, indicating that, by comparison with carnivore occupation, human occupation had been, at most, infrequent and sporadic. An analysis of the material from Henri-Martin's excavations supports these conclusions.

Faunal remains from her excavations were stored in the Musée d'Archéologie Nationale in Saint-Germain-en-Laye. Material counted and described in her report (Henri-Martin 1957) was found together in one location, and many of these specimens were apparently selected because she erroneously believed them to be tools. The remainder of the material was stored in a separate building in boxes marked variously as unidentified, unidentifiable, "cooking debris," and so on. However, many of these specimens were clearly identifiable, and it was apparent that not all material had been saved (for example, larger specimens were almost certainly overrepresented). For this reason, many of the usual kinds of zooarchaeological analyses were not feasible and statistical analysis was not possible.

However, a sample of 511 herbivore limb bones was examined for traces of human action. Probable cut marks could be observed on only 4 of 476 specimens (on the other 35 specimens, the surface was in some way obscured). There were questionable marks on 9 specimens, and on 15, there were a large number of light scratches scattered about the surface, which probably indicate sediment movement or possibly trampling.

Green-bone fractures, which may be produced either by percussion or by pressure – in other words, by either human hammers or carnivore teeth – yielded more ambiguous evidence (Dibble et al. 2006). The percentage of bones with this kind of fracture varied with the depth at which they were found (Table 12.1). The highest frequency was 32.1 percent, found on bones marked as coming from near the opening of the Diverticule. Henri-Martin interpreted this area as a carnivore den because of the lack of evidence of human occupation. We could not check this interpretation because she did not record the horizontal provenience of her artifacts, but if it were correct, it would point to carnivores as the primary producers of green-bone fractures.

Both Henri-Martin (1957) and Paletta (2005) reported shed antlers from Henri-Martin's excavations. Although Paletta believes that

Figure 12.1
Photograph of the base of a chimney at the back of the currently accessible portion of the cave. In 1999, fine sediments from the chimney were gradually burying the rubble-strewn surface left after Henri-Martin's excavations.

Table 12.1. Bones from Henri-Martin's excavations with green-bone fractures

Bed*	N	Percentage		
		Yes	No	?
E0	2	12	81	7
E1'	23		100	
E1''	65	30	70	
E2'	85	20	68	12
E2''	81	15	81	4
DIV-51	107	32	60	7

*Inferred from depths marked on bones.

some of these show evidence of human modification, data from dens without human occupation show that carnivores do collect antlers (Stiner 1991:113).

Overall, for both Henri-Martin's excavations and ours, the percentage of specimens with clear evidence of human action was very low, indicating that the bulk of the faunal remains are attributable to natural causes and that human occupation of the site was sporadic.

In addition, as noted previously, the redeposition of fossilized material from the overlying plateau supports the sedimentological evidence.

Origin of the lithics

A comparison of the lithic material of Henri-Martin's collection and our own (see Chapter 11) shows some differences in the overall sizes of worked artifacts, suggesting that she tended to save the larger pieces. Other than that, few significant differences exist between the artifacts recovered by her and those recovered during the 1994–1998 excavations. However, her collection also includes a large number (almost 65%) of pieces that were totally unworked. In other respects, the two collections are virtually identical, which argues against an initial concern of ours that she had completely excavated the artifact-bearing deposits and stopped excavating only when the archaeological deposits ended. Rejection of this possibility is important because it means that the results of our analysis of the stone tools can be extended to the entire site. As discussed in Chapter 11, the combined collections are easily attributed to the Tayacian, given that it is a flake-dominated industry, with little Levallois, no bifaces, and no other distinguishing characteristics. Therefore, the results presented here have relevance to other similar assemblages that may be attributed to this particular industry.

One feature of this combined assemblage is the rarity of retouched pieces. The material from Fontéchevade is dominated by types 46–49, which collectively are flakes with irregular retouch on both the interior and exterior surfaces (Fig. 12.2). These "types" have been for some time interpreted as edge-damaged artifacts and not as deliberately retouched artifacts, with the damage being the result either of use or, more often, of depositional processes (see Debénath and Dibble 1994). Among the pieces with retouch that is generally considered deliberate, the dominant types are notches and denticulates, followed by scrapers of various types.

It is important to emphasize, however, that deliberately retouched pieces are extremely rare in either collection. Henri-Martin's collection contains only 111 such pieces. We estimate that she excavated 750 m³ of sediment, which means she found one retouched artifact per 6–7 m³. Our own excavations yielded only 55 retouched pieces in 19 m³ or roughly three pieces per cubic meter. The fact that our artifact densities are greater than hers is not surprising, given the differences in excavation methodology and the size bias noted in her collection. Nonetheless, the overall density of retouched artifacts is extremely low in both collections. For comparison, recent excavations at Pech de l'Azé IV and Roc de Marsal, which used identical methods, resulted, respectively, in 88 and 101 retouched lithics per cubic meter.

Given that the sedimentological evidence suggests that the bulk of the sediments entered the cave through openings, the major question for the lithic assemblage is whether it, too, entered the cave in the same

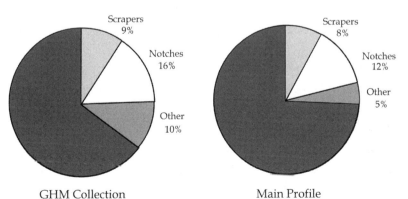

GHM Collection

Main Profile

Figure 12.2
Basic breakdown and comparison of major tool classes (including types 46–49, which are essentially edge-damaged pieces) from the 1994–1998 excavations (Main Profile, N = 418) and those of Henri-Martin (N = 369).

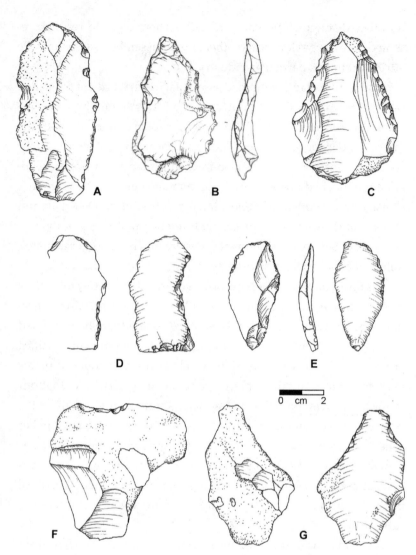

Figure 12.3
Selected artifacts from
the Main Profile of the
new excavation showing
the degree of damage,
which is highly prevalent
in the industries. A, B, E:
Level 3A; C: Level 3D; D,
F, G: Level 5.

manner; that is, whether it washed in with the sediments. If so, then
to what extent could site-formation processes explain the character
of the Tayacian industry? Our focus is on three aspects of the material
related to site formation: damage, size distributions, and orientations.

DAMAGE

Movement, displacement, or redeposition of lithic artifacts through
geological processes often, although not always, produces damages
along their edges, where they are mechanically most vulnerable
(Gifford-Gonzalez et al. 1985; Schiffer 1987). Figure 12.3 illustrates
damaged pieces from the excavations. Figure 12.4 summarizes edge
damage at three sites, with material from the two excavations at

Fontéchevade shown separately. Material from all three sites was analyzed by the authors following a consistent methodology. The assemblages can be assigned to two major groups:

1. Asemblages from Pech de l'Azé IV (Levels 2A, 5A, 6A-B, and 8; McPherron and Dibble 2000; McPherron, Soressi, and Dibble 2001), show relatively little overall damage, and what damage does occur is usually on one surface only.
2. A second group of assemblages, which contains both collections from Fontéchevade, shows considerably more damage, and damage is present on both surfaces significantly more often. Regarding the lithic assemblage from Level I1 at Cagny-l'Epinette, the material was deposited by fluviatile action (Dibble et al. 1997), and there are clear indications that Levels 5B and 7 from Pech

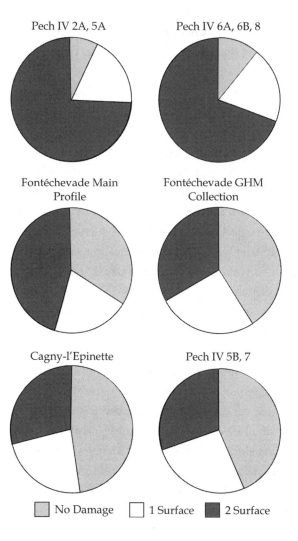

Pech IV 2A, 5A

Pech IV 6A, 6B, 8

Fontéchevade Main Profile

Fontéchevade GHM Collection

Cagny-l'Epinette

Pech IV 5B, 7

☐ No Damage   ☐ 1 Surface   ■ 2 Surface

Figure 12.4
Pie diagrams indicating the kind and extent of damage on pieces from various sites. The material from Cagny-l'Epinette and Pech de l'Azé IV (Levels 5B and 7) are known, on the basis of other studies, to have been significantly disturbed, and this is reflected by the high percentages of both one-sided and two-sided damage. The other material from Pech de l'Azé IV comes from contexts that show no other signs of disturbance. The material from both Fontéchevade collections indicates relatively severe disturbance.

de l'Azé IV have been subjected to mass movement, particularly solifluction (P. Goldberg, personal communication). The extent of damage at Fontéchevade is closely comparable to that found in these collections and is consistent with a depositional model that entails significant movement of the material.

Although some damage is easily recognized as such, other damage resembles retouch (Bordes 1953, 1961:46; Bordes and Bourgon 1951; Dibble and Holdaway 1993; McBrearty et al. 1998). Among these are types 46–49, already discussed, which represent the most prevalent "type" in these collections. The next most common types are notches and denticulates, which can also be the product of both mass movement of sediments and trampling (Bordes and Bourgon 1951; Flenniken and Haggerty 1979; Nielson 1991). Although these pieces may reflect human retouch, their high frequency and their association with very large numbers of pieces that are clearly naturally damaged suggest that these were also the product of sediment movement.

SIZE DISTRIBUTIONS

The products of flintknapping inevitably include a wide range of sizes, from large flakes, tools, and cores; through smaller retouch or preparation flakes; to microscopic particles. Several quantitative replicative experiments (see Amick and Mauldin 1989; Newcomer 1971; Shott 1994) have shown that, in an undisturbed flintknapping assemblage, as the size of objects decreases, their frequency increases. This rule seems to hold true in spite of differences in technology or in degree of core reduction (although the upper size limit may vary). When the distribution of archaeological materials does not fit this pattern, however, there are several possible explanations, particularly when the smallest objects are underrepresented. First, it might be that very little lithic reduction took place on the site; tools and flakes may have been brought to the site and discarded without significant tool production or maintenance. Second, certain natural processes, especially flowing water, can alter the undisturbed distribution by selectively removing small flakes. As flow increases, water is capable of transporting increasingly heavy sediment loads, which means that increasingly larger flakes will be removed, or winnowed, from an assemblage and redeposited downstream as the flow energy eventually diminishes (Behm 1983; Schick 1986; Stein and Teltser 1989).

Third, it is possible that neither flintknapping nor tool use occurred at the site but that the assemblage was created by the redeposition of allochthonous artifacts. In this case, the size distributions of artifactual and non-artifactual material are likely to be similar, because the same processes were responsible for their deposition.

It is clear from Figure 12.5 that the size distributions of the artifacts from Fontéchevade do not match the expected distribution for an assemblage representing in situ stone tool reduction, as Henri-Martin had suggested. Although this figure only displays percentages of pieces larger than 2.5 cm in maximum dimension (the cutoff size limit for artifacts in the analysis), the number of smaller pieces increases much less steeply than would be expected. Moreover, in terms of the material recovered from wet-screening through 5-mm mesh (not included in this figure), there was less than one small flake per 7-liter bucket of sediment. In other words, very small flakes are virtually non-existent. This finding is inconsistent with an undisturbed workshop or occupation site in which core reduction was taking place.

Figure 12.5 also shows that the size distribution of the worked artifacts more or less matches the size distribution of unworked chert and other clasts (primarily quartz). This finding implies that both worked and unworked artifacts were deposited by similar processes.

Figure 12.5
Comparison of weight distributions of artifacts (worked flint and chert), natural clasts (including quartz), and unworked chert from the 1994–1998 excavations in the Main Profile. The similarity in the distributions suggests that all three classes of material had a common origin and/or were subject to the same post-depositional processes.

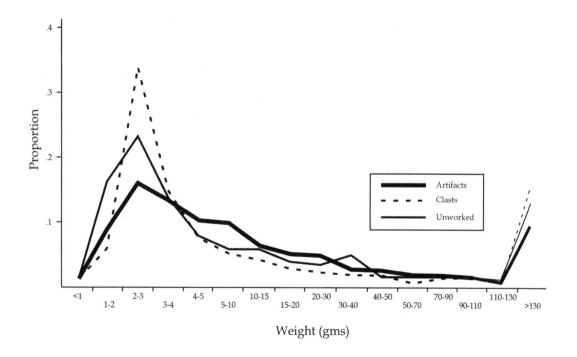

Given that the sediments were brought in through chimneys at the back of the cave (Chapter 3), the same would appear to be true of the lithics. A similar relationship between the sizes of artifacts and non-artifactual material has previously been shown for the Acheulian site of Cagny-l'Epinette (Dibble et al. 1997), where both artifacts and gravel were deposited by stream action.

ORIENTATIONS

Various studies have shown that the orientations of clasts can provide good information about depositional processes (see Lenoble and Bertran 2004; McPherron 2005 and citations within). At Fontéchevade, artifact orientations were recorded and analyzed using the methods described by McPherron (2005). Unfortunately, the exceedingly low artifact densities meant that samples from most of the levels were insufficient for this kind of analysis. Of the levels included, Level 1A is at the top of the sequence, just under the present-day surface of the deposits, and is thought to have been disturbed in recent times. Levels 2A, 3A, and 5 represent different portions of the main Tayacian deposits that nearly traverse the width of the cave. At the edges of the cave, however, there is a complete vertical break in the stratigraphy that is represented here as Level X.

When there is little post-depositional disturbance and artifacts are lying randomly on a flat surface, the Schmidt diagrams show a continuous distribution of points along the outer edge of at least half the diagram. Disturbances are indicated by artifacts that plot near the center of these diagrams (indicating artifacts that are nearly vertical) or by modalities in the patterning. The results from Fontéchevade are presented in Figure 12.6. Of the levels shown here, all but 3A show modalities to some extent, and Level 3A has a sample size of only 29. The patterning is weakest in Level 1A and strongest in Level X.

This finding is summarized in the Benn diagram, which is based on a kind of principal components analysis of the three-dimensional orientations. Artifacts oriented randomly in three dimensions will produce equally weighted components and plot toward the isotropic corner of the diagram. Randomly oriented artifacts on a flat surface will have two components with high loadings and plot near the planar corner, whereas artifacts that point in only one direction will have a single component with high loadings and will plot in the linear corner (Benn 1994). Based on comparative data (Lenoble and Bertran 2004; McPherron 2005), the Fontéchevade levels plot at the limit between (a) areas that at other sites are indicative of some post-depositional movement, in particular debris flow, and (b) areas that are indicative of limited post-depositional movement.

Origin of the quartz cobbles

In both the collections of Henri-Martin and those resulting from the 1994–1998 excavations, a large number of quartz cobbles were found.

Figure 12.6
Schmidt diagrams (lower half) and Benn diagram of artifact orientations. The Fontéchevade grid is oriented such that the 0–180 degree axis is aligned with the cave and 180 degrees is toward the cave entrance.

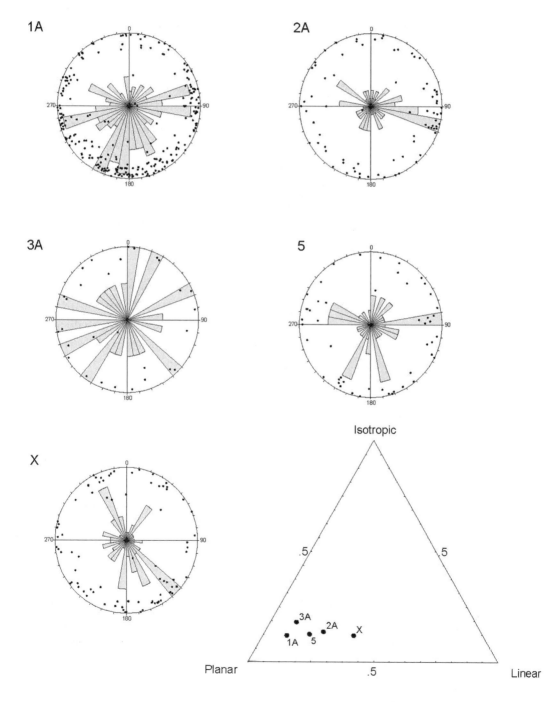

Again, these cobbles are not part of the bedrock formation of the cave and so must have been introduced into the sediments through either human or natural agencies. As discussed in Chapters 1 and 3, Henri-Martin interpreted their presence as reflecting their selection and importation into the site for use as hammerstones.

As stated previously, cobbles, pebbles, and granules are very numerous, and most are smaller than 30 mm. Cobbles of this size would not be particularly useful as hammerstones, and in fact, only six of them show any damage that would suggest such use. Moreover, in our excavations, where we exercised care to recover all of the cobbles, there are almost twice as many quartz cobbles ($N = 605$) as there are blanks (complete or proximal flakes or tools) made in the local material ($N = 344$). Because one hammerstone is sufficient to produce many thousands of flakes, having more hammerstones than flakes is not an expected pattern for a raw material exploitation site. Finally, the size distribution of these cobbles is fairly even (Fig. 12.7) and shows no modalities that would be expected if they were being selected for use as hammerstones, in which case some patterning according to preferred size would be expected. This same pattern holds even for the overlying Bronze Age deposits when hammerstone use was, perhaps, less likely.

For all of these reasons, the quartz cobbles most likely originated from the same process as the sediments and the rest of the lithic assemblage. Given that the plateau over the site is littered with quartz cobbles, and therefore represents the probable source of these objects, this is the only reasonable conclusion possible.

Summary of the evidence

All these lines of evidence point to the conclusion that the Tayacian assemblages at Fontéchevade are primarily the result of natural formation processes. These processes probably introduced some modified artifacts into the site. They clearly also produced pseudo-artifacts that were originally interpreted as artifacts.

Two natural processes were acting more or less simultaneously. The first was the movement of sediments and other materials from the overlying plateau through one or more openings in the back of the cave. The amount of damage on the flint artifacts and the similarity in the size distributions of artifacts and non-artifacts indicate that movement from the plateau is also the most likely source of the flint artifacts. Although there are no known Paleolithic sites on the plateau, it is clear that, after more than a half-million years of occupation, a light-density background of Paleolithic artifacts is found everywhere – what archaeologists sometimes call the "scatter between the patches" (Stern 1991, 1993).

The second natural process was the dissolution of the bedrock of the cave walls and ceiling, which released chert nodules into the sediments. These nodules tended to break apart, sometimes when they fell but more often through frost action. The cave sediments are filled with pseudo-artifacts in this material. It is sometimes difficult to tell the difference between these "geofacts" and intentionally produced flakes, which is perhaps why the Henri-Martin collection contained so many unworked pieces. After deposition, all of these artifacts were then subject to the same natural processes that were moving sediment through the cave system.

Taking all these lines of evidence together, the Tayacian of Font-échevade cannot be interpreted as the result of hominin behavior. It is best interpreted as the mixed accumulation of non-artifactual material and artifacts redeposited from elsewhere.

IMPLICATIONS

The processes by which sediments, fauna, and lithics arrived in the cave deposits have implications for our understanding of the site, of

Figure 12.7
Comparison by weight classes of quartz cobbles and pebbles from Henri-Martin's collection, the newly excavated material from the Main Profile, and material excavated from the Bronze Age deposits. All three contexts show a similar distribution and have no evidence of selection for particular size classes to be used as hammerstones.

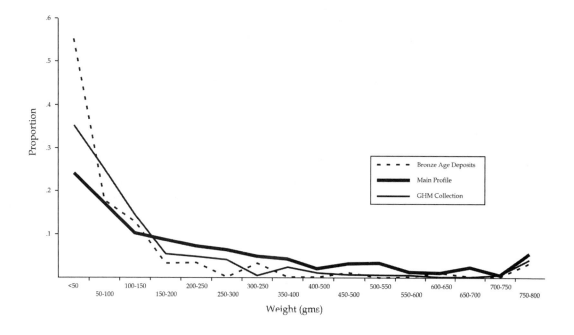

the Tayacian industry, and of human occupation and activities at the site.

Implications for the concept of the Tayacian

As described in more detail in Chapter 1, the Tayacian was first recognized early in the twentieth century by Denis Peyrony at the site of La Micoque (Dordogne) (Peyrony 1938). However, Henri-Martin's excavations at Fontéchevade produced a larger assemblage, which she documented more fully. As a result, Fontéchevade became the reference site for the industry.

The Tayacian at La Micoque came from a series of levels underlying the "Micoquian" horizons uncovered by Hauser (Peyrony 1938). The new assemblages consisted of large flakes and rough flake tools and lacked the refined bifaces from the Micoquian (Peyrony 1938). Although the existence of an industry without bifaces underlying the Mousterian ran contrary to a strictly unilineal scheme for the Paleolithic (Mortillet 1869, 1883), the parallel phyla scheme proposed by Breuil and Lantier (Breuil 1932; Breuil and Lantier 1959) allowed the Tayacian to be interpreted as intermediate between the Clactonian and the Levalloisian.

In subsequent years, Tayacian industries were discovered over a wide geographic area, from France to the Levant to North Africa (Dibble et al. 2006). At the same time, there was considerable controversy about the homogeneity of the industry. Fitte (1948) suggested two facies, one focused on large flakes and the other on small, thick, and irregular flakes. Others, such as Bourgon (1957), assigned pieces to the Tayacian assemblages with a typological emphasis on notches, denticulates, and Tayac points (convergent denticulates), as well as pieces with abrupt and alternating retouch. Eventually, the heterogeneity of the industry became so great that Rolland (1986:124) described it as being in "a state of classificatory limbo" (but see also Bordes and Bourgon 1951; Peyrony 1950). Moreover, various scholars proposed new names – for example, "Tabunian" (Howell 1959) and "Shamshi" (Solecki 1968) – for essentially the same phenomenon.

Not everyone was convinced, however, that the Tayacian reflected only human modification. Bordes himself (1953, 1984; Bordes and Bourgon 1951) believed that at least some of the typological nature of the industry, especially the abrupt and alternating retouch, was a result of post-depositional processes that damaged the material.

Indeed, at many of the sites mentioned previously, layers that exhibited such assemblages were also shown to be geologically disturbed. Bordes (1953; Bordes and Bourgon 1951:17) also showed by experimental trampling (cf. McBrearty et al. 1998) that it was very easy to produce such "tools" naturally. In fact, one of the categories of "tools" organized by Henri-Martin and stored presently in the Musée d'Archéologie Nationale at Saint-Germain-en-Laye was labeled by Bordes as "podoliths."

The preceding analysis of the Tayacian material at Fontéchevade throws considerable doubt on the validity of the Tayacian as an actual industrial variant with behavioral significance. Yet, it has always been the case that the Tayacian appeared so heterogeneous as to throw doubt on its reality. In addition, many Tayacian assemblages seemingly owed at least part of their appearance to naturally occurring factors rather than to human intent. Our work at Fontéchevade, arguably the most important Tayacian site, supports this conclusion. Therefore, the term "Tayacian" should no longer be used as an industrial variant.

The analysis of lithics from both Henri-Martin's collection and the 1994–1998 excavations, reported in Chapter 11, produced several findings that are of great importance to our understanding of the Tayacian. These findings were equally apparent in both collections.

- The density of lithic artifacts was extremely low.
- The percentage of retouched pieces was very low. The most common Bordian type was the combined abrupt and alternating retouch on thin or thick flakes (type 48 in our terminology), which are essentially edge-damaged pieces.
- A very high proportion of artifacts exhibited edge damage.
- There was a very high frequency of unworked pseudo-artifacts caused by thermal fracturing of flint derived by weathering from the cave walls. These pseudo-artifacts were often hard to distinguish from true artifacts. Approximately 65 percent of Henri-Martin's collection consisted of unworked flints.

The taphonomic evidence indicates that the Tayacian assemblage at Fontéchevade cannot be considered an industry. It consisted of (1) material redeposited from the surface above the cave, much of it damaged in the process; (2) flint derived naturally from the cave walls and subsequently damaged either by thermal fracture or sediment movement; and (3) a very small percentage of material actually worked in situ by humans – much of this undoubtedly also damaged.

These facts shed a great deal of light on the nature of the Tayacian in general. The assemblages that have been assigned to the industry share two characteristics. First, taken together, they produce only an ill-defined whole. Second, they all share a high percentage of crude and ill-defined artifact types and of types that actually represent natural damage. Thus, all lines of evidence point to the same conclusion. Bordes was right in suspecting that the "Tayacian" was in fact a chimera, a set of assemblages produced, altered, or damaged by natural processes, rather than a valid lithic industry (Dibble et al. 2006).

The data from Fontéchevade also serve as yet one more reminder that the word "culture" must be used with caution when applied to lithic assemblages. If the word is taken to mean no more than "assemblages that resemble one another," then the Tayacian can be called a culture. However, there are many ways in which sets of similar assemblages may be formed. At the most elaborate end of the spectrum, the forms of artifacts may have had symbolic meaning for their makers and may have been prescribed by cultural norms (Byers 1994, 1999; Chase 1991, 2006:136–144). However, at a less elaborate level, the similarities may have no symbolic meaning but simply reflect the fact that youngsters learn to knap by watching their elders, and therefore tend to make similar artifacts (Chase 2006:136–144; see also Sackett 1973, 1982, 1985). Similarities may also reflect nothing more than the intensity of raw material use – the degree to which artifacts are reused and resharpened (Dibble 1984, 1987a, 1988; Dibble and Rolland 1992; Rolland 1981). Finally, as in the case of the Tayacian, the similarities may result from purely natural processes. Remember that Dart's osteodontokeratic "culture" turned out to be no more than this (Brain 1967, 1969, 1981; Dart 1957). Because readers will usually take the word "culture" to have strong symbolic, normative implications, the term should be avoided unless less elaborate explanations of the assemblages are explicitly impossible.

Implications for human activities and occupation at Fontéchevade

Henri-Martin (1957:231–240) believed that Fontéchevade was occupied permanently, with perhaps occasional absences, by people who were exploiting its flint. She thought that the lithics and at least the bulk of the faunal remains reflected this occupation, and that the quartz cobbles common in the sediments were brought into the site as hammerstones. In addition, she reported finding hearths and clearly defined zones of flintknapping, and she presented plans of these for four different levels within Bed E. There are reasons to be skeptical about all of these conclusions.

First, as has been seen in Chapter 8, the faunal remains from both Henri-Martin's excavations and ours show very little evidence of human activity. Although some animals or parts of animals were undoubtedly brought into the site and consumed by humans, the bulk of the faunal assemblage was produced by (or consisted of) carnivores. In addition, some of the assemblage was apparently entirely allochthonous.

The same can be said of the lithic assemblage. In fact, because this assemblage was much larger and necessarily better preserved, lithics provide a much stronger basis for reaching these conclusions. As reported previously in this chapter, the lithic assemblage was not produced by in situ knapping. Most of the lithics in the site are either redeposited from the surface or are the product of frost fracturing.

There is also reason to be skeptical of her plots of hearths and of knapping areas. First, if we compare her stratigraphic drawings with the stratigraphy we found, there is little reason to believe that her Figure 75 (Henri-Martin 1957) represents carefully measured plots. Moreover, she does not plot artifacts, which would make it possible to evaluate her impression that artifact concentrations were real. In fact, she did not record the horizontal proveniences of any artifacts. Moreover, the sedimentary processes in the cave were such that they would probably have destroyed any such concentration. Pristine spatial patterning is rare in Lower and Middle Paleolithic sites (Pettitt 1997). In a site where sediments were subjected to mass movement in the cave, it is hard to see how such features could have survived.

Nonetheless, Henri-Martin's claim of hearths is harder to evaluate directly, because we found none in our excavations. In the Witness Section in the front of the cave, we encountered patches of darkly stained lenses of sediments (Fig. 12.8), but these were concentrations of manganese, which occurs in very high quantities in the sediments. Chemical test of the soils on the plateau have revealed concentrations

Figure 12.8
Photo of manganese stain
in the Witness Section.

of manganese high enough to affect the kinds of crops that could be grown there. Given that sediments from the plateau were entering the cave through the chimney, and given the presence of manganese in our own excavations, it is possible that Henri-Martin mistook these stains for hearths. This mistake has been made at other Paleolithic sites (Genty et al. 1997; Goldberg et al. 2001; Hill 1982; Shahack-Gross, Bar-Yosef, and Weiner 1997).

Henri-Martin (1957:234–244) does report on thermal analysis of samples of flint taken from these "hearths" and of comparative samples from outside of them, which apparently showed heating to as much as 820°C. These thermal analyses are so incompletely reported, however, that they are impossible to evaluate, though heating to such a high temperature seems unlikely enough that the results may be questionable. There was only rare and even then often inconclusive evidence of burned bone in her collections. Of the stone tools, only 25 of 12,385 specimens showed possible evidence of heating, and more than half of these were non-artifactual pieces of flint. Thus, given all of these lines of evidence, the safest and most prudent conclusion is that Fontéchevade should be removed from the list of sites that provide evidence for hominin use of fire (cf. James 1989).

In short, Henri-Martin's interpretation of how hominins used the site during the "Tayacian" is not supported by the evidence. Yet, this does not reflect negatively on the quality of her work. The basis for our reinterpretation is a large body of research on site-formation processes and taphonomy that post-dates her report. However, it does remind us that, as a discipline, archaeology progresses and that old interpretations based on old excavations must be reevaluated by modern methods.

13

Summary and Conclusions

This monograph reports the results of new excavations at Fonté-chevade, one of the most important and best-known Paleolithic sites in Western Europe. The new excavations, which took place between 1994 and 1998, followed those of Germaine Henri-Martin, who worked there for many years during the middle part of the twentieth century. Although the meticulous reporting by Henri-Martin and her collaborators on the site's fossils and archaeological industries had a tremendous influence on the field of paleoanthropology, the new work has radically altered virtually every aspect of the earlier interpretations.

The Fontéchevade Cave, which is located near the town of Montbron in the southeastern part of the Department of the Charente, France, is a long, narrow, tunnel-like formation that extends back some 30 m from its north-facing mouth. When Henri-Martin started excavating in 1937, following relatively brief excavations by others since the turn of that century, the cave itself was almost completely full of sediment. However, after almost 20 years of work, with interruptions because of World War II, she had removed about 750 m³ of sediment. The main deposits of the site that were the focus of Henri-Martin's excavations were a relatively thick (up to 7 m) series of sediments that contained an industry called the Tayacian. These deposits preceded overlying industries of Mousterian and Upper Paleolithic, most of which had already been removed by the earlier excavations. The Tayacian deposits were subdivided on the basis of depth, rather than natural stratigraphy, into beds labeled E0 through E2'''. She excavated all these deposits from the front half of the presently accessible part of the cave, including talus deposits in front of the cave. All the overlying Mousterian and Upper Paleolithic deposits were removed, including those in the back half of the cave. Some Bronze Age material remained in burials that she recognized and, as it turned out, in deposits she did not reach. Our excavations, therefore, are relevant to an understanding of the deposits she assigned to the Tayacian, which are also the deposits for which the site is best known.

THE ORIGINAL INTERPRETATIONS OF FONTÉCHEVADE

In their reports, Henri-Martin and her collaborators stressed four major topics:

1. the nature of the hominin remains
2. an assessment of their age
3. the nature of the associated lithic assemblage
4. the nature of hominin occupation at the site

At the time of publication, their interpretations appeared to be sound. It was only later, in the light of new advances in taphonomy and archaeological methodology, and with better dates for the European fossil record, that questions inevitably arose that could only be answered by new excavations.

The human remains consisted of two cranial fragments, one a portion of frontal bone and the other a much larger portion of both parietals. The parietals, referred to as Fontéchevade II, are relatively thick and in many respects resemble individuals, such as the fossil from Swanscombe, which were thought to be relatively old – in fact, older than Neanderthal remains known at that time. Fontéchevade I, the frontal, is very different. In terms of the thinness of the bones and the lack of a supraorbital torus, it resembles modern *Homo sapiens*. Henri Vallois (1958) interpreted these two finds as representatives of a single "presapiens" population, ancestral to modern humans, that was distinct from contemporary and later Neanderthal populations. When Piltdown – the most famous presapiens of all – turned out to be a hoax, Fontéchevade became the key site for this hypothesis.

However, this interpretation is based on the assumptions that the two individuals are of the same geological age (they were both discovered at the top of main Tayacian deposits) and that both are older than known Neanderthal populations. Henri-Martin (1957) estimated that the Tayacian deposits (her Bed E) belonged to the last interglacial (Riss-Würm or OIS 5e). She based this hypothesis mainly on the associated temperate fauna and pollen, but also on the stratigraphic position of the Tayacian relative to the Mousterian. Alimen (1958) generally concurred, citing correlations of bedrock terraces to those of the classic alpine sequence. Later, a number of authors noted the presence of colder climate species in the upper part of Bed E and suggested an even earlier OIS 6 or Riss interstadial age. Either date would mean that Fontéchevade I was older than many European Neanderthals. In addition, if Fontéchevade I represents a modern population, it fits very badly with all the other evidence available today about the arrival of anatomically modern humans in Europe.

The Tayacian, which was originally defined at the French site of La Micoque only a few years before Henri-Martin began excavating at Fontéchevade, is a lithic industry characterized by its crudeness and lack of diagnostic elements. It has very few formal tools such as scrapers, no bifaces, but some choppers and chopping-tools made on quartz cobbles, and it lacks any specialized technology such as Levallois. With its presumed age placing it before the Mousterian, such crudeness appeared very reasonable, and soon similar assemblages were found in many sites throughout the Old World. Thus, as the industry associated with fossil presapiens, it earned a place in the systematics of Paleolithic assemblage groups. Eventually, some instances of Tayacian assemblages, or ones that shared many of its features, were shown to be associated with dynamic sedimentary contexts that suggested relatively high levels of disturbance. However, Fontéchevade retained its position as the de facto type site of the industry.

Henri-Martin believed that people occupied the site more or less permanently, exploiting the flint contained in the cave bedrock. She believed that both the lithics and the faunal remains were overwhelmingly the product of this occupation and that the quartz cobbles common in the sediments had been imported as hammerstones. She also believed that she could identify such features as hearths (many associated with cave bear bones), concentrations of bone, and flintknapping areas.

In sum, for Henri-Martin, Fontéchevade was a relatively old site that attracted groups of ancestral modern hominins because of the abundant raw material there. The crude character of their lithics was only a reflection of their antiquity, but in other respects, the use of the cave reflected essentially modern kinds of behavior.

MAJOR FINDINGS OF THE 1994–1998 EXCAVATIONS

The goals of the current excavation were to test – using new techniques of excavation, analysis, and dating – the four principal findings of Henri-Martin's work: the nature, origins, and age of the Tayacian industry there, and the dates of the hominin remains.

Our work took place in three separate areas. The primary excavation continued where Henri-Martin left off in the middle of the cave, at what we call the Main Profile. We also did more limited testing in two other areas. We enlarged one of her test pits in the very back of the cave (the Test Pit) and carried out limited excavation in a bench of sediment near the front that she had intentionally left for future archaeologists (the Witness Section). Altogether, the new project excavated about 19 m^3 of sediment, resulting in a collection of more than 1300 worked lithic remains and about the same number of faunal remains. Three new human fragments were also discovered: two teeth and a very small piece of parietal (described in Chapter 6).

One of our primary goals in studying the Tayacian industry was determining the degree to which it was a result of natural formation processes as opposed to deliberate behavior on the part of hominins. Therefore, the methods of excavation and analysis that we used at the site had to be especially relevant to questions of taphonomy. All objects found during the work, including bone, worked chert or flint, quartz cobbles, and even unworked pieces of the local chert, were point provenienced, with X, Y, and Z coordinates recorded. On elongated pieces, two measurements were taken – one on either end of the object – so that their orientations could be evaluated. In addition, all of the sediments were screened to recover small fragments of lithics or bone. Also important for this work were the various sedimentologic and geologic studies designed to reconstruct the origin of the cave sediments.

Several lines of evidence converged into a single and unified conclusion: Both the sediments and a major portion of archaeological lithic material entered the site through a chimney or chimneys in the rear of the cave. One such chimney is accessible and still active in the back of the cave and was identified through electrical resistivity. Another is visible at the end of the side passage that Henri-Martin called the Diverticule. Others were suggested by the electrical resistivity survey and by anecdotes of the local inhabitants concerning sinkholes on the plateau overlooking the site.

A dynamic movement of sediment and artifacts leaves many signatures on lithic assemblages. In every respect, the analysis of the
objects recovered during the excavation expressed these signatures,
ranging from a high incidence of edge damage, to a pronounced
winnowing of smaller pieces of lithic debris, and to orientations of
the elongated objects (see Chapter 12). The quartz cobbles that were
present in the cave sediments also exist in abundance on the plateau,
and it is difficult to demonstrate that any were purposefully brought
into the site.

One of the defining characteristics of the Tayacian is its general
crudeness. However, at Fontéchevade, the chert that occurs in the
cave suffered a very high degree of mechanical and, especially, thermal fracture. In fact, in both our own excavations and in the collection
excavated by Henri-Martin, entirely naturally produced "flakes" and
other chert debris that closely resembled intentional artifacts were
extremely common. In Henri-Martin's collection, over half of the
objects were found to be unworked. The inclusion of such "geofacts"
in a collection would, of course, make the resulting lithic "assemblage" appear much cruder than it really was. The same is true of the
high degree of damage on the Fontéchevade specimens.

Because most of our excavation concentrated on remaining sediments that were well inside the cave, the possibility existed that our
data would not be comparable to Henri-Martin's, which came mostly
from the area in front of the dripline. However, extensive analysis on
the totality of her collection showed that, in virtually all respects, the
two collections were identical, with the exception that she appeared
to have saved pieces that were larger overall. What this means is that
our results and interpretations can be extended to hers with a sufficiently high degree of confidence.

Analysis of the faunal remains from our excavations point to three
conclusions. First, there are a few indications of human exploitation
of fauna at the site. Second, such traces are rare; the great bulk of
the faunal material in the cave owes nothing to human occupation.
Third, a few specimens were probably redeposited from the overlying
plateau, specimens that entered the cave along with and as a part of
the sediments. Finally, it should be noted that it is clear from the
literature that the fauna from Henri-Martin's excavation in her Bed
E was not homogeneous, that species indicative of colder climates
were more common near the top of those deposits.

Henri-Martin's recognition of horizontal spatial patterning of
both lithics and fauna and her interpretation of some of them as

knapping areas must be questioned. The fact that both sediments and lithics were derived, for the most part, from the overlying plateau and the evidence that the bulk of the faunal remains were not present because of human activity invalidate any behavioral interpretation of such patterning. Moreover, the movement of sediments through the cave from the chimneys where they entered makes it unlikely that any artifact patterns would have been preserved.

We found no traces of hearths in our excavations. Only 25 lithics (less than 1 percent of the total), most of which were unworked pieces of flint, showed any evidence that might indicate burning. In the Witness Section – precisely in the area where she indicated the presence of an exceptionally large hearth – there was clear evidence of manganese staining. Given that such stains have often been mistaken for evidence of hearths, this represents the most parsimonious explanation for the other hearths that she believed she had found.

The absence of burned lithics and of faunal remains from our own excavations prevented us from obtaining a complete absolute chronology for the sequence. The magnetic susceptibility analysis reported in Chapter 4 could not help because we were unable to correlate the stratigraphy of the Test Pit, where the study was done, with those of the Main Profile or Witness Section (see discussion in Chapter 3). We were, however, able to date material from Henri-Martin's excavations that were stratigraphically associated with the two human fossils. All of the ESR dates and all but one of the radiocarbon dates indicate that the upper part of Bed E dates to OIS 3. Although either Fontéchevade I or Fontéchevade II may have been redeposited, this date would be unsurprising for in situ remains. This, of course, has direct bearing on the presapiens interpretation of these remains, indicating that there are no chronological grounds for interpreting Fontéchevade I as a Middle Pleistocene presapiens. Though it is still possible that it represents an immature Neanderthal, given the new dates it is not impossible that it represents an early modern human.

CONCLUSIONS

Based on the 1994–1998 research and excavation at Fontéchevade, it is clear that many of the original interpretations of this site, its industries, and its human fossils were in error. As a consequence, many of the apparent implications of Fontéchevade are also false. This is not the first time that new work at a site has overturned the results of previous excavations and analysis, and it will undoubtedly not be the last. It is, after all, a natural consequence of the continuing development of both method and theory in archaeology, and an important part of the overall process in the scientific study of our past.

Although these findings do not support the interpretations of Henri-Martin, they do not detract in any way from the quality of the work that she did at the site. Rather, they only show how far archaeology as a discipline has come in the 50 years since the publication of the original Fontéchevade report. Her work was undertaken in a time when archaeologists paid little attention to alternative, non-human explanations for the accumulation and distribution of material found in caves when those caves also contained unambiguous artifacts and, in this case, hominin remains.

Nevertheless, there are two important implications of this reevaluation of Fontéchevade. First, if the Tayacian of Fontéchevade is the product of natural processes, at how many other Tayacian sites is this the case – especially given that their industries often were defined as Tayacian based on comparisons with Fontéchevade? Obviously, the answer will require more detailed taphonomic studies of these sites, although similar arguments have already been put forward for some sites where relatively dynamic sedimentary contexts, including fluvial transport, karstic slumping, and other kinds of mass movement, may have created these assemblages or contributed significantly to their character. At this point, however, it would seem fair to conclude that, unless the contrary can be explicitly demonstrated, Paleolithic stone tool assemblages comparable to the "Tayacian" of Fontéchevade should not be considered as unambiguous reflections of prehistoric behavior. Furthermore, we conclude that the use of the term "Tayacian" should be dropped.

Finally, the Fontéchevade I specimen almost certainly dates to OIS 3. Thus, its modern appearance is no longer either an anomaly nor evidence of a presapiens population, although it may represent a rather early specimen of anatomically modern *Homo sapiens* in Europe.

References

Abbazzi, L., F. Fanfani, M. P. Ferretti, L. Rook, L. Cattani, F. Masini, F. Mel-
legni, F. Negrino, and C. Tozzi. 2000. New human remains of archaic
Homo sapiens and Lower Palaeolithic industries from Visogliano (Duino
Aurisina, Trieste, Italy). *Journal of Archaeological Science* 27: 1173–1186.

Alimen, H. 1958. Les formations quaternaire autour de Fontéchevade.
Archives de l'Institut de Paléontologie Humaine Mémoire 29: 164–184.

Amick, D. and R. Mauldin, (eds.). 1989. *Experiments in Lithic Technology.*
British Archaeological Reports, Oxford.

Arambourg, C. 1958. Les gros mammifères des couches tayaciennes. *Archives
de l'Institut de Paléontologie Humaine Mémoire* 29: 185–229.

Ballesio, R. 1979. Le gisement pléistocène supérieur de la grotte de Jaurens
à Nespouls, Corrèze, France: Les carnivores (Mammalia, Carnivora). 1.
Canidae et Hyenidae. *Nouvelles Archives du Museum d'Histoire naturelle
de Lyon* 17: 56–65.

Banerjee, S. K. 1996. Sediment reveals early Holocene climate change in
China. *EOS, Transactions, American Geophysical Union* 77: 3 and 5.

Bastin, B. 1976. Etude palynologique des couches E2, D et Bs de la grotte
de Fontéchevade (Charente, France). *Bulletin de la Société Royale Belge
d'Anthropologie et de Préhistoire de Bruxelles* 87: 15–27.

Baumler, M. 1988. Core reduction, flake production, and the Middle Paleolithic industry of Zobiste (Yugoslavia). In *Upper Pleistocene Prehistory of
Western Eurasia*, edited by H. L. Dibble and A. Montet-White, pp. 255–
274. University Museum, University of Pennsylvania, Philadelphia.

Behm, J. A. 1983. Flake concentrations: Distinguishing between flintworking
activity areas and secondary deposits. *Lithics Technology* 12: 9–16.

Behrensmeyer, A. K. and A. P. Hill. 1980. *Fossils in the Making: Vertebrate
Taphonomy and Paleoecology.* University of Chicago Press, Chicago.

Benn, D. I. 1994. Fabric shape and the interpretation of sedimentary fabric
data. *Journal of Sedimentary Petrology* 64: 910–915.

Biberson, P. 1961. *Le Paleolithique Inferieur du Maroc Atlantique.* Public Service
des Antiquites du Maroc 17, Rabat.

Bon, F. and P. Bodu. 2002. Analyse technologique du débitage aurignacien.
In *L'Aurignacien de la Grotte du Renne: Les fouilles d'André Leroi-Gourhan*

à Arcy sur Cure (Yonne), edited by B. Schmider, pp. 115–133. Gallia Préhistoire, XXXIVe Supplément, Paris.

Bonatti, E. 1966. North Mediterranean climate during the last Würm glaciation. *Nature* 209: 984–985.

Bonifay, M. F. 1971. Carnivores quaternaires du Sud-Est de la France. *Muséum d'Histoire Naturelle de Paris, Mémoires, série C* 21: 43–377.

Bonnichsen, R. and M. H. Sorg, (eds.). 1989. *Bone Modification*. Center for the Study of the First Americans, Institute of Quaternary Studies, University of Maine, Orono.

Bordes, F. 1947. Étude comparative des différentes techniques de taille du silex et des roches dures. *L'Anthropologie* 51: 1–29.

———. 1952. Stratigraphie du loess et évolution des industries paléolithiques dans l'ouest du bassin de Paris. II. Évolution des industries Paléolithiques. *L'Anthropologie* 56: 405–452.

———. 1953. Essai de classification des industries 'moustériennes'. *Bulletin de la Société Préhistorique Française* 50: 457–466.

———. 1961. *Typologie du Paléolithique Ancien et Moyen*. Centre National de la Recherche Scientifique, Paris.

———. 1984. *Leçons sur le Paléolithique, Tome I. Notions de Géologie Quaternaire.* Cahiers du Qaternaire No. 7 (CNRS), Paris.

Bordes, F. and M. Bourgon. 1951. Le complexe Mousterien: Mousterien, Levalloisien et Tayacien. *L'Anthropologie* 55: 1–23.

Bordes, J.-G. 2005. La séquence aurignacienne du nord de l'Aquitaine: Variabilité des productions lamellaires à Camindade-Est, Roc-de-Combe, Le Piage et Corbiac-Vignoble II. In *Productions lamellaires attribuées à l'Aurignacien: Chaînes opératoires et perspectives technoculturelles. XIVe Congrès de l'UISPP, Liège, 2–8 septembre 2001*, pp. 123–154. Archéologiques 1, Luxembourg.

Bordes, J.-G. and F. Bon. Unpublished. Analyse techno-typologique de l'industrie lithique de la grotte Dufour (Corrèze, France): Anciennes fouilles, nouvelles données. Paper presented at the international colloquium *El Centenario de la Cueva de El Castillo: El Ocaso de los Neandertales*, Santoña, September, 18–20 2003.

Bottema, S. 1994. The prehistoric environment of Greece: A review of the palynological record. In *Beyond the Site: Regional Studies in the Aegean Area*, edited by P. N. Kardulias, pp. 45–68. University Press of America, Lanham, Maryland.

Bourdier, F. 1967. *Préhistoire de France*. Flammarion, Paris.

Bourgon, M. 1957. *Les industries mousteriennes et pre-mousterniennes du Perigord*. Archives de l'Institut de Paleontologie Humaine Memoire 27. Masson, Paris.

Bouvier, J.-M., M. Cremades, and L. Duport. 1987. *L'abri Paignon à Montgaudier (Montbron, Charente). Art et industrie, analogies et relations. Préhistoire de Poitou-Charentes. Problèmes actuels*. Editions du CTHS, Paris.

Brace, C. L. 1964. The fate of the 'Classic' Neanderthals: A consideration of hominid catastrophism. *Current Anthropology* 5: 3–43.

Brain, C. K. 1967. Hottentot food remains and their meaning in the interpretation of fossil bone assemblages. *Scientific Papers of the Namib Desert Research Station* 32: 1–11.

———. 1969. *The Contribution of the Namib Desert Hottentots to an Understanding of Australopithecine Bone Accumulations. Scientific Papers of the Namib Desert Research Station* 39.

———. 1981. *The Hunters or the Hunted?* University of Chicago Press, Chicago.

———. 1985. Interpreting early hominid death assemblages: The rise of taphonomy since 1925. In *Hominid Evolution: Past, Present, and Future*, edited by P. V. Tobias, pp. 41–46. Alan R. Liss, New York.

Brennan, B. J., H. P. Schwarcz, and W. J. Rink. 1997. Simulation of the gamma radiation field in lumpy environments. *Radiation Measurements* 27: 299–306.

Breuil, H. 1932. Les industries à éclat du Paléolithique ancien, I: Le Clactonien. *Préhistoire* 1: 125–190.

Breuil, H. and R. Lantier. 1959. *Les Hommes de la Pierre Ancienne*. Payout, Paris.

Bunn, H. T. 1983. Comparative analysis of modern bone assemblages from a San hunter-gatherer camp in the Kalahari Desert, Botswana, and from a spotted hyena den near Nairobi, Kenya. In *Animals and Archaeology 1. Hunters and their Prey*, edited by J. Clutton-Brock and C. Grigson, pp. 143–148. B.A.R. International Series S163, Oxford.

Byers, A. M. 1994. Symboling and the Middle-Upper Palaeolithic transition: A theoretical and methodological critique. *Current Anthropology* 35: 369–400.

———. 1999. Communication and material culture: Pleistocene tools as action cues. *Cambridge Archaeological Journal* 9: 23–41.

Chaline, J. 1972. *Le Quaternaire: L'Histoire humaine dans son environnement*. Doin, Paris.

Chase, P. G. 1991. Symbols and Paleolithic artifacts: Style, standardization, and the imposition of arbitrary form. *Journal of Anthropological Archaeology* 10: 193–214.

———. 2006. *The Emergence of Culture: Evolution of a Uniquely Human Way of Life*. Springer, New York.

Chase, P. G., A. Debénath, H. L. Dibble, S. P. McPherron, H. P. Schwarcz, and T. W. J. Stafford. 2007. New dates for the Fontéchevade (Charente, France) *Homo* remains. *Journal of Human Evolution* 52: 217–221.

Chase, P. G. and H. L. Dibble. 1987. Middle Paleolithic symbolism: A review of current evidence and interpretations. *Journal of Anthropological Archaeology* 6: 263–296.

Chiotti, L. 2000. Lamelles Dufour et grattoirs aurignaciens (carénés et à museau) de la couche 8 de l'abri Pataud, Les Eyzies-de-Tayac, Dordogne. *L'Anthropologie* 104: 239–263.

———. 2003. Les productions lamellaires dans l'Aurignacien de l'abri Pataud, Les Eyzies-de-Tayac, Dordogne. *Gallia Préhistoire* 45: 113–156.

———. 2006. La production d'éclats dans l'Aurignacien ancien de l'abri Pataud, Les Eyzies-de-Tayac, Dordogne. In *Actes de la Table ronde 'Autour des concepts de Protoaurignacien, d'Aurignacien initial et ancien: Unité et variabilité des comportements techniques des premiers groupes d'hommes modernes dans le Sud de la France et le Nord de l'Espagne', Toulouse, 27 février-1er mars 2003. Espacio, Tiempo y Forma, Serie I, Prehistoria y Arqueología, Madrid* 15: 195–214.

Clark, G. A. 1988. Some thoughts on the Black Skull: An archaeologist's assessment of WT-17000 (*A. boisei*) and systematics in human paleontology. *American Anthropologist* 90: 357–371.

Clot, A. 1980. *La grotte de la Carrière (Gerde, Hautes-Pyrénées). Stratigraphie, et paléontologie des carnivores.* Thèse, 3ème cycle, Université Paul Sabatier.

Commont, V. 1910. *Les différents niveaux de l'industrie de l'Age du Renne dans les limons du Nord de la France.* Congrès Préhistorique de France, Tours.

———. 1913. Les hommes contemporains du renne dans la vallée de la Somme. *Memoire de la Societe des Antiquaires de Picardie* 7: 207–646.

Corruccini, R. S. 1975. Metrical analysis of Fontéchevade II. *American Journal of Physical Anthropology* 42: 95–98.

Cruz-Uribe, K. 1991. Distinguishing hyena from hominid bone alterations. *Journal of Field Archaeology* 18: 467–486.

Dart, R. A. 1957. *The Osteodontokeratic Culture of Australopithecus prometheus.* Transvaal Museum Memoirs, no. 10, Pretoria.

Darwin, R. L., C. R. Ferring, and B. B. Ellwood. 1990, Geoelectric stratigraphy and subsurface evaluation of Quaternary deposits at Cooper Basin, northeast Texas, *Geoarchaeology* 5: 53–79.

David, P. 1933. Communication. *Bulletin et mémoires de la Société Archéologique et Historique de la Charente* 23: 84–86.

Debénath, A. 1969. Le gisement prehistorique de La-Chaise-de-Vouthon (Charente). In *Livret guide excursion A4, VIIIeme Congres INQUA,* pp. 66–71, Paris.

———. 1974. *Recherches sur les terrains quaternaires charentais et les industries qui leur sont associées.* Docteur ès Sciences, Université de Bordeaux I.

———. 1976. Les gisements préhistoriques de la Chaise de Vouthon, commune de Vouthon. In *L'excursion A 4, Sud-Ouest (Aquitaine et Charente), IXe Congrès de l'UISPP, Nice 13–18/09/1976,* edited by J.-P. Rigaud and B. Vandermeersch, pp. 141–144.

Debénath, A. and H. L. Dibble 1994. *The Handbook of Paleolithic Typology. Vol. I. The Lower and Middle Paleolithic of Europe.* The University Museum. University of Pennsylvania, Philadelphia.

Debénath, A. and L. Duport. 1986. Le Mousterien de la grotte de Montgaudier (Charente), note préliminaire. *Bulletin de la Société Anthropologique du Sud-Ouest* 21: 5–9.

Delagnes, A., J.-F. Tournepiche, D. Armand, E. Desclaux, M.-F. Diot, C. Ferrier, V. Le Fillâtre, and B. Vandermeersch. 1999. Le gisement Pléistocène moyen et supérieur d'Artenac (Saint-Mary, Charente): Premier bilan interdisciplinaire. *Bulletin de la Société Préhistorique Française* 96: 469–496.

Demars, P.-Y. L'industrie aurignacienne de la couche 2 de la grotte Bourgeois-Delaunay. In *Les gisements paléolithiques de La Chaise-de-Vouthon (Charente),* edited by A. Debénath. Forthcoming.

Demars, P.-Y. and P. Laurent. 1989. *Types d'outils du paléolithique supérieur en Europe.* Cahiers du Quaternaire 14. Editions du CNRS, Bordeaux.

Denton, G. H. and W. Karlén. 1973. Holocene climatic variations – their pattern and possible cause. *Quaternary Research* 3: 155–205.

Dibble, H. L. 1984. Interpreting typological variation of Middle Paleolithic scrapers: Function, style, or sequence of reduction? *Journal of Field Archaeology* 11: 431–436.

———. 1987a. The interpretation of Middle Paleolithic scraper morphology. *American Antiquity* 52: 109–117.

———. 1987b. Measurement of artifact provenience with an electronic theodolite. *Journal of Field Archaeology* 14: 249–254.

———. 1988. Typological aspects of reduction and intensity of utilization of lithic resources in the French Mousterian. In *Upper Pleistocene Prehistory of Western Eurasia*, edited by H. L. Dibble and A. Monte-White, pp. 181–187. The University Museum. University of Pennsylvania, Philadelphia.

———. 1995. An assessment of the integrity of the archaeological assemblages. In *The Middle Paleolithic Site of Combe-Capelle Bas (France)*, edited by H. L. Dibble and M. Lenoir, pp. 245–258. University Museum Monograph 91.

Dibble, H. L., P. G. Chase, A. Debénath, W. R. Farrand, and S. P. McPherron. 2006. Taphonomy and the concept of Paleolithic cultures: The case of the Tayacian from Fontéchevade. *PaleoAnthropology* 2006: 1–21.

Dibble, H. L., P. G. Chase, S. P. McPherron, and A. Tuffreau. 1997. Testing the reality of a "living floor" with archaeological data. *American Antiquity* 62: 629–651.

Dibble, H. L. and S. Holdaway. 1993. The Middle Paleolithic of Warwasi Rockshelter. In *The Paleolithic Prehistory of the Zagros*, edited by D. Olszewski and H. L. Dibble, pp. 75–99. The University Museum. University of Pennsylvania, Philadelphia.

Dibble, H. L., S. Holdaway, M. Lenoir, S. P. McPherron, B. J. Roth, and H. Sanders-Gray. 1995. Techniques of excavation and analysis. In *The Middle Paleolithic Site of Combe-Capelle Bas (France)*, edited by H. L. Dibble and M. Lenoir, pp. 27–40. The University Museum. University of Pennsylvania, Philadelphia.

Dibble, H. L. and S. P. McPherron. 1989. On the computerization of archaeological projects. *Journal of Field Archaeology* 15: 431–440.

Dibble, H. L. and S. P. McPherron. 2006 The missing Mousterian. *Current Anthropology* 47: 777–803.

Dibble, H. L. and S. P. McPherron 2007. Truncated-faceted pieces: Hafting modification, retouch, or cores? In *Tools versus Cores Alternative Approaches to Stone Tool Analysis*, S. McPherron, editor, pp. 75–90. Cambridge Scholars Publishing, Newcastle.

Dibble, H. L., S. P. McPherron, P. G. Chase, W. R. Farrand, and A. Debénath, 2006. Taphonomy and the concept of Paleolithic cultures: The case of the Tayacian from Fontéchevade. *Paleoanthropology* 4: 1–21.

Dibble, H. L. and N. Rolland. 1992. On assemblage variability in the Middle Paleolithic of Western Europe: History, perspectives, and a new synthesis. In *The Middle Paleolithic: Adaptation, Behavior, and Variability*, edited by H. L. Dibble and P. Mellars, pp. 1–20. The University Museum. University of Pennsylvania, Philadelphia.

Drennan, R. 1956. Note on the morphological status of the Swanscombe and Fontéchevade remains. *American Journal of Physical Anthropology* 14: 73–83.

Duport, L. 1969. Le gisement préhistorique de Montgaudier (Charente). In *Livret-Guide de l'Excursion A4, VIIIe Cong. d'INQUA.*

———. 1976. La grotte de Montgaudier, commune de Montbron, Cahrente. In *Livret-Guide de l'Excursion A4,. IXe Congrès de l'UISPP, Nice,* pp. 151–158.

Efremov, I. 1940. Taphonomy: A new branch of paleontology. *Pan-American Geologist* 74: 81–93.

Eisenmann, V. 1991. Les chevaux quaternaires européens (Mammalia, Perissodactyla). Taille, typologie, biostratigraphie et taxonomie. *Geobios* 24: 747–759.

Ellwood, B. B. and W. A. Gose. 2006. Heinrich H1 and 8,200 year B.P. climate events recorded in Hall's Cave, Texas. *Geology* 34: 753–756.

Ellwood, B. B. and F. B. J. Harrold. 1993. Unusual electrical resistivity effects associated with fast-growing trees, Rio Maior, Portugal. *Geoarchaeology* 8: 157–162.

Ellwood, B. B., F. B. Harrold, S. L. Benoist, L. G. Straus, M. Gonzalez-Morales, K. Petruso, N. F. Bicho, Z. Zilhão, and N. Soler 2001. Paleoclimate and intersite correlations from Late Pleistocene/Holocene cave sites: Results from Southern Europe. *Geoarchaeology* 16: 433–463.

Ellwood, B. B., F. B. Harrold, S. L. Benoist, P. Thacker, M. Otte, D. Bonjean, G. L. Long, A. M. Shahin, R. P. Hermann, and F. Grandjean. 2004. Magnetic susceptibility applied as an age-depth-climate relative dating technique using sediments from Scladina Cave, a Late Pleistocene cave site in Belgium. *Journal of Archaeological Science* 31: 283–293.

Ellwood, B. B., F. B. Harrold, and A. E. Marks 1994. Site identification and correlation using geoarchaeological methods at the Cabeço do Porto Marinho (CPM) locality, Rio Maior, Portugal. *Journal of Archaeological Science* 21: 779–784.

Ellwood, B. B., F. B. J. Harrold, K. M. Petruso, and M. Korkuti. 1993. Electrical resistivity surveys as indicators of site potential: Examples from a rock shelter in southwestern France and a cave in southern Albania. *Geoarchaeology* 52: 137–150.

Ellwood, B. B., D. E. Peter, W. Balsam, and J. Schieber 1995. Magnetic and geochemical variations as indicators of paleoclimate and archaeological site evolution: Examples from 41TR68, Fort Worth, Texas. *Journal of Archaeological Science* 22: 409–415.

Ellwood, B. B., K. M. Petruso, and F. B. Harrold. 1996. The utility of magnetic susceptibility for detecting paleoclimatic trends and as a stratigraphic correlation tool: An example from Konispol Cave sediments, SW Albania. *Journal of Field Archaeology* 23: 263–271.

Ellwood, B. B., K. M. Petruso, F. B. Harrold, and J. Schuldenrein. 1997. High-resolution paleoclimatic trends for the Holocene identified using magnetic susceptibility data from archaeological excavations in caves. *Journal of Archaeological Science* 24: 569–573.

Ellwood, B. B., J. Zilhão, F. B. Harrold, W. Balsam, B. Burkart, G. J. Long, A. Debénath, and A. Bouzouggar. 1998. Identification of the Last Glacial Maximum in the Upper Paleolithic of Portugal using magnetic susceptibility measurements of Caldeirão Cave sediments. *Geoarchaeology* 13: 55–71.

Fassbinder, J. W. E., H. Stanjek, and H. Vali. 1990. Occurrence of magnetic bacteria in soil. *Nature* 343: 161–163.

Fitte, P. 1948. Note sur le Tayacien. *Bulletin de la Société Historique Naturelle du Vaucluse* 1: 3–7.

Flenniken, J. and J. Haggerty. 1979. Trampling as an agency in the formation of edge damage: An experiment in lithic technology. *Northwest Anthropological Research Notes* 13: 208–214.

Fosse, P. 1995. Le role de l'hyène dans la formation des assemblages osseux: 150 ans de controverses. *Paléo* 7: 49–84.

———. 1997. Variabilité des assemblages osseux créés par l'Hyène des cavernes. *Paléo* 9: 15–54.

Garrod, D. and D. M. A. Bate. 1937. *The Stone Age of Mount Carmel. Volume I.* Clarendon Press, Oxford.

Genty, D., Y. Dauphin, G. Deflandre, Y. Quinif, and C. Miskovsky. 1997. Exemples de particules d'origine anthropique piegees dans les lamines de croissance de stalagmites; interet pour la reconstitution des environnements humains anciens. In *Karst et archéologie*, pp. 149–157, 341–342. Colloque de l'UMR 5590 du CNRS et de l'Association Française pour l'Etude du Quaternaire 8.

Giaccio, B., I. Hajdas, M. Peresani, F. G. Fedele. and R. Isaia 2006. The Campanian ignimbrite tephra and its relevance for the timing of the Middle to Upper Paleolithic shift. In *When Neanderthals and Modern Humans Met*, edited by N. J. Conard, pp. 343–378. *Tübingen Publications in Prehistory*, Tübingen.

Giacobini, G. 1990–1991. Hyenas or cannibals: Fifty years of debate on the Guattari Cave Neandertal cranium. In *The Fossil Man of Monte Circeo. Fifty Years of Studies on the Neandertals in Latium*, edited by A. Bietti and G. Manzi, pp. 593–604. Quaternaria Nova, Rome. I.

Gifford, D. P. and D. C. Crader. 1977. A computer coding system for archaeological faunal remains. *American Antiquity* 42: 225–238.

Gifford-Gonzalez, D., D. B. Damrosch, D. R. Damrosch, J. Pryor and R. L. Thunenl. 1985. The third dimension in site structure: An experiment in trampling and vertical dispersal. *American Antiquity* 50: 803–818.

Gilot, E. 1984 Datations radiométriques. In *Peuples chasseurs de la Belgique préhistorique dans leur cadre naturel*, edited by D. Cahen and P. Haesaerts, pp. 115–125. Institut royal des science naturelles de Belgique, Bruxelles.

Goldberg, P., S. Weiner, O. Bar Yosef, Q. Xu, and J. Liu. 2001. Site formation processes at Zhoukoudian, China. *Journal of Human Evolution* 41: 483–530.

Gradstein, F., J. Ogg, and A. G. Smith. 2004. *A Geologic Time Scale 2004.* Cambridge University Press, Cambridge.

Grimaud, D. 1982. *Evolution du pariétal de l'Homme fossile.* Museum National d'Histoire Naturelle, Mémoire 15, Paris.

Guadelli, J.-L. 1987. *Contribution à l'étude des zoocénoses préhistoriques en Aquitaine (Würm ancien et interstade würmien).* Thèse de doctorat, Université de Bordeaux I.

Guérin, C. 1980. *Les Rhinocerotidae (Mammalia, Perissodactyla) du Miocène supérieur au Pléistocène terminal en Europe occidentale. Comparaisons avec les espèces actuelles.* Doctorat d'Etat ès Sciences, Université de Lyon I.

Hahn, J. 1988. Fiche sagaie à base fendue. *Fiches typologiques de l'industrie osseuse préhistorique* 1.*Cahier I : Sagaies*, Commission de nomenclature sur l'industrie osseuse de l'os préhistorique de l'UISPP, Publication de l'Université de Provence, Aix-en-Provence, pp. 1–21.

Harrold, F., B. P. Ellwood, P. Thacker, and S. Benoist. 2004. Magnetic susceptibility analysis of sediments at the Middle-Upper Paleolithic transition for two cave sites in northern Spain. In *The Chronology of the Aurignacian and of the Transitional Technocomplexes. Dating, Stratigraphies, Cultural Implications*, edited by J. Zilhão and F. D'Errico, pp. 301–310. Trabahos de Arqueologia 33. Instituto Português de Arqueologia, Lisboa.

Heberer, G. 1951. Grundlinien in der pliestocänen Entfaltungsgeschichte der Euhomininen. *Quartär* 5: 58–78.

———. 1955. Die geographische Verbreitung der fossilen Hominiden (auszer Eusapiens) nach neuerer Gruppierung. *Die Naturwissenschaften* 42: 85–90.

Heller, F. and M. E. Evans. 1995. Loess magnetism. *Reviews of Geophysics* 33: 211–240.

Henri-Martin, G. 1951. Remarques sur la stratigraphie de la grotte de Fontéchevade (Charente) et les conditions dans lesquelles les échantillons des ossements fossiles de Fontéchevade ont été prélevés, afin d'être soumis au "test" de la fluorine. *L'Anthropologie* 55: 242–247.

———. 1953. Un niveau de Châtelperron de la grotte de Fontéchevade (Charente). *Bulletin de la Société d'Etudes et de Recherches Préhistoriques des Eyzies* 2: 35–36.

———. 1957. *La Grotte de Fontéchevade. Première Partie: Historique, Fouilles, Stratigraphie, Archéologie.* Archives de l'Institut de Paléontologie Humaine 28. Masson et Compagnie, Paris.

———. 1965. La Basse-Tardoire grottes et abris paléolithiques. A. Fontéchevade. *Bulletin de l'Association Française pour l'Etude du Quaternaire* 2: 211–216.

Herberer, G. 1951. Grundlinien in der pliestocänen Entfaltungsgeschichte der Euhomininen. *Quartär* 5: 58–78.

Hervet, S. 2000. Tortues quaternaires de France: Critères de détermination, repartitions chronologique et géographique. *Mésogée* 58: 9–47.

Hill, A. P. 1978. Taphonomical background to fossil man. In *Geological Background to Fossil Man*, edited by W. W. Bishop, pp. 87–101. Geological Society of London, Scottish Academic Press, Edinburgh.

Hill, C. A. 1982. Origin of black deposits in caves. *NSS Bulletin* 44: 15–19.

Howell, F. C. 1951. Place of Neanderthal man in human evolution. *American Journal of Physical Anthropology* 9: 379–416.

———. 1957. The evolutionary significance of variation and varieties of Neanderthal man. *Quarterly Review of Biology* 32: 330–347.

———. 1958. Upper Pleistocene men of the Southwest Asian Mousterian. In *Hundert Jahre Neanderthaler, 1856–1956*, edited by G. H. R. von Koenigswald, pp. 185–198. Kemink en Zoon, Utrecht.

———. 1959. Upper Pleistocene stratigraphy and early man in the Levant. *Proceedings of the American Philosophical Society* 103: 1–65.

Imai, T., T. Kanemori, and T. Sakayama. 1987. Use of ground probing radar and resistivity surveys for archaeological investigation. *Geophysics* 52: 137–150.

James, S. 1989. Hominid use of fire in the Lower and Middle Pleistocene: A review of the evidence. *Current Anthropology* 30: 1–26.

Jéquier, J.-P. 1975. *Le Moustérien alpin*. Eburodunum II. Institut d'Archéologie Yverdonoise, Yverdon.

Joussaume, R., B. Joffroy, G. Henri-Martin, and J.-L. Heim. 1975. Sépulture collective de l'Age du Bronze de la Grotte de Fontéchevade (Charente). *Bulletin et Mémoires de la Société d'Anthropologie de Paris* 2, ser XIII(61–86):62–86.

Keller, G. and F. Frischknecht. 1966. *Electrical Methods in Geophysical Prospecting*. Pergamon Press, New York.

Klien, R. G. 1986. Carnivore size and Quaternary climatic change in southern Africa. *Quaternary Research* 26: 153–170.

Klien, R. G. and K. Scott. 1989. Glacial/interglacial size variation in fossil spotted hyenas (*Crocuta crocuta*) from Britain. *Quaternary Research* 32: 88–95.

Knowles, F. 1911. The correlation between the interorbital width and the other measures and indices of the human skull. *Journal of the Royal Anthropological Institute* 41: 318–349.

Kolfschoten, T. V., Gifford, D. P. and D. C. Crader. 1977. A computer coding system for archaeological faunal remains. *American Antiquity* 42: 225–238.

Kolfschoten, T. V. and W. Roebroeks. 1985. Maastricht-Belvédère: Stratigraphy, palaeoenvironment and archaeology of the Middle and Late Pleistocene deposits. *Mededelingen Rijks Geologische Dienst* 39: 1–121.

Kurtén, B. 1957. The bears and hyenas of the interglacials. *Quaternaria* 4: 69–81.

Lartet, E. 1861. Nouvelles recherches sur la coexistence de l'homme et des grands mammifères fossiles réputés caractéristiques de la dernière période géologique. *Annales des Sciences naturelles. II. Zoologie, 4ème série* XV: 177–253.

Lartet, E. and H. Christy. 1865–1875. *Reliquiae Aquitanicae, Being Contributions to the Archaeology and Palaeontology of Périgord and the Adjoining Provinces of Southern France*. Williams & Norgate, London.

Laville, H. 1982. On the transition from 'lower' to 'middle' palaeolithic in south-west France. In *The Transition from Lower to Middle Palaeolithic and the Origin of Modern Man*, edited by A. Ronen, pp. 131–135. BAR International Series 151. BAR, Oxford.

———. 1988. Recent developments on the chronostratigraphy of the Paleolithic in the Perigord. In *Upper Pleistocene Prehistory of Western Eurasia*, edited by H. L. Dibble and A. Montet-White, pp. 147–160. University Museum Symposium Series, Vol. I. The University Museum. University of Pennsylvania, Philadelphia.

Laville, H., J.-P. Rigaud, and J. R. Sackett. 1980. *Rock Shelters of the Perigord: Geological Stratigraphy and Archaeological Succession*. Academic Press, New York.

Laville, H., J. L. Turon, J.-P. Texier, J.-P. Raynal, F. Delpech, M. Paquereau, F. Prat, and A. Debénath. 1983. Histoire paléoclimatique de l'Aquitaine et du Golfe de Gascogne au Pléistocène supérieur depuis le dernier interglaciaire. *Bulletin de l'Institut Géologique du Bassin de l'Aquitaine, Bordeaux* 34: 219–241.

Le Grand, Y. 1994. Approche méthodologique et technologique d'un site d'habitat du Pléistocène moyen: La grotte no. 1 du Mas des Caves (Lunel-Viel, Hérault). *Préhistoire Anthropologie Méditerranéennes* 3: 205–207.

Lenoble, A. and P. Bertran. 2004. Fabric of Palaeolithic levels: Methods and implications for site formation processes. *Journal of Archaeological Science* 31: 457–469.

Leroi-Gourhan, A. 1964. *Les Religions de la Prehistoire*. Presses Universitaires de France, Paris.

Lumley, H. d. 1960. Clactonien et Tayacien dans la région méditerranéenne française. *Compte-Rendu Académie des Sciences de Paris* 250: 1887–1888.

Lyman, R. L. 1987. Archaeofaunas and butchery studies: A taphonomic perspective. *Advances in Archaeological Method and Theory* 10: 249–337.

———. 1994. *Vertebrate Taphonomy*. Cambridge Manuals in Archaeology. Cambridge University Press, London.

Marseiller, E. 1937. *Les dents humaines, morphologie*. Gauthier-Villars, Paris.

McBrearty, S., L. C. Bishop, T. Plummer, R. Dewar, and N. J. Conard. 1998. Tools underfoot: Human trampling as an agent of lithic artifact edge modification. *American Antiquity* 63: 108–129.

McPherron, S. J. P. 2005. Artifact orientations and site formation processes from total station proveniences. *Journal of Archaeological Science* 32: 1003–1014.

McPherron, S. P. and H. L. Dibble. 1987. Hardware and software complexity in computerizing archaeological projects. *Advances in Computer Archaeology* 4: 25–40.

———. 2000. The lithic assemblages of Pech de L'Aze IV (Dordogne, France). *Préhistoire Européene* 15: 9–43.

———. 2002. *Using Computers in Archaeology: A Practical Guide*. McGraw-Hill, New York.

McPherron, S. P., M. Soressi, and H. L. Dibble. 2001. Deux nouveaux projets de recherche á Pech de l'Azé (Dordogne, France). *Préhistoire du Sud-Ouest* 8: 11–30.

Mortillet, G. d. 1869. Essai d'une classification des cavernes et des stations sous abri, fondée sur les produits de l'industrie humaine. *Matériaux pour servir à l'histoire primitive de l'homme* V: 172–179.

———. 1883. *Le Préhistorique: Antiquité de l'Homme*. C. Reinwald, Paris.

Mullins, C. E. 1977. Magnetic susceptibility of the soil and its significance in soil science – a review. *Journal of Soil Science* 28: 223–246.

Nash, D. and M. Petraglia. 1987. *Natural Formation Processes and the Archaeological Record*. British Archaeological Reports, International Series, Oxford, 352, Oxford.

Neuville, R. 1951. Le site Clacto-Abbevillien, Tayacien, Acheuléen et Micoquien de Sidi-Abderrahman (Maroc); histoire d'un classement. *Bulletin de la Société Préhistorique Française* 48: 101–108.

Newcomer, M. 1971. Some quantitative experiments in handaxe manufacture. *World Archaeology* 3: 85–94.

Nielson, A. 1991. Trampling the archaeological record: An experimental study. *American Antiquity* 56: 483–503.

Nishiaki, Y. 1985. Truncated-faceted flakes from Levantine Mousterian assemblages. *Bulletin, Department of Anthropology, University of Tokyo* 4: 215–226.

O'Brien, S. R., P. A. Mayewski, L. D. Meeker, D. A. Meese, M. S. Twickler, and S. I. Whitlow. 1995. Complexity of Holocene climate as reconstructed from a Greenland ice core. *Science* 270: 1962–1964.

Oakley, K. P. and C. R. Hoskins. 1951. Application du test de la fluorine aux crânes de Fontéchevade (Charente) avec remarques sur la stratigraphie de Fontéchevade. *L'Anthropologie* 55: 239–247.

Olivier, G. 1960. *Pratique anthropologique.* Vigot Frères, Paris.

Palacky, G. 1988. Resistivity characteristics of geologic targets. In *Electromagnetic Methods in Applied Geophysics – Theory Volume 1,* edited by M. Nabighian and J. Corbett, pp. 53–129. Society of Exploration Geophysicists, Tulsa.

Paletta, C. 2005. *L'Evolution des comportements de subsistance des hommes du moustérien au solutréen dans la région Poitou-Charentes (France).* Ph.D. thesis, Musée National d'Histoire Naturelle.

Perpère, M. and B. Schmider. 2002. L'outillage lithique. In *L'Aurignacien de la grotte du Renne,* edited by B. Schmider, pp. 143–195. Supplément à Gallia-Préhistoire. Vol. 34. Editions du CNRS, Paris.

Perrot, J. 1968. La préhistoire palestinienne. *Supplément au dictionnaire de la Bible VIII* 43: 286–446.

Pettitt, P. B. 1997. High resolution Neanderthals? Interpreting Middle Paleolithic intrasite spatial data. *World Archaeology* 29: 208–224.

Peyrony, D. 1938. La Micoque, les fouilles recentes, leurs significations. *Bulletin de la Société Préhistorique Française* 6: 257–288.

———. 1950. Qu'est-ce que le Tayacien? *Bulletin Société Préhistoire Française* 47: 102.

Pickering, T. R. 2002. Reconsideration of criteria for differentiating faunal assemblages accumulated by hyenas and hominids. *International Journal of Osteoarchaeology* 12: 127–141.

Potts, R. 1988. *Early Hominid Activities at Olduvai.* Aldine de Gruyter, New York.

Prat, F. 1968. *Recherches sur les équidés pléistocènes de France.* Thèse de sciences naturelles, Université de Bordeaux I.

Quiles, G. 2003. *Les Ursidae du Pléistocène moyen et supérieur en Midi méditerranéen: Apports paléontologiques, biochronologiques et archéozoologiques.* Thèse de doctorat, Musée National d'Histoire Naturelle.

Rink, W. J. 1997. Electron spin resonance (ESR) dating and ESR applications in Quaternary science and archaeometry. *Radiation Measurements* 27: 975–1025.

Rolland, N. 1981. The interpretation of Middle Paleolithic variability. *Man* 16: 15–42.

———. 1986. Recent findings from La Micoque and other sites in southwestern and Mediterranean France: Their bearing on the "Tayacian" problem and Middle Paleolithic emergence. In *Stone Age Prehistory,* edited by G. N. Bailey and P. Callow, pp. 121–151. Cambridge University Press, Cambridge.

Ruddiman, W. F. and A. C. Mix. 1993. The North and Equatorial Atlantic at 9000 and 6000 yr B.P. In *Global Climates since the Last Glacial Maximum,* edited by J. Wright, H.E., J. E. Kutzbach, T. I. Webb, W. F. Ruddiman, F. A. Street-Perrott, and P. J. Bartlein, pp. 94–124. University of Minnesota Press, Minneapolis.

Sackett, J. R. 1973. Style, function, and artifact variability in Palaeolithic assemblages. In *The Explanation of Culture Change: Models in Prehistory*, edited by C. Renfrew, pp. 317–325. University of Pittsburgh Press, Pittsburgh.

———. 1982. Approaches to style in lithic archaeology. *Journal of Anthropological Archaeology* 1: 59–112.

———. 1985. Style, ethnicity, and stone tools. In *Status, Structure and Stratification: Current Archaeological Reconstructions*, edited by M. Thompson, M. T. Garcia, and F. J. Kense, pp. 277–282. University of Calgary, Calgary.

Schick, K. D. 1986. *Stone Age Sites in the Making: Experiments in the Formation and Transformation of Archaeological Occurrences.* British Archaeological Reports International Series 319, Oxford.

Schiffer, M. B. 1987. *Formation Processes of the Archaeological Record.* University of New Mexico Press, Albuquerque.

Schwarcz, H. P. and B. Blackwell. 1983. 230Th/234U age of a Mousterian site in France. *Nature* 301: 236–237.

Schwarcz, H. P., B. Blackwell, and A. Debénath. 1983. Absolute dating of hominids and Paleolithic artifacts of the Cave of La Chaise de Vouthon (Charente), France. *Journal of Archaeological Science* 10: 493–513.

Sergi, G. 1967. Morphological position of the "Prophaneranthropi (Swanscombe and Fontéchevade)." In *Ideas on Human Evolution 1949–1961*, edited by W. W. Howells, pp. 507–520. Harvard University Press, Cambridge.

Sergi, S. 1953a. I profaneratntropi di Swanscombe e di Fontéchevade. *Rendiconti dell'Accademia Nazionale dei Linei* ser. 8, 15: 601–608.

———. 1953b. Morphological position of the "Prophaneranthropi" (Swanscombe and Fontéchevade). In *Actes du Congrès International du Quaternaire* INQUA, pp. 651–665.

Shahack-Gross, R., O. Bar-Yosef, and S. Weiner. 1997. Black-coloured bone in Hayonim Cave, Israel: Differentiating between burning and oxide staining. *Journal of Archaeological Science* 24: 439–446.

Sheriff, R. E. 1980. *Seismic Stratigraphy.* International Human Resources Development Corporation, Boston.

Shipman, P. 1981. *Life History of a Fossil.* Harvard University Press, Cambridge.

Shott, M. J. 1994. Size and form in the analysis of flake debris: Review and recent approaches. *Journal of Archaeological Method and Theory* 1: 69–110.

Simonet, P. 1991. *Contribution à la connaissance des grands mammifères du Pléistocène supérieur de Belgique et de Bretagne.* Thèse, Université de Liège.

Singer, M. J. and P. Fine. 1989. Pedogenic factors affecting magnetic susceptibility of northern California soils. *Soil Science Society of America Journal* 53: 1119–1127.

Solecki, R. S. 1968. The Shamsi industry, a Tayacian related industry at Yabroud, Syria. Preliminary report. In *La Préhistoire: Problèmes et tendances*, pp. 401–410. Eds du CNRS, Paris.

———. 1970. A new secondary flaking technique at the Nahr Ibrahim Cave site, Lebanon. *Bulletin du Musée de Beyrought* 23: 137–142.

Sonneville-Bordes, D. de. 1972. Environnement et culture de l'homme du Périgordien ancien dans le sud-ouest de la France: Données récentes.

In *The Origin of* Homo sapiens. *Proceedings of the Paris Symposium, 2–5 September*, edited by F. Bordes, pp. 141–146. UNESCO, Paris.

Sonneville-Bordes, D. de. and J. Perrot. 1954. Lexique typologique du Paléolithique supérieur, I. II. *Bulletin de la Société Préhistorique Française* 51: 327–333.

———. 1955. Lexique typologique du Palolithique supérieur III. *Bulletin de la Société Préhistorique Française* 52: 76–79.

———. 1956a. Lexique typologique du Paléolithique supérieur V. VI. VII. VIII. IX. *Bulletin de la Société Préhistorique Française* 53: 547–558.

———. 1956b. Lexique typologique du Paléolithique supérieur. IV. *Bulletin de la Société Préhistorique Française* 53: 408–412.

Stafford, T. W. Jr., P. E. Hare, L. Currie, A. J. T. Jull, and D. J. Donahue. 1991. Accelerator radiocarbon dating at the molecular level. *Journal of Archaeological Science* 18: 35–72.

Stanjek, H., J. W. E. Fassbinder, H. Vali, H. Wägele, and W. Graf. 1994. Evidence of biogenic greigite (ferrimagnetic Fe3S4) in soil. *European Journal of Soil Science* 45: 97–103.

Stein, J. K. and P. A. Teltser. 1989. Size distributions of artifact classes: Combining macro- and micro-fractions. *Geoarchaeology* 41: 1–30.

Stern, N. 1991 *The Scatters between the Patches: A Study of Early Hominid Land-Use Patterns in the Turkana Basin, Kenya*. Unpublished Ph.D. dissertation, Harvard University.

———. 1993. The structure of the Lower Pleistocene archaeological record: A case study from the Koobi Fora formation. *Current Anthropology* 34: 201–226.

Stiner, M. C. 1991. The faunal remains from Grotta Guattari: A taphonomic perspective. *Current Anthropology* 32: 103–117.

Sullivan, A. and K. Rosen. 1985. Debitage analysis and archaeological interpretation. *American Antiquity* 50: 755–779.

Sutcliffe, A. J. 1970. Spotted hyena: Crusher, gnawer, digester and collector of bones. *Nature* 227: 1110–1113.

Tite, M. S. and R. E. Linington. 1975. Effect of climate on the magnetic susceptibility of soils. *Nature* 256: 565–566.

Tournepiche, J.-F. 1996. Les grands mammifères pléistocènes de Poitou-Charentes. *Paléo* 8: 109–141.

Trinkaus, E. 1973. A reconsideration of the Fontéchevade fossils. *American Journal of Physical Anthropology* 39: 25–36.

Trinkaus, E., O. Moldavan, S. Milota, B. A., L. Sarcina, S. Athreya, S. Bailey, R. Rodrigo, G. Mircea, T. Higham, C. B. Ramsey, and J. Van Der Plicht. 2003. An early modern human from the Peştera Oase, Romania. *Proceedings of the National Academy of Sciences* 100: 11231–11236.

Tuffreau, A. 1982. The transition Lower/Middle Palaeolithic in Northern France. In *The Transition from Lower to Middle Palaeolithic and the Origin of Modern Man*, edited by A. Ronen, pp. 137–149. BAR International Series. BAR, Oxford.

Tuffreau, A. and J. Sommé. 1988. *Le Gisement paléolithique moyen de Biache-Saint-Vaast (Pas-de-Calais). Stratigraphie, environnement, Etudes archéologiques*. Mémoires de la Société Préhistorique de France, t. 21, Paris.

Vail, P. R., R. M. Mitchum, and S. Thompson. 1977. Chrono-stratigraphic significance of seismic reflections. *American Association of Petroleum Geologists Memoirs* 26: 99–116.

Valladas, H., N. Mercier, J. L. Joron, S. P. McPherron, H. L. Dibble, and M. Lenoir. 2003. TL dates for the Middle Paleolithic site of Combe-Capelle Bas, France. *Journal of Archaeological Science* 30: 1443–1450.

Vallois, H. 1949. The Fontechevade fossil man. *American Journal of Physical Anthropology* 7: 339–362.

———. 1958. *La Grotte de Fontéchevade. II: Anthropologie.* Archives de l'Instut de Paléontologie Humaine 29, Paris.

Valoch, K. 1968. Le remplissage et les industries du Paléolithique moyen de la Grotte Külna en Moravie. *L'Anthropolgie* 72: 453–466.

Verosub, K. L., P. Fine, M. J. Singer, and J. TenPas. 1993. Pedogenesis and paleoclimate: Interpretation of the magnetic susceptibility record of Chinese loess-paleosol sequences. *Geology* 21: 1011–1014.

Villa, P. 1982. Conjoinable pieces and site formation processes. *American Antiquity* 47: 276–290.

Weiner, J. and B. Campbell. 1964. The taxonomic status of the Swanscombe skull. In *The Swanscombe Skull*, edited by C. D. Ovey, pp. 175–209. Occasional Papers 20. Royal Anthropological Institute, London.

Wendorf, F. and R. Schild. 1974. *A Middle Stone Age Sequence from the Central Rift Valley, Ethiopia.* Zaklad Narodowy Im. Ossolinskich Wydawnictwo Polskiej Akademii Nauk, Wroclaw, Poland.

Weymouth, J. W. 1986. Geophysical method of archaeological site surveying. *Advances in Archaeological Method and Theory* 9: 311–396.

Williams, J. M. 1984. A new resistivity device. *Journal of Field Archaeology* 11: 110–114.

Wolliard, G. 1978. Grande Pile peat bog: A continuous pollen record for the last 140,000 years. *Quaternary Research* 9: 1–21.

Zohdy, A., G. Eaton, and D. Mabey. 1974. *Applications of Surface Geophysics to Groundwater Investigations: Techniques of Water Resources Investigations.* Book 2, Chapter D1. U.S. Government Printing Office, Washington, D.C.

Index